Skid row

Skid row

An introduction to disaffiliation

HOWARD M. BAHR

New York
OXFORD UNIVERSITY PRESS
London   Toronto   1973

Still, to some people death is very welcome. If they've spoiled their piece of goods, I'm sure many would rather be dead.

SAUL BELLOW, *Mr. Sammler's Planet*

To be rooted is perhaps the more important and least recognized need of the human soul. . . . A human being has roots by virtue of his real, active, and natural participation in the life of a community, which preserves in living shape certain particular treasures of the past and certain particular expectations for the future.

SIMONE WEIL, *The Need for Roots*

Then I came to realize that men build themselves personalities as they build houses—to protect themselves from the world. But once they have built a house, they are forced to live in it. They become its prisoners.

COLIN WILSON, *The Outsider*

Preface

In writing this book I have drawn upon materials collected during an eight-year program of research on homelessness conducted at the Bureau of Applied Social Research and supported by three separate awards to Columbia University: a one-year contract with the City of New York, a three-year grant from the National Institute of Mental Health ("Homelessness: Etiology, Patterns, and Consequences: MH-10861), and a subsequent two-year grant from the same source ("Disaffiliation Among Urban Women": MH-15637). Theodore Caplow was the principal investigator for all three projects; I was the project director on the last two.

I have also used memoranda and source files accumulated while continued analysis of these data was supported in part by funds provided for biological and medical research by the State of Washington Initiative Measure No. 171 and by Project 1960, Department of Rural Sociology, Agriculture Research Center, College of Agriculture, Washington State University.

My greatest debt is to Theodore Caplow, whose research on homelessness spans my entire lifetime. He first interested me in disaffiliation as a research topic, and he trusted me, an unseasoned new Ph.D. at the time, to help direct a large-scale project in an unfamiliar city. Most important, he provided the necessary encouragement, guidance, and quality control to bring that research project to fruition. Special thanks are also due to Stanley K. Henshaw and Gerald R. Garrett, who directed major portions of the Columbia studies on homelessness. Garrett is the co-author of Chapter 6, and my description of Camp LaGuardia draws heavily upon Henshaw's work. Project reports prepared by George Nash and Patricia Nash during the first year of the Columbia studies have also been useful, and their contributions are acknowledged with gratitude. I am also grateful to my wife, Rosemary, whose patience and support during evenings and weekends for longer than I care to remember made this book possible.

Brigham Young University   H.M.B.

Contents

Skid row

1 | Introduction

This introduction to skid row begins with glimpses of life there. These sketches, not representative in any statistical sense, depict life in a public shelter, an encounter in an off-Bowery restaurant, and three skid row street scenes. Following these views of skid row is a more general treatment of skid row men as a minority community.

Nobody bothers me . . .

If he was like other little boys, his mother told him not to go out in the rain without his galoshes. But that was about 50 years ago. Now it didn't matter any more. It was 5 A.M. on the Bowery and beneath the lamps the frigid rain gleamed on the pavement. Up at the Weather Bureau the instruments said it was 33 degrees and the wind was 12 miles an hour, gusting to 22. The man lay face up on the sidewalk near East Houston St. and the wind and the wet and the near-freezing cold were busy working at what was left of him. He had five minutes to live, right there on his back in the street with no shoes on. Just a pair of black socks and khaki pants, a blue shirt and an open wool jacket, incongruously cheery with its orange, white and brown checks. The girl was out walking her dog when she found him. The lips moved over his toothless upper gums. He was muttering something about an attack, about someone taking his shoes. The lips twisted again and for the last

time, and the girl heard him call, "Police." And then he lay silent and
still, right there on the street by the "No Parking" sign. When the
squad car from the Ninth Precinct arrived, the girl and her dog were
still with him. The girl was bent over the body, crying because she
thought if she found him just a few minutes earlier, she might have
saved him.

. . .

The body on the street was taken to the Medical Examiner's morgue
where fingerprints were taken to be used in an effort to establish an
identity. The man poses a mystery. No, not his name. That really
doesn't matter so much. But those missing—perhaps stolen—shoes. To
know exactly the reason for their absence, the manner of their disappearance would be to know with unprecedented precision the condition
of life in this city.[1]

City of New York, Department of Social Services. The Men's Shelter
on East 3rd Street . . . A familiar East Village landmark, it is always
party time in front of the Shelter as if the men were at a Hilton hotel
convention in hell. The men think of it as "God's open arms," "The
Muney," society's wino charity, a public men's club.

. . .

The original, noble idea of the Muney was to help men get back on
life's turntable. That was a long time ago. All right, all right. Show time
in The Big Room. High ceilinged, arched floor to ceiling windows give
the impression of a townhouse ballroom. It is very bright with modern
lights. Folding camp cots, plastic turquoise arm chairs blanket the
room. Now it is two in the morning and 72 men are home for the night.
Sprawled on the stone floor, in chairs, cots, men slept and tried to sleep.
Ate, drank, laughed, talked with friends and made connections. One
man washed his short-sleeved white shirt and white arm sling. WPAT
type of music, rock radio music mingle with snores, cries for "mama!"
A few nightmares telegraph the same code: "No! no!" "Stop. Stop it!"
"HELP!" A man vomits in a corner, his head moving like a contestant
at the Eat'm Up banquet, and, as if to top him, a comfortable cot man
raises up, turns on his side. Vomit showers the floor in healthy heaves.
Naturally, the stoned men nearest him take no notice. Fifteen minutes
later they are indifferent as comfortable cot fights a man who is trying
to steal his 1940 sport coat. Occasionally, the staff looks in through the

glass squares of the two double doors. Checking. There are two guards. One, looks like a jolly, fat grandfather. But he smells sadistic, acts as if he were a quick study for a Buñuel film. The lean young guard walks as if he were in church. No, he is not a guard. At least in The Big Room. Perhaps he is taking care of things at Rockland State, in Recife. Let's review a bottle snatch happening. Two pug types have the pint. They are laughing, taunting the pint loser, who is now on his feet, executing brave dying soldier routines. Protesting. But the B film pugs are killing wine in the john. The loser makes it to the john entrance as they exit. Loser stammers: "I, I, I wan . . ." Champions break pint on stone floor. The sound of glass becomes brief, shrill music. Young church-stepping guard enters. He wants to know what the hell is going on. Speaking softly, and from the stomach, he says: "All right. You guys pipe down." Then he looks at the two prize wine snatchers and then at the loser. The young guard tells loser to sit down or get out. The Buñuel guard has his henchmen, who look like extras in a very good, old-fashioned western (two Puerto Ricans, one Negro, and another who pretends to be Puerto Rican, and one Gentile camp follower). They are the gentlemen of law and order. The voices to smother an uncool scene. I know the following line will not surprise you: The henchmen are the bullies of The Big Room. They kick men out of cots for the simple reason that they are cotless or their followers are cotless. A few fast left-rights into the face of a chair sleeper. He smelled, one of them said. They beat up others because they have no wine, money, nothing worth taking. Drunken sadists, they beat up others for pleasure. "Please. Don't beat him up," a youngish man pleads, nodding toward his frozen-eyed, trembling friend. "He just got out of the hospital and I'm ill too. We're just trying to get a little sleep." They were awarded fast timed slaps and kept chair changing without saying a word.

. . .

Dark-haired Martel berths in the crevice of an arched window facing the room. He drapes the clean trench coat around his shoulders, turns up the collar, drops his head and tries to sleep. But a giant of a drunk, wearing white collar worker suit and tie, staggers into The Big Room, crouched like a TV Munster quarterback. He lands against Martel and passes out. Martel looks up slowly like a cold early morning Mexico City street Indian, and executes an act of art. There's no doubt about it, he is living on the soles of his feet; he is pickpocketing a drunk in the Bowery Men's Shelter. Any fool knows the man was clipped before arrival. But Martel with now-you-see-now-you-don't-see hands expertly goes through the four trouser pockets, the two jacket pockets and extracts a tobacco brown wallet. He slips the wallet back in to left jacket pocket in the manner that you will raise a cup to your lips or open them to love. Disgusted, he rises, straightens the trench coat collar, and sits down in a chair in the row ahead of me. Silently, we exchange glances. Martel closes his eyes.[2]*

On the street, as in the rooms, crime is a major problem on the Bowery. It worsens in the winter, if only because everything worsens there in the winter. "You can't even sleep in the park now," said one man. "You always got to have one eye open or you wouldn't have the shoes on your feet." Tony swore, recalling the sight last winter of a man sleeping in the snow completely naked. "They stole his clothes right off him while he slept," he said. To Tony, "they" were the true "bums"—a word used rarely on the Bowery and only to describe men who prey on helpless alcoholics. He said he remembered the days when a man could stagger from bar to bar, clutching a sheaf of dollar bills in his hand. "Now," he added, "you can get cut up for holding a pint, or even for nothing." He said he wasn't prejudiced but believed the blame lay with "these guys who come up from the South."[3]†

I saw . . . Ben run to the police call box at the corner of Bowery and Rivington Street. Ben got his hand inside the box, a young Puerto Rican boy named Lefty ran up to the box and closed it on Ben's hand. Ben started to walk away and a Negro man named Duke came up and threw a bone he had been chewing which hit Ben square in the face. Duke and Lefty roughed Ben up and told him not ever to "rat" on them again.

. . .

I walked over to Ben and asked him what had happened. He told me that Duke had held him and that Lefty had gone through his pockets to see if he had any money. He hadn't any and they left him alone. As Lefty and Duke walked off, I noticed that there was a small Puerto Rican boy about ten years old with them. They looked into a bar, but kept going. Presently, they spotted their victim. Duke picked out a sixty year old man named Charles who was walking north on the

* Reprinted by permission of *The Village Voice*. Copyrighted by The Village Voice, Inc., 1968.

† Copyright © 1964 by The New York Times Company. Reprinted by permission.

Bowery. Despite the fact that it was seven o'clock in the evening and still quite light, and despite the fact that there were at least twenty people within a hundred feet of Charles, Duke walked up to him and pinned his arms behind his back. Lefty then proceeded to go through Charles' pockets one by one. When he came to his wallet, he opened it and took out what money was there. Then he put the wallet back into Charles' pocket, handed the money to the small boy, and the three walked off. Charles told me they had taken thirty dollars from him. Not one of the numerous people who saw what had happened complained, cried out or made any attempt to discourage Duke and Lefty. Charles made no complaint to the police. Later that evening, I saw Lefty and the small boy walking by themselves on the west side of the Bowery. Lefty would walk into a group of men, hit one fellow and take his money and then walk on. No effort was ever made to stop him. At my request, the police later picked up Duke and Lefty. It proved impossible to find Charles, the complainant and they had to be let go. I talked to Lefty the following day and he told me that he had made four hundred dollars the preceeding evening. He was a presentable, even handsome fellow and I asked him, "Why are you looking to get in trouble?" He wasn't a thief, he told me, "just a hustler."[4]

On Second Avenue near 5th Street is an old toad of a woman, monstrous, fat, unpleasant, ugly inside. She used to sit on a box in front of a delicatessen there, like some earth-bound gargoyle. Sometimes she helped out behind the counter. One night, an old derelict came in while I was getting cigarettes. He was sober and he actually wanted to buy coffee and a roll. The old toad screamed at him to get out. He held the change in his hand and said, "But mam, I've got money, I just want coffee and a roll—see mam, here's the money," and she screamed again for him to get out, and he, proud that he was sober, proud that he had money in his hand, proud that he wanted coffee and a roll, backed through the door still treating the woman as if she were royalty, very gently holding out his hand and repeating, "But mam, the money is here, I only want coffee and a roll." The fight was gone from him and only dignity was left.[5]*

These incidents happened in New York City. They might have happened in any skid row area in the nation. Everyone bothers the skid row man; it is always open season on the homeless. The policeman, the jackroller, the welfare worker, the employment agent,

* Reprinted by permission of *The Village Voice*. Copyrighted by the Village Voice Inc., 1968.

other skid row men, and the poor white playing a desperate game of one-upmanship by treating the skid row resident as a child, a criminal, or an animal—all may prey with relative impunity on the human being stigmatized as derelict.

Yet the homeless men and their apologists continue to mouth the fiction that men live on skid row because of the freedom it offers. Thus, the former president of a company that runs a chain of hotels on the Bowery summarized the motivation of his customers: "A man lives in a Lyons house because that is the place he is comfortable. . . . He comes here to get away from people who ask questions, actually from people who care."[6] One skid row researcher used the term "responsibilitilessness" to characterize the condition of the men she interviewed. When asked about their reasons for living in lodging houses, a surprising number of her respondents said "no one bothers me" or that they were "free to come and go."[7] It was also suggested that the average citizen's apparent enmity toward the homeless might reflect resentment about his own "mandatory responsibility" and a certain envy for the lot of the homeless man:

Perhaps, it is responsibilitilessness that the average citizen, with his overly developed status set and resulting weight of obligations, most dislikes. He senses that the homeless man has a carefreeness that the average citizen can never hope to recapture.[8]

One of the theses of this book is that the homeless man's oft-repeated affection for skid row facilities, and the ready repetition of those sentiments by the non-homeless, serve as guilt-reduction devices for the average citizen, as well as for the rehabilitation agent. If skid row men prefer the quality of life which characterizes skid row, then the rest of us are absolved of guilt. The same kind of rationalization that has served so well in race relations—"they like things that way," "that's the way they are," "they're happy, carefree people"—then serves to reduce the dissonance that awareness of the actual physical conditions of skid row would otherwise create. To repeat: skid row men are preyed upon, either physically or psychically, by almost everyone they meet. But if they like to be preyed upon, then they deserve it.

It is true that certain perceived social costs may be reduced by a move to skid row. For example, one may be able to drink heavily there without fearing the sanctions of one's spouse or relatives. But the freedom from specific constraints which may accompany a move to skid row is likely to be more than counterbalanced by the increased costs linked to repeated exposure to the "revolving door" of arrest, incarceration, release, and arrest again; the increased probability of contracting tuberculosis and other diseases; and the costs to self-esteem which derive from interacting with and living among representatives of the most stigmatized subculture in our society.

In the paragraphs that follow I refer to skid row men as a "tribe," and use terminology sometimes employed in descriptions of primitive peoples. I do not mean to suggest that they are more primitive than representatives of any other subculture; rather, the intent is to cast the study of the homeless into the context of ethnic pluralism and majority–minority relations. To some extent, the relationships between skid row men and representatives of the "outside" may be viewed as an example of internal colonialism.

Skid row men as a tribal population

The skid row men are a little-known tribe who live in seclusion in small urban enclaves. There are more than 150 distinct bands, each having its own land base and unique institutions. The skid row men have been at times quite numerous, but now students of the tribe speak of its imminent extinction. Certainly the record of the past decade suggests that the tribe is dying out. In one recent three-year period, more than 1500 members of one Eastern band disappeared. This amounted to a loss of about 7 per cent per year, and if this rate of loss would continue, the band could survive only for another generation or so.

For many years explorers, traders, missionaries, and political officials from the outside have worked among the skid row men. These outsiders have often had opposing opinions about the members of the tribe; they have labored diligently to achieve their various and often contradictory aims. Some have worked to destroy the tribal homelands and to resettle them where their identity as a tribe would be diminished. Many of the persons advocating relocation honestly feel that members of the tribe would be happier if they were separated from each other and were living under different circumstances; others have been motivated by disgust at the primitive conditions of native life. Some outsiders feel that the land the tribe occupies could be put to better, more civilized use.

Among those who understand the natives best are the traders. Some enmity exists between them and the politicians and missionaries who want to disperse the skid row men, perhaps because the traders say that the best thing for the tribe is to leave them alone and let them live in their own way, thus continuing their reliance on the traders for lodging facilities, food, and other essentials. Some of the traders have been harassed by other outsiders, mainly political officials, and recently their profits appear to have decreased considerably; some have abandoned their posts and returned to their homes. But most of the traders are dedicated men resolved to continue to serve the tribesmen until they have been dispersed. The traders are convinced that they serve the men better and more efficiently than do the missionaries and political officials.

The traders have received much bad publicity. For one thing, they make their living among the skid row men, while public officials and missionaries are supported by outside sources and thus ostensibly have no personal interest in the continued subjugation of the tribe. Some traders have been accused publicly of prolonging the inferior status of the tribesmen to protect their own profits. Nevertheless, the traders appear to have won the respect and confidence of the tribesmen to a greater extent than either the missionaries or the politicians. The traders seem to accept the tribesman as he is, and to deal with him on a man-to-man basis.

To the public as a whole, the tribe has been an object of curiosity, derision, and considerable animosity. In fact, there is such prejudice against them that members of the tribe who can pass as outsiders often lie about their addresses to avoid identification as skid row men. Even some of the traders are loath to admit that they work among the tribesmen.

Like many other "primitive" tribes living in close contact with more "civilized" peoples, the skid row men are objects of discrimination. Their personality characteristics and values often are criticized. A journalist's description of the New Zealand Maori fits the skid row man perfectly: "With few exceptions he is said to be lazy, dirty, have loose morals, be ignorant, irresponsible, over-fond of drink and addicted to ridiculous, unbecoming customs. . . ." Although they are criticized for being dirty, lazy, immoral, and alcoholic, they have made valuable economic contributions to several major industries, such as providing cheap labor for restaurants or hotels.

Their propensity to invent stories about themselves has often been exaggerated; some investigators have even gone so far as to suggest that there is a special class of priesthood among them who approach outsiders who visit the reservation and spin wildly improbable tales about themselves, usually just the sort of tales the visitor came seeking. While there may be individual men who engage in such activities, the suggestion that these individuals are so numerous as to form a separate contingent of the population or well organized enough to propagandize any but a small proportion of the visitors to the reservation seems absurd.

The skid row men are of interest because in many respects their ideas and customs are the antithesis of much that the "civilized" American sees as valuable and sacred. Yet every year many outsiders join the tribe, and after a short time they cannot be distinguished from the natives. Further, they and several related tribes located on reservations in other areas of the country have been recognized as problems and objects of social action for many years. In general, the basic question has been: "Is it better to leave the tribesmen alone on their reservation or shall we disperse them and try to socialize them into the dominant population?" As with other minority populations, the public has been concerned with the problem of assimilating the tribesmen, often against their will, into more profitable uses.

The tribe is overwhelmingly male. Since there are so few women, one of the interesting things about the tribe is its manner of self-perpetuation. Despite the abhorrence the public manifests for the tribesmen, the tribe is fascinating and in some ways attractive. Every year men from the outside join the skid row men. Experts are not yet sure just how the process of recruitment operates, but it is speculated that recruits are mainly of two kinds: men who are rejected by other societies first and then come to find peace and human association among the skid row men, and men who are integrated in other cultures but at the same time become involved in habits more compatible with life on skid row than with the customs of their home neighborhoods. Such "recruits" may live on the edge of both worlds for many years before renouncing the skid row men's way of life or fully accepting it.

It is the process of recruitment that outside political and religious leaders have tried to interrupt. One of the arguments for dispersion of the tribesmen is that they will find it more difficult to pass on their way of life if separated, and hence will be less likely to provide opportunities for others to be recruited.

Despite the threatened extinction of the tribe, some of the outsiders who have worked among them are convinced that even if the reservation is "cleaned up" and the tribesmen dispersed, there will be concentrations of skid row men and their ilk as long as civilization exists. A number of minority groups like the skid row men are scattered across the United States. Some are concentrated in reservations, others are widely dispersed. Those in reservations have the advantage of some social support for their way of life. Many of those dispersed throughout the cities are unaware of the numerous others who share their economic and social situation, and to some extent, their attitudes and values.

Members of these minorities often are seen as threatening the general public, and there is considerable animosity toward the tribes on reservations. Isolated members of the minority groups of homeless persons are less often perceived as a threat, and very little is known about them. Public ignorance about them prevents "the establishment" from knowing the extent to which, if at all, they are a threat to the present social order. It can only be said that wherever they congregate, wherever a "reservation" of the homeless minority becomes visible, the larger society seems to perceive them as a threat and acts to disperse the tribesmen to as great an extent as possible, and to resocialize them into patterns of life that, if they do not actually change the tribesmen's attitudes and values, at least make them less visible to the majority.

The study of the skid row men and similar tribes is of value because it not only provides information about the tribesmen on their reservations, but also gives us ideas about the far more numerous members of the minority that are never studied due to their anonymity and isolation. If society sees the concentrations of tribesmen as a problem, it needs to be awakened to the greater problem of the dispersed, unattached individuals who have no tribal affiliation.

Structure and basic themes

In addition to this introductory chapter, this book contains seven chapters that treat selected dimensions of homelessness, the character of skid row and its men, and the interaction between the men of skid row and other elements of society. Chapter 2 identifies the skid row man as one species of the genus homeless, defines skid row, and summarizes its history. It also introduces one of the dominant arguments of the book, the idea that one of the main distinguishing features of the skid row man, and a fundamental key to many of his problems, is his powerlessness. That powerlessness is identified as an inevitable consequence of disaffiliation. Freedom from the restraints of stable affiliative ties is accompanied by a loss of control over one's environment, both social and non-social. The natural consequence of powerlessness (or of its synonym, minimal personal influence) is that in encounters with others the skid row man rarely gets his way. When he does it is usually a situation of no contest: He seeks resources or facilities for which there is little competition, e.g., tiny, noisy, filthy hotel rooms. It is suggested that even the stigmatization he suffers flows, in part, from the nature of his powerlessness. If one has little power, his function or contribution to society is likely to be seen as minimal. Interaction with him, from a social exchange point of view, is apt to be costly to the non-skid-row person, who has much to lose and little to gain in the encounter.

Chapter 3 is devoted to a topic that has received little attention in previous works on skid row: the way the skid row men are perceived by outsiders. We examine the components of the stereotype, "skid row man," and present data from content analyses of newspaper articles and magazine cartoons about the homeless, from surveys of national and local populations about attitudes toward alcoholism or reasons for "losing" in life, and from the writings and statements of experienced observers with first-hand experience of skid row people and life. Chapter 3 presents one of the main objectives of this book, an attempt at combining the results of the numerous social scientific studies of skid row with relevant material from other sources. The synthesis of data representing a variety of methods of data collection and diverse professional and disciplinary perspectives is intended to produce a composite, correlated picture of the organization, population, and social context of skid row, and to reflect the diversity and scope of the voluminous published literature relevant to skid row and homelessness.

Chapter 4, "Who's on Skid Row?," represents a distillate of the results of numerous surveys of skid row men conducted during the past two decades. The characteristics considered include the family status and family background, economic status, employment, personal problems, age, race, educational attainment, nativity, and mobility of skid row men. Then several influential typologies of skid row dwellers are introduced and compared, and the imputed defectiveness of skid row men is singled out as the underlying characteristic of the men. Stigmatization as a defective and unsalvageable person, it is proposed, stems from the homeless man's occupying, or being thought to occupy, several stigmatized statuses at once, e.g., he has an unsightly or broken body, a presumably bad character, he is dependent on welfare or charity, is aged and impoverished, and is possibly an alcoholic. His imputed defectiveness is augmented by his powerlessness which itself derives from his disaffiliation, and the combination of these traits prevents rehabilitation efforts from being taken seriously either by the man himself or by the agents of social control who go through the motions of working with him. His defectiveness and powerlessness combine with his other negative characteristics, real or imagined, and predispose him to involvement in a vicious circle of negative encounters which serve to bind him to skid row, lower his self-esteem, and make social fact what was at first mere definition—that he is hopeless and unsalvageable.

Chapter 5 considers the familiar institutions of skid row, focusing on hotels and lodging houses, gospel missions, and bars as the dominant facilities but also considering employment agencies, blood banks, junk dealers, public shelters, and other formal organizations. The last half of the chapter discusses the informal relationships on skid row. Considered at length are the well-known "bottle gang" and the nature of friendship on skid row; treated more briefly are informal racial discrimination and the distinctive style of interaction at the "thieves' market."

A little-known element of the skid row population, the homeless women, is discussed in Chapter 6. Results of original studies of the clients of the Women's Emergency Shelter in New York City are presented along with a review of previous studies of institutionalized or impoverished female alcoholics. It is noted that while male homelessness seems linked primarily to specific occupations and only secondarily to marital history, for women, work history has little bearing on homelessness but marital history seems critical.

Throughout the book the problem of alcoholism is confronted

more directly than in many other studies of skid row; this is particularly so in Chapter 7, which describes the shift from vagrancy to alcoholism as the dominant deviance ascribed to homeless men, and summarizes control and rehabilitation programs and proposals for both pathologies. Encounters between homeless men and the law are described, as well as the infamous "revolving door." The discussions of the kinds of therapies and treatment programs includes recognition of the widespread deficiencies in program evaluation and of their general ineffectiveness with skid row men. It is proposed that the manner of providing treatment is at least as important as the type of treatment. Most evidence suggests that in terms of number of men "cured," no treatment at all is probably just as effective as the costly programs now in progress.

Chapter 8 reviews the book, sets forth some generalizations about skid row and homelessness, and stresses that the crucial problem in rehabilitation of skid row men is interrupting the vicious circle which continually confirms a man's defectiveness. This last point is really a plea for a more sociological approach to treatment programs, with increased attention to symbolic interaction, to reversing the "self-fulfilling prophecy," and to the definitions of self and situation that skid row men and the representatives of respectable society bring to their encounters.

2 | Homelessness, affiliation, and skid row

"Homelessness is a condition of detachment from society characterized by the absence or attenuation of the affiliative bonds that link settled persons to a network of interconnected social structures."[1] It takes many forms, depending on the type of detachment involved. Beggars, refugees, migratory workers, outlaws, religious mendicants, and skid row men are all homeless to some degree. Most of this book is about one kind of homeless man, the skid row resident. But before we narrow the scope let us consider some of the historical context and concepts related to homelessness.

In addition to pointing out some correlates of the condition of homelessness—among them the religious ideal of mendicancy and poverty, the overrepresentation of those with lower-class backgrounds among recruits to homelessness, the salience of certain occupations as avenues to homelessness, and the link between disaffiliation and skid row residence—we shall introduce one of the important themes of this work. It is that a distinguishing characteristic of the homeless is their powerlessness, and that much of the social abhorrence for skid row men is due to their powerlessness, itself a derivative of their disaffiliation or lack of social ties. The chapter concludes with a definition of skid row and a brief history of skid rows in the United States.

Homelessness: context and dimensions

The twentieth century has been called "the century of the homeless man,"[2] but homelessness must not be viewed as a distinctly modern phenomenon. Some forms of disaffiliation may be more prevalent now than in the past, but there have always been vagabonds, beggars, refugees, and religious mendicants.[3] For example, there seems to have been no shortage of beggars in Greek cities. Although Athens had a system of "state aid" for its needy, only citizens were eligible and so numerous migrants and resident "aliens" may have been reduced to begging.[4] One of Homer's characters complains to the swineherd who has conducted the disguised Odysseus to Ithaca: "Why did you bring this fellow to town? Haven't we already got enough tramps and bothersome beggars?"[5]

Homelessness seems most prevalent during periods of social change and the disorganization that inevitably follows. There were few beggars in Rome until the foreign wars had dislodged large segments of the rural population, who descended on the city in hordes. There, unemployed and demoralized, they were made beggars by the "corn and games" of the politicians, and as the disintegration of the empire proceeded, the number of beggars in Rome increased.[6]

Various historical institutions can be associated with homelessness. A case in point is the institution of slavery, which fostered homelessness by "tearing" individuals from their former network of social relations and transplanting them in another system.[7] Flight from slavery meant that ties to the new system were dissolved, often irrevocably. Fugitive slaves were among the most disaffiliated of men.

There have always been refugees from wars, and plagues and famines have always left some persons desolate and alone. Other social and political changes that fostered homelessness were the crusades, the discovery and colonization of new lands, the dissolution of feudal bonds, and the Industrial Revolution.[8]

Gilmore's discussion of "our mendicant heritage," for example, claims that despite the difficulties of travel during the Middle Ages, and despite the typical relationship between lord and serf, there was a "floating population" including robber bands, camp followers with the armies, and residents in marginal areas who never became serfs or lords. Persons dislodged from the regular feudal system augmented the unattached group.

While conditions of life were hard and the death rate was high, the population did undoubtedly increase and this meant a gradual overcrowding of the older settled areas, which necessitated some leaving the older manors. The tendency of natural increase to produce an oversupply of nobility has been widely recognized and blamed for many of the ills of the period, such as the mercenary armies and the robber gangs. While less obvious, this same process undoubtedly deprived many in the lower classes of their birthright. As a result of this overcrowding, some of the serfs might have found it impossible to meet their tenure obligations and been forced to surrender their right to the use of the land. Thus they were dispossessed of their source of livelihood and forced to migrate unless some substitute could be found.

While this forced migration due to overpopulation was more or less continuous, there were mass migrations which occurred occasionally. . . . In addition . . . there were individuals who for personal reasons fled the manor or were forced off. Criminals, socially disgraced persons, maladjusted individuals, and even some insane persons departed for many reasons other than economic ones.

Besides these foot-loose groups there were the bona fide travelers who might take to the road for any of a number of reasons.[9]

In the thirteenth and fourteenth centuries, the declining amount of land available for clearing and cultivation combined with an increase in the amount of money in circulation and an increase in trade to release many workers from the land. These changes, along with the social and economic disorganization that accompanied the Black Death, operated to weaken the lower classes' attachment to the soil and created circumstances that favored migrancy and vagrancy. For a time there was a shortage of laborers, and governments reacted to widespread vagrancy by passing repressive laws against it. But by the sixteenth century the labor shortage was succeeded by a labor surplus, and problems of caring for the poor became increasingly serious. Inadequate poor laws often stimulated vagrancy and begging.[10]

The social and economic changes accompanying the Industrial Revolution have also encouraged homelessness. There have been massive migrations, not only between continents or countries, but also within countries, particularly in the movement of rural population to the cities. Migration is almost always accompanied by the social and economic dislodgement of many persons; it involves a cutting away of old ties, and sometimes the old social network is not replaced. In addition, rapid technological change has eliminated many occupations and created others, so that it has been possible for a person who did not migrate geographically to find himself "left behind" occupationally, perhaps impoverished and jobless because his skills have become obsolete.

Homelessness as a religious ideal. Homelessness as an ideal is a recurrent theme in many religions. The ancient Greeks encouraged kindness to beggars and vagrants, teaching that Zeus was the "god of strangers" and "the gods do haunt these mortal cities, variously disguised as foreigners while taking in the hubris and lawfulness of men."[11]

The Christian ascetic ideal and the tradition of the virtue of poverty are exemplified in statements such as "lay not up for yourselves treasures on earth" and "foxes have holes, and birds have nests, but the Son of Man hath not where to lay his head."[12] O'Conner asserts that "Christ was a propertyless vagrant, and in that cardinal legend or fact rests the source of the ethos of the vagrant tradition. . . ."[13] The ideal of renunciation of property and earthly affiliations was continued and augmented by medieval monastic orders, especially the Franciscans and their imitators.[14]

Homelessness is idealized in Islam. Moslems regard beggars as holy men; one of the great commandments, often repeated in mottoes is "Give alms before you die." Buddhism also exalts the homeless state. The desirable state of "non-attainment" of the Zen Buddhist refers to the lack of both material goods and knowledge.

Emptiness, another word for poverty, is devoutly desired because the spirit can then stand naked, free, with no defiling material trappings.[15]

The Chinese terms for becoming a monk or nun means "to leave home," while ordinary members of secular society are "those who live at home."[16] A similar correspondence to the term "homeless" is the description of early Buddhist mendicants in India as persons who had gone "from a house to a houseless state" and had voluntarily detached themselves from the hindrance of worldly ties so that they might more readily pursue their ideal.[17]

Those who seek monastic seclusion may already have experienced partial detachment from normal society. Thus, a history of Chinese Buddhism records that the residents of Buddhist monasteries frequently were orphans put in the care of a monastery, young men fleeing the world because of personal or social crises, criminals and others who "made themselves impossible in society," sick persons who entered monasteries in hope of healing or to be cared for in their infirmity, or aged and lonely people who came to find a place of peace and security during their declining years.[18]

Sjoberg comments on the universality of religious mendicants:

Segments of the clergy within all the major religions—e.g., those in medieval Europe, the Muslim Middle East, Hindu India, the Buddhist Far East—have been distinguished by their emphasis upon contemplation and asceticism, including subsisting by begging alms, living as hermits, and/or engaging in self-flagellation or other forms of self-immolation. Olufsen describes the dervishes of Bokhara who abjured worldly goods, wandering almost naked and maintaining life through begging; and mendicant priests have been an accepted part of the urban scene over much of Asia. Although some cultural variations on this theme appear, the basic form is surprisingly general.[19]

He suggests that the generality of religious idealization of homelessness is due, in part, to the need for balance within the religious system and fulfillment of its contradictory functional requirements:

Because some clerics enjoy positions of influence and privilege—a desideratum if the religious organization is to maintain its power and authority in the society or city—others in the system must indulge in extreme self-denial in order to sustain in the eyes of the populace the other-worldly ideals of behavior that are propounded by, and essential to, the religion.[20]

Although the religious mendicants were prominent in many pre-industrial cities, they accounted for only a small percentage of the disaffiliates there.

Social class and affiliation. In the preindustrial city the lower classes, particularly the outcast groups, often contained sizable numbers of homeless persons. The outcasts were a universal feature of the preindustrial city; the various outcast types—slaves, prostitutes, entertainers, members of lowly or "unclean" professions—usually lived in segregated areas.[21]

Of course, many of the outcasts could not be considered disaffiliates; some had their own families, occupational responsibilities, and perhaps even recreational or cultural organizations. The point is that true disaffiliates also were considered outcasts. Apparently entry into outcast status was fairly easy; a lower-class woman who had lost her family ties might enter prostitution, or a child of poor parents might be sold into slavery.[22]

Among preindustrial populations, the urban lower-class and outcast groups, as well as rural families, are much less able to maintain close family ties than urban elites.[23] The extended family forms the "prime security agency" in the preindustrial city; members of the lower-class and outcast groups are unable, with some exceptions, to maintain large households. Relatives in these classes still seek to assist one another where possible, but bonds among several small family units are not nearly as strong as those among family members residing in a single household.[24] Thus the lower classes and outcasts are particularly prone to disaffiliation:

Some of the poor may even find themselves isolated from any family unit, driven to begging or scavenging as a means of eking out a bare subsistence or, more probably, a slow death through starvation and disease. A woman isolated from her kinship system is readily reduced to prostitution, and children, most often girls, orphaned or from poor families, are not infrequently sold to buyers who turn them into servants, entertainers, or prostitutes—as in traditional China and Japan.[25]

Sjoberg has noted that "inherent in industrialization are processes that steadily eliminate the various outcaste roles."[26] If outcast populations are prone to disaffiliation, we might predict that with industrialization would come a decline in disaffiliation, alienation, and homelessness.

The relationship between sustenance problems and homelessness continues in industrial society. Two types of pressures—poor economic conditions and isolation from community institutions—dominate the lives of the lower class,[27] and often produce a vicious circle in which economic insecurity contributes directly to early termination of education (i.e., disaffiliation from educational institutions) which in turn prevents low-status persons from achieving vertical mobility and thus escaping economic insecurity. In addition, the inferior status of those with whom the lower-class individual associates in his early life may contribute to a low self-concept which further prevents attempts to "get ahead in the world."[28]

Lower-class families participate in few community or social organizations; their church affiliation is often nominal, and religion generally plays an unimportant part in their lives. These patterns of minimal attachment to community institutions continue from generation to generation.[29]

Some maintain that much of the isolation of the lower classes is "self-imposed."[30] Low status, according to this view, creates a type of "mental isolation" which limits sources of information, retards development of efficient judgement and reasoning, and confines attention to trivial interests.[31]

Cohen and Hodge have observed that in comparison with other strata, the "social network" of the lower-lower class is "shrunken," and the few relationships which are sustained are based on kinship and propinquity.[32] They also report that more than any other class, the lower-lower class prefers the familiar and is extremely reluctant to enter into new situations or to meet new people. They assert that a member of this class is uncomfortable and anxious in unfamiliar situations because "he lacks confidence in his ability to say and do 'the right things.' "[33] The "style of life" of the lower-class person has not prepared him for new and unfamiliar situations. Because of this lack of adaptability, members of the lower class are particularly vulnerable to disaffiliation during periods of rapid social change.

The economic insecurity which characterizes most lower-class families may lead to their concentration in certain neighborhoods. In this respect, the isolation of the lower class may be similar to that of outcast groups.[34] The social and spatial isolation of the lower-lower class, like that of racial and ethnic groups, breeds negative attitudes toward the general community. Knupfer refers to the suspicion and dread of the foreign, "the definition of foreign being more or less inclusive," as a corollary of social isolation. There is much support for this "corollary." For example, "pessimism" and "misanthropy" are said to be major elements in the lower-lower class character[35]; August Hollingshead, among others, has highlighted the "deep-seated distrust of authority figures" which pervades the lower-lower class. Politicians, police, teachers, doctors, public health nurses, social workers, clergymen, and other official representatives of "society" are subjects of fairly general hostility.[36]

Some maintain that determining the degree to which social isolation is voluntary is a vital theoretical issue,[37] and in doing this it may be impossible to separate the effects of societal rejection and exploitation of the lower class from those of rejection of the rest of society *by* the lower class. In any event, it is evident that a portion of the disaffiliation of lower-class persons derives from their own attitudes. Many aspects of social isolation continue to be problematic, but more than three decades of research has supported the Lynds' hypothesis about the relation between affiliation and social class:

Progressively as one comes down the social scale, the chance of becoming a lost individual, not united in any active sense to community-wide life and values, increases. One "lives in a town," "makes money there," is part of its "available labor supply" rather than necessarily being an integral part of the town.[38]

Refugees. One of the dominant forms of homelessness in the twentieth century is the refugee. The essential quality of being a refugee seems to be displacement from one's own normal social context, usually "as a result of political events in that country which rendered . . . continued residence impossible or intolerable." The definition is sometimes extended to include persons who migrate because of actual or threatened persecution because of race, religion, political convictions, or any reason related to war.[39] One writer distinguishes between the "refugee" who flees voluntarily for one reason or another, and the "expellee" who does not leave his home voluntarily but rather is driven out.[40]

The problems of disaffiliation are most severe for the "hard-core" refugees who are both homeless and stateless; no government assumes responsibility for these persons.

For them the uncertainties of today are matched only by the *homelessness* of tomorrow. International protection for them is an urgent day-to-day need and emergency assistance to many of them is their alternative to starvation. They are men and women of all ages and many nationalities. They are children of no nationality, who were born refugees. They have skills and professions that they cannot practice. They have the will to work, but the law denies it. They cannot travel because they have no passport. They cannot work because they have no labor permits. They sometimes cannot marry because they lack some necessary document. It is even difficult for them to die legally. They are often thought of as peculiar people and, in a sense, they are. It must be peculiar to be in the world and not of it—to pass years of life extruded from community is a state of suspended animation.[41]

Occupations associated with homelessness. Some occupations are associated with homelessness and begging. One writer lists as "isolated types" the sailor, peacetime soldier, miner, logger, cowboy, hobo, hired man, and "bunkhouse man."[42] Another list includes assorted "street" occupations: street sellers, street buyers, street performers, street dancers and musicians, street laborers and cleaners.[43] In China, the ricksha men were particularly liable to homelessness; the low income and relatively short working life of the men left them dependent on the community, and in some cities it was necessary to establish special shelters for them.[44]

Among the medieval occupational guilds, and to some extent down to the present day, homelessness has been a stage in the career of the craftsman. For example, in Germany there was the tradition of the journeyman or wandering workman who moved from town to town, staying and working a few days and then going on. Most of these wanderers eventually settled down. After wars or economic crises the number of such persons on the road usually increased.[45] One of the objects of tramping from town to town and working for a time in many places was "to acquire experience in the craft or mystery in which the traveler was engaged by seeing the different methods of work in various parts of the country."[46]

The largest group of "occupationally homeless" persons in the United States are the migratory workers for whom "home is where the crops are ripe."[47] In many cases the excessive mobility of these groups tends to strengthen rather than weaken familial and cultural bonds among themselves,[48] but they are severely isolated from the communities in which they work. They occupy the lowest level of any major group in the American economy[49] and may be considered modern equivalents of the outcast groups of the preindustrial city.

The migrant is a minority within a minority. The components of the general migrant population belong to racial or ethnic minorities. In addition, each in turn within his own ethnic group occupies a place at the very bottom of the social and economic hierarchy. He meets the most discrimination, does the hardest work, earns the least money; he has the least job security, the least formal schooling, the lowest status. His migrancy separates him from the larger community; his minority status aggravates the separation. Migrancy reduces to zero the chance to develop the feeling of belonging to a stable community.[50]

Unattached urbanities and skid row. Another dominant form of homelessness in modern times is the unattached urbanite.

Every metropolis has its Hobohemia populated by homeless and often jobless males who live in barren rooms and eke out a drab existence. These Hobohemias are areas of last resort for the socially uprooted, men who are unable, for one reason or another, to have a normal family life. Higher in the social and economic scale is a veritable army of unattached men and women who reside in rooming houses, bachelor apartments, residential hotels, or "Y" dormitories. Probably most of the younger unattached men and women on the higher social levels eventually marry, but the middle-aged and older persons will likely "go it alone," whether by choice or necessity.[51]

Of these unattached urbanites, the men on skid rows have received the most attention. In fact, disaffiliates who do not live on skid rows have sometimes been excluded from the category of homeless persons by definitions which limit the phenomenon to participants in "skid row subculture."[52]

We have noted elsewhere that the common unifying element in the multiplicity of definitions which have been used to describe homeless, unattached, or skid row men is their "detachment from society characterized by the absence or attenuation of the affiliative bonds that link settled persons to a network of interconnected social structures."[53] Such detachment or attenuation may conveniently be subsumed under the concept "disaffiliation." This book is about one type of disaffiliated man, the skid row man, whose other labels include homeless man, derelict, unattached man, urban nomad, vagrant, and tramp.

Most cities in the United States have one or more sections where such people are concentrated. Nevertheless, there are residents of skid row neighborhoods who are not disaffiliated, and, of course, many disaffiliated people live elsewhere.

There are many kinds of skid row men. They are stereotyped as alcoholic derelicts, urban nomads, the lost. Yet about one-fifth of them are tee-totalers, between one-fifth and one-half either were born in the city where they now reside on skid row or have lived there more than twenty years, and perhaps 40 per cent of them are employed. Part of the objective of this book is to portray the skid row residents accurately, including all of them, not merely the derelicts who fit the public stereotype. Gleason has aptly stated part of the problem:

They [people from The Outside] simply can't believe that a well-groomed, neat man could be a resident of Skid Row trying to panhandle thirty cents from a priest. The reason, of course, is that they have been conditioned to think of a West Madison Street man as a bum. If the man is not dirty, smelly, unshaven, beat up, and drunk, he can't be from Skid Row. The visitor from The Outside finds it difficult to concede that a man on The Street is human and that he has occasional triumphs as well as frequent failures.[54]

The particular kind of disaffiliate we shall be concerned with in this book may or may not live on skid row, but he manifests a lifestyle compatible with the institutions found there. We shall be talking about clients of missions, shelters, persons incarcerated for vagrancy or public drunkenness, lodgers in cheap hotels, and, in a few cases, samples of the population of entire skid row neighborhoods. Among the characteristics which most clearly define the population we shall be considering are alcohol and powerlessness, and included in powerlessness are elements of poverty, isolation, and impermanence.

Power, affiliation, and homelessness

Despite the importance of power in human affairs, in social analysis it has remained a vague and ill-defined variable, and theories attempting to explain it are notoriously unsatisfactory. Not only have empirical studies sometimes floundered for want of a satisfactory theoretical base, but there has been a tendency for students to concentrate their attention on only one end of the continuum of power: to study only the powerful and to neglect the powerless. To understand power we must study its absence as well as its presence, and the circumstances in which minimal as well as maximal power is exercised.

Power has been defined as "the ability of persons to move goods and services toward defined goals," or as "capacity for effective action." In various sociological studies it is "the ability to exercise influence in a decision-making process," the capacity to realize one's will even against the resistance of others, or "the ability to influence the thoughts and behavior of others." Both Hawley and MacIver have treated power in social relations as analagous to energy in the physical world.[55]

It is often observed that power has a worth in itself, and commands respect merely because it exists. Thus, Weber remarks that power may be valued for its own sake, and striven for because of the "social honor" which accompanies the holder of power. Similarly, MacIver writes that "Power has thus its own worthiness, its value-in-itself, in various degrees according to its extent and its effectiveness."[56] If we view power as distributed along a continuum, with a continuum of "social honor" alongside it, the question of "scoring" the social honor continuum is worth considering. While there can be, by definition, no negative value for power (e.g., its complete absence is zero power, and any power at all results in a positive value), honor and esteem have a negative side—the continuum does not begin at a zero point denoting the absence of honor or total lack of esteem, but instead runs from negative values "dishonor" and "ill esteem" through the zero point of neither honor nor dishonor to the many degrees of honor and respect. An attempt to identify compatible points on the continua of power and honor suggests that a lack of power may provoke abhorrence and disrespect rather than a neutral reaction. In other words, referring specifically to the homeless population, society at large may fear and abhor the residents of skid row in part *because of their powerlessness.*

Powerlessness is tolerated in some statuses, notably infants, the very sick, and the mentally retarded. But since power is, in Hawley's phrase, "the capacity to produce results,"[57] and social life depends for its existence on the production of results, there are limits to the amount of powerlessness a social system can tolerate. The negative attitude of the general population toward skid row men may be based, in part, on the social abhorrence of powerlessness.

Power may be viewed as a property of social systems. Hawley says that "whatever power an individual might appear to possess is in effect *attached to the office he occupies in a system.*" Presthus makes the same point: "Individual power is always worked out within some larger framework of institutional power. . . . Men are powerful *in relation* to other men." He goes on to say that an individual derives his power from the social subsystems of power to which he belongs.[58] The connection between power and organization is specific. The powerless are persons without relations to other men or persons lacking offices within a system. In short, power derives from affiliations; the powerless are the disaffiliated.

There is empirical support for these statements. Studies of community power generally have shown that the most powerful persons are also the most active in organizations, that is, they tend to have more affiliations, or affiliations of greater scope, than their fellows. For instance, Barth and Abu-Laban were told that community leaders became leaders because of their activity in organizational work, and their respondents indicated that if such activity ceased, the top leadership positions would quickly be lost to others.[59] Leaders identified in community studies typically have high positions in the economic organization of their communities and often also are leaders in other areas. The implications of these findings for the power of the disaffiliated are clear. Activity and affiliation breed power and esteem. Inactivity and disaffiliation merit not merely low status, but negative status.

The link between effective goal-directed action and social affiliation has been noted before. In a recent study, a psychiatrist began with the idea that purpose in life was a crucial factor in mental health, and that people suffering from "existential frustration" or purposelessness would withdraw from interaction with others. He demonstrated that students with high scores on a Purpose-in-Life Test were more likely to belong to two or more formal organizations than students with low scores.[60] Robert E. Park made essentially the same point forty-five years earlier when he concluded that although social organization develops "in locomotion," the highly mobile hobo has few memberships because his mobility is without destination or firm goal; it is expressive, not instrumental.[61] In other words, mobility with destination is (or may be) an affiliating process; mobility without destination is likely to be a disaffiliating one.

Power is control over environment—both the physical and the social environment. In a real sense, power represents survival: Unless the individual can exercise a certain minimal level of control he is at the mercy of other people and of external forces. Without power he cannot satisfy his desires and needs, and his continued existence depends on the largesse of others more powerful than he. Power is a central, vital concept, one that needs little explanation to be seen as critical to life.

The concept of affiliation is less primary than that of power. Say that a man is powerless and at once we appreciate his plight and recognize the issue of survival; say that he is without affiliations and his status is obscure. Yet the two conditions are alike in their consequences.

Power is difficult to measure, but affiliations can be conceived as reflections of power. In summary: we are really talking about power, but power is manifest through organizations. We shall talk about disaffiliation, always recognizing that affiliations are so vital to social life because power is wielded through them. Organizations are the instruments by which men control the world, and their own destinies.

A homeless man lacks the power to influence others or to mold his own future. It is an unenviable, and at the same time, a threatening condition. Skid row is reputed to be full of men in this state.

A brief history of skid row

Homelessness may be as old as civilization, but skid row is an American invention. It is one century old, and its place of birth is clearly recorded. Jerry McAuley, "the first person in the world to open the doors of a religious institution every night of the year specifically for outcasts of society," began his Water Street Mission

in New York City in October 1872.[62] A year later the Reverend
John Dooley opened the first cheap Bowery lodging house. With
the appearance of these two dominant institutions, the gospel mission and the lodging house, skid row was born.

Of course there had been charitable work among the outcasts of
society before, but most of the institutions had catered to homeless
women or children or to particular occupational groups. Before
1850, several missions for seamen had been established on New
York's Lower East Side. The Five Points House of Industry, a mission where "wretched females" were given work, was established
in 1852, and by 1861 the institutions aimed at rescuing fallen
women or homeless children included The Howard Mission and
Home for Little Wanderers and The Midnight Mission.[63] But these
early institutions for the wretched and homeless cannot be cited as
literal ancestors of skid row because they did not cater to a male
clientele. McAuley's mission was the first aimed primarily at the
homeless man. A 1931 report stated that "the Water Street institution is known as the Mother of Missions, and can point to a dozen
or more missions in the city and over the country that may trace
their origin to 'old Water Street'."[64] As for Dooley, his first dormitory for homeless men soon became the Bowery branch of the
YMCA.[65]

Concentrations of facilities which catered to homeless men came
to be called "skid rows," the name deriving from the skidways on
which lumberjacks in the Northwest transported logs. In Seattle the
lodging houses, saloons, and other establishments were contiguous
to the "skid road" running from the top of the ridge down to
Henry Yesler's mill, and the term "skid road" was applied to the
community of the homeless. Transferred to other urban enclaves
of homeless men, it became "skid row."

In keeping with that origin, most researchers have identified skid
rows by virtue of the predominance of facilities for the homeless in
a given neighborhood. Bogue, for example, defined skid row as

. . . a district in the city where there is a concentration of substandard
hotels and rooming houses charging very low rates and catering pri-

marily to men with low incomes. These hotels are intermingled with numerous taverns, employment agencies offering jobs as unskilled laborers, restaurants serving low-cost meals, pawnshops and second-hand stores, and missions that daily provide a free meal after the service. Perhaps there are also barber colleges, burlesque shows or night clubs with strip tease acts, penny arcades, tattoo palaces, stores selling men's work clothing, bakeries selling stale bread, and unclaimed freight stores. Most frequently the Skid Row is located near the Central Business District and also near a factory district or major heavy transportation facilities such as a waterfront, freight yards, or a trucking and storage depot.[66]

Wallace's definition is that skid row is "an isolated and deviant sub-cultural community expressing the features of a distinct and recognizable way of life,"[67] and Blumberg, Shipley, and Moor add that

The Skid Row men are the dominant land-use population (although not the only one); that is, Skid Row men "live" there—it is *their* territory. The other land users in the area "live" elsewhere.[68]

Blumberg, Shipley, and Moor reject what they call the "categorical definition" of skid row. Instead, they emphasize the integration of skid row with other parts of a city, the similarity of its residents to people in other institutions, that people of skid row have counterparts in other parts of the city, and that many people who resemble skid row residents—who are "skid-row-like"—live elsewhere. Their frank intent is to define skid row in a way that will assist public policy and planning, and they emphasize that the differences between the skid row population and other poor and powerless people in metropolitan areas of the United States are not great. "Skid row is not so much a place as a human condition," they say, and to be a "skid row person" is to be poor, to live outside "normal" family relationships, to live in extremely low-cost housing, to have high probabilities of coming to police attention for behavior related to alcohol use, to be more vulnerable to victimization than other destitute people, to have a superficial style of social relations, and to have a prognosis for continued low status or even downward mobility.[69]

Home for the homeless: Reginald Marsh's "East Tenth Street Jungle" (1934).

There are thus two dominant approaches: the traditional view of skid row as a section of a city, a geographic place with coordinates in space and time, and the more recent perspective on skid row as a human condition. Blumberg, Shipley, and Moor's opting for the latter usage may make sense from a social labeling and policy point of view; stop labeling an area skid row and we may remove some of the stigma associated with its residents. No one denies that there are homeless people who live off skid row nor that there are bars, cheap hotels, and gospel missions elsewhere which serve non-skid-row people. We may agree with Blumberg, Shipley, and Moor that the differences between these "skid-row-like" people and the residents of the "natural area" of skid row are slight, but there is one very decisive distinction: The skid row people live on skid row territory, the others do not. In terms of the ecology of the city, the concentration of institutions and persons with homeless characteristics creates a neighborhood, a context, which is different from other regions of the city both in terms of symbolic nature (how people think about it, treat its residents, and relate to it) and in terms of population composition. Skid row may reflect a state of mind. But it is also a place, an area of the city, and those who frequent it are aware of its distinctive identity.

At least three dominant historical processes combined to produce the conditions leading to the establishment of skid rows in the United States. The first of these was the Civil War. Like all wars, it created homelessness on a vast scale, and many of those uprooted by the war—the orphaned, the impoverished, the widowed, the discharged soldiers—were drawn to the nation's cities. Second was the continuing European immigration. The poor and familyless migrants increased the pool of potentially homeless persons and the need for cheap lodging facilities in major cities. Third, there was the panic of 1873 and the depression which followed. During the depression the idea of setting up cheap dormitories or lodging houses caught on, and when prosperity returned the facilities created to serve the unemployed and outcast continued as fixed features of urban life.[70]

Other important historical processes which affected skid row were the closing of the frontier, a gradual decline in the need for unskilled labor, and collective upward mobility of whole occupational groups as they became unionized. Skid row reached its maturity around 1900, just as the frontier norms were passing from the American scene. For perhaps thirty years, these urban centers for the homeless enjoyed a ripe and sometimes energetic maturity. Skid rows were employment centers, recreational areas, supply and outfitting places, homes for seasonal and casual workers, and refuges for the deviant.

After the turn of the century this collection of employment, recreation, service and charitable institutions fused into a distinctive configuration characterized by a distinguishing set of life styles which constituted a new community form in America. The dominant life style was that of the hobo or migratory casual worker, and the flamboyant world of hobohemia flourished in urban skid-row areas and on the open road from approximately 1900 until 1930 when great numbers of disconsolate unemployed men invaded skid row and changed its character.[71]

Many of the homeless men who appeared on skid rows during the 1930's were temporarily, accidentally homeless, and did not want to maintain the status of homelessness any longer than was necessary. Skid row culture was diluted by the sudden intrusion of thousands of the temporarily homeless, and skid row never really recovered. In the year ending September 30, 1931, over one million lodgings were provided in Chicago. Estimates of the number of homeless persons in 1933 ranged from one and a half million to five million. But within a decade they were gone, lured away by new jobs in a recovering economy, fighting in a new world war.

By this time many of the hobos of the 1910's and 1920's were aging or gone, and there were new men to replace them. The veterans returned from the war, and their transition to civilian status was eased by a variety of imaginative federal programs. In contrast to the aftermath of previous wars, relatively few of them became permanent residents of skid row. The men who did drift there no longer were migratory workers, but instead were permanent residents, many of them local men. The role of migratory occupations as fields of recruitment for the homeless declined, and instead welfare institutions came to play a dominant role.

The political organizers of the earlier decades disappeared, and with them went interest in politics. Voting became an expression of indifference and apathy, an act sold for the price of a meal or a day's wine. Left behind were men who could not make it anywhere else, "losers" who blamed themselves for their failures rather than the workings of an imperfect economic system. The prevailing mood of skid row was no longer wanderlust, freedom, or protest, but instead acquiescence, passivity, and inertia. Even the hobo newspapers, songs and poems, and soapbox orators disappeared.[72]

In 1965 Wallace summed up the decades of change in the statement that skid row's function had shifted from employment pool to old age rest home. A few years later Rooney said that the aged, the ill, and the disabled seemed to be locating elsewhere and that in the future the primary function of skid row would be to serve as an open asylum for alcoholics and the psychically disabled.[73]

Whatever the final result, it is certain that over the past three decades the traditional skid row areas have steadily lost population. There may be temporary fluctuations linked to business recessions, but the general trend toward a gradual disappearance of skid rows will probably continue. Among the concomitants of the decline in the skid row population will be an increase in the number of multiple-problem persons there, higher rates of mental illness, alcoholism, and violent crime, and fewer clients for social control agents. The clients who remain will have more severe problems, or a wider variety of problems, and the chances of successful treatment will decline. Consequently, disappointment and frustration among social control agents on skid row can be expected to increase.[74]

Although the traditional skid rows may lose population, there is no evidence that the number of homeless persons in metropolitan areas will decline. Homeless persons will be "deprived" of their skid row subculture, and the "support" it provided. Presumably the skid row men in dispersion will be more likely to view themselves in terms of "normal" society's definitions. This may have positive consequences both for the treatment of homelessness and the problems associated with it.

Thus, some of them will not only appear sicker, but will also believe themselves to be sicker. In turn, away from the stigma of skid row, they will be more likely to look for help and more likely to get a profit from it. Similarly, again because of the gradual disappearance of skid row and some of its typical services, it will be increasingly harder for them to "make it" or to "get by" as homeless men.[75]

3 | Attitudes about homeless men

What do people think about skid row men? Surprisingly, in light of the large-scale investments in "control" of derelicts indicated by the high rates of arrest and imprisonment for public drunkenness, we cannot answer this question in any descriptive empirical sense. Little is known about the common man's rank order of degradation, or about which point on that scale is reserved for the skid row resident. Not that there is no evidence in *behavior*. The consequences of public behavior toward the homeless have been thoroughly documented. We might, from that behavior, make inferences about general attitudes toward the homeless. My own assessment of those attitudes, inferred from the treatment accorded and the mildness of public response to "the screams of the unwashed"[1] is that they consist of about five parts indifference, one part hostility, one part annoyance, and one part an amalgam of revulsion and morbid curiosity.

But I commit a grave sociological error. One of the well-attested findings of modern social psychology is that there is no one-to-one correspondence between behavior and attitudes. The relationship between them is very complex, affected by such things as the milieu in which the behavior occurs, its visibility, and the social constraints affecting the actor. If we cannot infer attitudes from behavior, then we must admit that, at present, the question which began this chapter cannot be answered with any confidence.

We can present some attitudes toward the homeless by drawing upon research about characteristics which skid row men are reputed to share with other segments of the population, e.g., studies of attitudes toward alcoholism, or by distilling from journalistic and literary accounts statements reflecting a writer's perceptions about the homeless. We will also draw upon some previously unpublished exploratory research. Following a brief statement about the components or underlying bases of attitudes toward homeless men—which include elements of attitudes toward alcoholics, disaffiliates, criminals, the poor, strangers, the disreputable, and the unredeemable—we shall consider in detail four perspectives, each relevant to the general topic of public attitudes about homeless men: 1. the essentially negative views of the experts who work among and treat skid row residents; 2. the more negative definitions in published statements by newspaper reporters and other professional writers and in community leaders' and institutional workers' responses to specific questions about homeless men and about "losers" ("people defeating themselves and failing"); 3. the themes apparent in magazine and newspaper cartoons; and 4. the public image of alcoholism as revealed in national and local surveys and in the pronouncements of advocates of the "disease concept."

Components of the stereotype

Even for persons most involved with the homeless, such as rehabilitation agents in treatment programs, the nature of attitudes toward skid row men remains largely unexplored. Existing studies tend to be illustrative and exploratory. This state of affairs reflects a dominant bias in social research on deviant behavior. Usually scientists have looked at the people marked as deviant, rather than at the "normal" representatives of society treating the "deviant" group, or even the general public. "People with problems" have been studied, but not those who treat them or those who pay for the treatment.

The emergence of labeling theory as a legitimate theoretical perspective has shifted the focus. Now questions about why certain behaviors are considered deviant, and by whom, are as valid as queries about why people "go astray" or how they commit forbidden acts. Unfortunately, the collection of systematic data to answer these questions lags far behind sociologists' excitement with the idea of asking them. Hence we must accept on faith statements like "No one is considered as beneath contempt by one and all as the 'Bowery Bum',"[2] although it does seem improbable that a majority of the general public would vote "Bowery Bum" the most reprehensible of a list of deviant statuses also including mass murderer, sex pervert, dope pusher, racist, pimp, and traitor.

There has been research about attitudes toward alcoholics. Of course most alcoholics are not homeless men. But the stereotype of chronic alcoholic *is* one of the stigma borne by skid row residents, and it is safe to assume that attitudes about skid row men are at least as negative as attitudes about alcoholics. Also available is a great deal of illustrative material revealing attitudes of professionals and other "experts" having personal experience with skid row. In a sense, every publication about skid row is a definition of the situation by an "expert." In addition, there are other valuable sources where revealing indications of attitudes about skid row or accounts of experience with the homeless may be found. Sunday School manuals, literary pieces, newspapers, and cartoons may make reference to the problems of vagrancy or homelessness.

Popular attitudes toward the homeless man, a relatively diffuse stimulus, are a melange of attitudes toward more specific stimuli, especially the outlaw, the hobo or migrant worker, the drunk, the derelict, and the stranger. There are some functional bases for the generalized distrust of the disaffiliate. It is not so much that he is a deviant as that he is outside the usual system of sanctions, and hence his behavior cannot be predicted with any certainty.

The stability of the larger system is threatened not by the continual forming and dissolution of bonds, but by the dissolution of bonds without the formation of new ones. The disaffiliate who does not reaffiliate moves beyond the power of particular organizations, and hence beyond that of society. He poses a threat because he has moved beyond the reward system; he is a man out of control. Being functionally if not actually devoid of significant others, property, and substantial responsibility, he is not subject to the usual social restraints. It is no threat to the fully disaffiliated man to threaten the forfeiture of his property, the imprisonment of his family, or the loss of his job. He has none of these. Perhaps the only sanction remaining is corporeal punishment, and in a system where the use of such punishment is minimized there is no way to control the retreatist *predictably*. He may go along with the rules, but there is no guarantee that he will do so, and because he is not part of the team, not privy to the conspiracy, he has no stake of any size in the continuance of the facade. He cannot be trusted.[3]

The threat which disaffiliation poses for a tightly organized social system is apparent in Mumford's description of personal survival and social attachment in the Middle Ages:

That unattached person during the Middle Ages was one either condemned to exile or doomed to death: if alive, he immediately sought to attach himself, at least to a band of robbers. To exist, one had to belong to an association: a household, a manor, a monastery, a guild; there was no security except in association, and no freedom that did not recognize the obligations of a corporate life.[4]

Another element in that composite "attitude toward the homeless" we are speculating about is one's attitude toward poverty, as poverty is by definition an attribute of the homeless. The propertied man is affiliated. At least he has ties with the keepers of his belongings. Mention of the relations between poverty and homelessness brings to mind Barnard Collier. Collier, a writer, hit the New York streets with sixty cents in his pocket and the assignment to write about how it felt to be down and out on the Bowery. At the end of the day, with three hours to kill before beginning a job, he decided to wait on a bench in Grand Central Station. He recorded his thought while sitting alone, thinking of himself as a bum and apparently being viewed as a bum by those around him.

I was thinking about how one's perception of people changes with circumstances. Many well-dressed men and many lovely women walked by as I sat there, but as a bum I must not notice them—out of self-defense. A bum is to be unnoticed and, more pertinent, unnoticing.[5]

Unnoticing, he was noticed. A policeman banged his night stick against the bench and asked what he was doing there. When Collier answered lamely that he was waiting for a relative, he was ordered out of the station. The police had never treated him that way before, even though he had let his beard grow, worn the same clothes, and been without money. Besides, he had recently bathed. Collier's perplexed question: "Does *thinking* poor emit radiations that summon the police?"[6] In answer, note the comments of a writer who several decades earlier had passed as a homeless woman in London and recorded her feelings about the radiations emitted by the poor:

By these, my own experiences, I learned how easy it is to form cruelly wrong conclusions from certain obvious facts. A straight glance of the eye, a clear tone in the voice, an assumed and ready bearing; these are but the manifestations of a well-fed life. Take away your regular meals, your comfortable bed, your sense of security, and you will find yourself like any other outcast, slinking along the pavement, shrinking from attention, utterly void of that self-confidence which is the hall mark of success.[7]

The "hopelessness" of the skid row man, the "non-redeemability" of his condition forms an important part of the public stereotype of the skid row resident. Skid row men refer to themselves as "forgotten men," the obvious implication being that they have been forgotten by members of the wider society because they are not worth remembering.

There is little expectation that anything can be done to make these men members of the "respectable" community again. The missions, the police, and the occasional nonreligious charity organizations have been left to do any "reforming" they can, and their small success is thought to affirm the impressions that these men are hopeless. In this, as in other stereotypes, there is just enough truth to make the whole stereotype appear convincing.[8]

Residents of skid row share the stereotype that the "true" skid row man is unredeemable, and so resist the identity of skid row man. Jackson and Connor observed that "being a skid row resident is not incorporated easily into the self-conception of the alcoholic." They saw the avoidance of self-definition as skid row man as critical to the potential for successful treatment. "Reaching bottom" was explicitly identified as a state of mind, a psychological crisis which occurred when the alcoholic recognized that his residence of skid row was not temporary, that he "belonged" there.[9]

The attitudes of experts

In a provocative paper entitled, "The Construction of Conceptions of Stigma by Professional Experts,"[10] Robert A. Scott notes that historically an assortment of defectives, including the mentally ill, the poor, and the disabled, have been stigmatized as moral inferiors, viewed as helpless dependents, ostracized from normal society, punished, and degraded. In the last century there has been a trend toward treating persons formerly stigmatized as defective and hopeless as if they were rehabilitable. Responsibility for care and definition of these defectives has moved from family and community to experts trained in rehabilitation. Accordingly, the defectives are now stigmatized not only by community definition but by the professional experts' ideas about the nature of their defectiveness. The experts' theories about the nature of the stigmatization, and the attempted operationalization of those theories by the clinicians, have become critical determinants of the self-concept of the one being rehabilitated and of society's reaction to him. But the accepted theories vary from place to place and time to time, demonstrating the social nature of definitions of so "simple" a phenomenon as blindness, let alone a more complex status such as alcoholism or homelessness.

In the United States most efforts at rehabilitation focus on the individual deviant. In some sense, the "deviant" is held responsible for his behavior. Rehabilitation methods aim at helping him understand himself, the assumption being that increased insight will allow him to solve his problems. Corrective efforts are "distinctly individualistic" and usually "normals" do not participate in organized rehabilitation efforts. Consequently such efforts tend to be unsuccessful. According to Scott,

. . . the origins of such (deviant) behavior lie not only in the personality and early socialization of the deviant but in the reactions that normals have to him as well. This growing body of research on labeling indicates that corrective measures are not likely to succeed if they are aimed only at the personality of the deviant, but do not attempt to modify the reactions that others have toward him.[11]

Professional experts' conceptions of stigma are not necessarily truer or more accurate than the notions of laymen, and they are shaped by numerous forces independent of empirical "reality." Scott discusses four of these external forces. First, there are the prevailing cultural values. Experts are members of society, they are exposed to the organizing ideas of their time, and their conceptions are necessarily related to the core values of their culture. Rehabilitation programs must have financial support from members of society and involve citizens other than the stigmatized. Accordingly, laymen's values affect the construction of expert meanings of stigma insofar as the laymen control the sources of funds, or are in other ways necessary as supporters of programs. In addition,

Stigma threatens the community and presents it with unpleasant problems it would rather not confront or think about. . . . A community's needs relating to stigmata may be to hide them from public view, or at least to dress them up in a way that makes them more palatable to laymen or at least less offensive to them.[12]

Thus, laymen's conceptions about homelessness and skid row help to determine the treatment of skid row residents.

Another factor affecting the construction of experts' meanings of stigma is the process of professionalization. Differences in ideologies persist, professional claims to expertise must be "staked out" or guarded against encroachment from other disciplines, and there must be an accommodation between the professionals and workers trained by practical experience. The former tend to be more flexible, the latter limited to expertise that is technique- and organization-specific. Organizational loyalties and self-interests of these experts combine to affect the meanings of stigma and the accepted modes of treatment: "untrained experts will evolve meanings that give primary emphasis to specific techniques and will guarantee the survival of the organization for which they work."[13]

The bureaucratic nature of the rehabilitation organization also has an impact upon expert conceptions of deviant behavior and societal reactions to it. Bureaucratic necessity spawns legal or administrative defintions of impairment, and then the legal definitions become the "real" definitions. Use determines reality; "thinking makes it so" in the world of definitions. The expert is supposed to know more about the client's "problem" than the client does, and if there are discrepancies between his definitions and the client's subjective reaction to his condition, the expert's definitions are likely to prevail. He is trained to help the impaired, and it follows that those who seek his aid must regard themselves as defective. The reshaping of a client's self-perception becomes a matter of doctrine: ". . . truly effective rehabilitation and adjustment can only occur after the client has squarely faced and accepted the 'fact' that he is, indeed, impaired."[14]

The clients themselves have some impact on the experts' notions of the nature of their stigmatization and the proper ways to deal with it. However, because the stigmatized client usually does not pay for the services he receives, he is comparatively powerless in changing the programs which serve him. Supposedly designed for him, the rehabilitation programs are more responsive to a variety of external interests and organizations than to the "deviant." The experts are free to tailor their definitions of the situation to bureaucratic, professional, and sociocultural pressures at the expense of the client.

Scott concludes that "expert meanings have little significance in preindustrial and developing nations" because there they are outweighed by the impact of traditional conceptions of stigma, but "in most highly industrialized nations they [experts' definitions] are posing a genuine challenge to traditional ideas about stigma," and in some countries the experts' views are now the dominant ones.[15] Another major conclusion is that, over time, the behavior of stigmatized persons comes to correspond with the assumptions and beliefs of the experts. The "self-fulfilling prophecy" creates deviant behavior congruent with the accepted social definitions of deviance.

The attitudes of professional rehabilitators toward skid row men and the corresponding attitudes of the men toward the rehabilitators have been highlighted by Wiseman.[16] Although skid row men would like to be helped and rehabilitators would like to help them, interaction breeds hostility rather than solidarity. The helper expects gratitude; the helped expect compassion. But the rehabilitators reserve compassion for the "worthy"—those whose situation is not their own fault, who respond in "acceptable" ways, and who manifest some improvement ("success") as a result of the help. The skid row men reserve gratitude for those helpers who give them gifts, as opposed to services which are theirs by right. In addition, each feels betrayed by the other; the skid row man because he is promised therapy or charity when there is none, and the rehabilitator because he is cheated and conned by an apparently insincere client.

Agents of social control view their clients with a combination of exasperation, anger, and despair. The skid row alcoholic sees the operators of the loop in which he is moving as heartless, insincere, and lacking in compassion for his problems.[17]

Maintenance of negative attitudes in a public shelter. Henshaw's description of relations between social workers and homeless men at the Men's Shelter in Manhattan illustrates how hostility is created and maintained between the skid row men and their "helpers." The negative attitudes of staff members toward their homeless clients are apparent both in how they treat the men they serve and what they say about them.

Most of the men who apply receive aid of some sort, but interviewers refuse men every day. The main reasons for being refused aid involve the client's failure to perform certain role obligations imposed by the shelter. These reasons include failure to seek other sources of support, such as unemployment benefits; failure to report to a clinic to which he was referred; being intoxicated to the extent that an interview is impossible; attempting to short-cut the shelter procedure by approaching an interviewer before being called; failure to report to an agency to which he was referred for a job, or failure to accept a job that was offered; and being abusive or disrespectful to the shelter staff.

· · ·

The procedure for obtaining aid normally takes a client from one and a half to three hours. He enters the first floor and depending on how crowded the social service area is, may be allowed to proceed to the third floor or may be required to wait in a large, bare room with a concrete floor and no chairs or benches. If many men are waiting, they may form a line. Periodically, the first twenty men in the line are escorted to the third floor. Once there, the client waits at one window to identify himself to the social worker. Then he sits down and waits for between one and two hours until his name is called. The waiting clients usually do not talk to each other; when they do, they are sometimes told to be quiet.

Eventually the client's turn comes, and he is interviewed at one of the windows like a bank customer standing at a teller's window. The clients' names are distributed randomly to the interviewers, so there is no continuity in the social worker–client relationship. The interviews average about three minutes, much of which time is spent by the interviewer in filling out forms. Often few questions are asked, it being understood by the interviewer that the client wants lodging and meals for thirty days. If the client has not been to the shelter for a period of time, however, he is asked how he maintained himself during the interim and why he cannot continue to do so. Frequently the interview assumes the tone of a cross-examination in which the client tries to justify himself and the interviewer attempts to force some kind of admission or catch him in a contradiction.

Relations between the social workers and clients are abrasive and sometimes hostile. Clients are expected to be respectful of the officials, accurate in the information given, sober, and well-behaved. One client was told to say "sir" when addressing the interviewers. Another client who had last come to the shelter in 1962 was severely reprimanded because he said he had never come before. One client, when asked how to spell his name, said brashly, "That's what you're here for, isn't it?" The interviewer became furious, said something like "you've shot your wad, buster" and refused him service. On one client's record, it was noted that one evening he came to the Shelter intoxicated and attacked a particular policeman. When he returned to the Shelter a year later, he was not served until he apologized to the police officer.

Several times a day, a loud argument arises between one or more interviewers and a client. Clients were never observed to support each other in an argument with the Shelter officials. On one occasion, an administrator called the supervisor on duty to object to the shouting of an interviewer. The administrator was evidently able to hear the incident from his desk at the far end of the floor. The supervisor admitted that shouting is not proper social procedure, but he defended the interviewer on the grounds that the incident was particularly frustrating to the interviewer.

By way of contrast, voices are never raised at the Case Unit, which is located by the desks of the shelter executives. Here the client sits by the social worker's desk rather than standing at the window. No incidents were observed in which the social workers were angry or the clients deviant at the Case Unit.

The social workers do not appear to feel much pressure to shorten the time a client must wait to be interviewed. If the waiting room is full, the interviewers need not worry because any additional men will be kept out of sight on the first floor. A rule is in effect that not more than twenty clients per interviewer on duty will be allowed to wait on the third floor. The general attitude was illustrated by one social worker when a loud argument broke out next to him. He walked away from his client in the middle of the interview and said, "I can't work under these conditions." He lit a cigarette and chatted with a researcher for about half an hour without showing any concern for the client who was standing at his window.

The long waiting period for clients serves the function of discouraging men who do not feel a strong desire for aid. When one social worker gave directions to a "first-timer" (a man who is applying for aid for the first time), he commented to a researcher, "He probably won't wait to get served. He'll wait through that line (to the receptionist's window) but when he sees that he will have to sit and wait with all these men, he will give up. Most first-timers do."

If the interviewers are harsh and demanding in their handling of the clients, this is partly because the clients frequently are stupid, hostile, demanding, deceptive, or otherwise difficult. One client, for example, gave his name as John Henry. The clerk could not find the right record, and the man was again asked his name. This time he mentioned that his last name was Jones, "But people mostly just call me John Henry. . . ." Some clients do not answer questions directly but just repeat confused stories and explanations. It frequently happens that a client will come to a window and ask to be served before his name is called. One client became angry and began shouting that he had been waiting for two hours, and that he was going to report them to the Department of Welfare at Church Street. After about fifteen minutes of yelling, he was ushered away by a policeman. Some clients refuse to leave the window if their demands are not satisfied. One case was observed in which the client tried to reach under the windows and grab the interviewer's papers; he did not leave until a policeman took him away.

Wherever possible, the official policy is to require a client to present proof of important facts. For example, if a man might be eligible for UIB (Unemployment Insurance Benefits), he will be given a meal ticket for one day and told that he must bring proof that he applied for UIB before being given more aid. When a decision on his UIB case is reached, he must show proof that he was rejected. In practice, however, the interviewers can give aid at their discretion, and they do not always follow the formal procedures for requiring proof. For example, one interviewer disburses change for carfare for men who need to take public transportation to a clinic, a government office, or an employment agency. The established procedure is for him to hold the client's meal ticket until the client returns and presents proof that he appeared at the clinic or office. However, in many, and perhaps most cases the interviewer does not hold the client's meal ticket. In another case, a man had been refused assistance four times over a period of three weeks because he could not produce proof that he had applied for UIB. However, he was given assistance on the fifth attempt, even though he still could not prove that he had applied for UIB.

Interpersonal friction between the social workers was also evident, and morale was low. Three of the social workers indicated to the researcher that they would transfer to Camp LaGuardia if personal considerations did not hold them in New York City. One interviewer refused to work on a Saturday even though his supervisor said that this might result in the imposition of a formal rotation system. Hostile jokes about their mental health and need for rehabilitation frequently pass between the officials. Some of the social workers like to create false case records with unusual names (for example, Frank Instein) in the hopes that other interviewers will call out the names before realizing that they have been fabricated. Fortunately, the interviewers are not particularly interdependent, and the interpersonal friction was not observed to interfere with the functioning of the department.

The interviewers also make disparaging comments to each other about the clients. One typical exchange went something like this: "Did you ever notice that these 5 by 8's smell like vomit?" "No, it's worse than that. Only our clients could smell that bad."[18]

Thus, the singularly consistent labeling of the skid row man as defective and unredeemable is common even among the professionals whose function is to treat the deviant. Therapists who treat problem drinking are described by Pittman and Gillespie as holding a two-category view of their clients. One category includes the problem drinkers who have disease and must be helped; the other contains the drunks or skid rowers who are hopeless and not worth treating. "This means that the public drunkenness offender cannot expect to find tolerance even among professionals who are reputed to be among the more tolerant groups in the field of alcoholism."[19]

"Reality Adjustment" among treatment staff. The failure of skid row men is contagious. Most attempts to reform the chronic alcoholic fail, and so professionals who work with them must modify their own definitions of what constitutes "success" or else be implicated in the homeless men's continued dereliction. Wiseman has described the "reality adjustment" of staff members in two treatment facilities: an outpatient therapy clinic linked to a county jail and a mental hospital. She documents how failure to achieve a program's original ideals and purposes leads to "protective" redefinition of the situation which allows the professional to maintain a positive image of himself and his methods.[20] Where blame must be assigned in the redefined situation, the homeless man's defective nature is a major target. Thus, the staff at the jail branch's outpatient clinic in Pacific City identified as one barrier to their success the "chronic drunk's lack of amenability to group therapy." In-

mates are described as insincere, apathetic, hostile, immature, and manipulative.[21]

At the mental hospital the allocation of blame toward the patients was somewhat more diffuse, in that the program explicitly acknowledged the incurability of alcoholism under present knowledge and treatment procedures.[22] Yet even when the lack of adequate knowledge for treatment is identified as the major element in the failure of a rehabilitation program, the client still is labeled defective. He is, for the present at least, *incurable*. Staff members are resigned to recidivism; in its effects on the patient, alcoholism is compared to cancer, and therapists are to be congratulated for controlling the symptoms of the disease. That permanent stigmatization is part of the therapist's view of the alcoholic he treats is clear in statements such as "alcoholism and the reaction to alcohol is a progressive disease which goes on whether they drink or not." Also, "you can expect to see these guys over and over. The best way to look at it is to be glad that you can do something for them to lengthen their lives."[23]

Another professional in contact with homeless men is the worker in the skid row mission. The assistant superintendent of a mission in Chicago is described as watching his charges file in "as a production manager might watch the assembly line, falcon-eyed for the alcoholic flaw." His face and bearing suggest that "mercy is not promiscuously squandered upon this alterant flock," and his attitudes about homeless men and the causes of homelessness are plain:

A good many of these are non-conformists. They've deliberately opted out. Their line of least resistance is to say "I don't need you or anything." A lot of them are weak-willed individuals all the same. They don't hold a job because they have no purpose in working except to exist. They're content to rest, to go into taverns, buy a few drinks and feel like a big shot for a moment.

They idealize themselves. They think there's romance in being on the road. They're picture book heroes in their own mind, that's the only way they can make something of themselves, by seeing themselves as gallant, bold individuals and by thinking they're showing their families that they're really roughing it out.

The trouble is that life's too easy here in America. In Europe and countries where food is hard to come by, every crumb of bread is of value. Here they scoff at it. Everywhere else in the world you have to struggle for existence. Here you can go anywhere and make it.

. . .

We treat them here like gentlemen. If they have any gumption at all, they want to get over the hump and we try to help them, to make them feel they are somebody. But a lot see themselves as tied down to the drudgery of factory machines and can't take it. They don't think about tomorrow. They just stop fighting. They're not ashamed about that. They don't see themselves as humble. They see themselves as big shots. Big shots on skid row.[24]

Professional views of alcoholism. Despite the lip service paid to the disease concept of alcoholism, or perhaps to the stigmatization which accompanies the disease, there is much evidence that professionals who treat alcoholics exhibit negative attitudes which counteract the possible benefits of the therapies they prescribe. A survey of social workers in New York City revealed that one out of four admitted feelings of annoyance when confronted by a drunken stranger. One-sixth were fearful, and one-ninth were "disgusted" by drunkenness. Social workers who had worked with alcoholics or knew them personally were likely to be more favorable in their attitudes, but even among these only about 40 per cent gave the socially positive response of sympathy or understanding when asked about their attitudes toward a drunken stranger. Recognizing the social desirability biases in these self-reports—it takes an exceptionally honest, self-aware social worker to deny that he is sympathetic and understanding—it is apparent that an inebriate's chances of receiving compassionate understanding from a social worker are much less than 50–50.[25]

When the social workers were asked to rate kinds of treatment for alcoholics, Alcoholics Anonymous received the largest number of favorable ratings, followed by group therapy, individual psychotherapy, and psychoanalysis. Fifty-eight per cent of the raters gave a favorable rating to AA, compared to 49 per cent, 43 per cent, and 32 per cent, respectively, for the modes of psychiatric treatment. Social casework was rated as a good treatment by one-fifth of the caseworkers, medical treatment was rated as good by one-eleventh of them, and pastoral counseling by only 6 per cent. However, when the respondents gave their opinions about the prognosis for alcoholics treated by those methods they had rated "good," no more than 30 per cent expected a favorable outcome from any of the methods. Of the almost 300 respondents who had worked with alcoholics and their families, only 16 per cent rated their own efforts as "moderately effective." The researchers summarized their findings:

They tended to regard nonpsychiatric treatment methods, with the exception of Alcoholics Anonymous, as relatively ineffective and to be pessimistic about prognosis, no matter what the treatment method. Few respondents rated social casework as an effective method, and those who had worked with alcoholics usually expressed frustration and disappointment at the limited results they felt they had achieved. This is not only a gloomy picture, but one far more extreme than authorities in the field of alcoholism, on the basis of their experience, believe to be warranted.[26]

Another study of social workers revealed more optimism about the efficacy of treatment. Approximately three-fifths of a sample of caseworkers from three family casework agencies in New York City agreed that "the majority of alcoholics can recover with treatment." Regarding treatment preferences, over 60 per cent of the caseworkers agreed that some form of "insight therapy" was necessary before an alcoholic could stop drinking and that such insight would lead directly to a decrease in drinking. As for motivation for treatment, approximately half agreed that motivation under external duress was often effective, and the same proportion blamed the alcoholic for failing to stay in treatment.[27]

Between one-third and one-half of these caseworkers held "moralistic" attitudes about alcoholism, in that they attributed excessive drinking to a lack of willpower, and stated that the alcoholic was responsible for his alcoholism.[28] Similar "anti-disease-concept" attitudes are held by many physicians and other health professionals who do not recognize alcoholism as an illness. There is research suggesting that physicians rely almost exclusively on physical symptoms in diagnosing alcoholic patients, and that they share the derelict image of the alcoholic.[29] One physician has summarized the dilemma facing most of the medical profession:

. . . the group for which the disease concept has created the most problems is the medical profession itself. "Alcoholism is a disease" may be a very nice statement for public consumption; but once something is declared a disease, then there is an implication that it is up to the doctor to treat it, and that the doctor will be able to treat it with some prospect of success. Here we have created a gap between society's definition of alcoholism as a disease and the doctor's willingness to deal with it. *The medical profession today is less ready to accept the disease concept than is the public at large.* Even though the executive of the American Medical Association has declared alcoholism a disease (the Canadian Medical Association has not), physicians by and large feel that the whole problem has been thrown into their laps without their wanting it.[30]

A positive view: skid row man as "the poor in spirit." Philip O'Connor devotes a chapter of his *Britain in the Sixties: Vagrancy* to a discussion of "Attitudes to Vagrants." He claims there is a general ambivalence among officials who must deal with vagrants, helping to "rehabilitate" them into active competition with their fellows, when at heart the officials may question the virtue or integrity of the competitive society they serve. The officials represent a particular stress point in the relationships between society and the homeless, for their position enables them to see that their clients are the "poor in spirit" and manifest the Christian ethic better than more "normal" members of society. O'Connor recognizes that the official role is a difficult one and points out that "we must also look for the martyr aspect of the officials, many of whom want to do good."[31]

"Happy Ex-C.P.A.," this photograph was titled. The subject, aged fifty-four, said he slept in doorways and gathered bottles. He had been beaten up the previous week. "I'm a C.P.A.," he told the photographer. "I got a license." (Bowery, New York City, 1963.)

The policy of officials of the National Assistance Board toward vagrants is that "self-helpers shall be helped." In practice, the officials tend to be tolerant, and the condition of vagrancy is viewed as something for which a man is not really to blame. Vagrants are seen as undesirable failures rather than wicked persons. Statements by officials frequently referred to the men as "misfits," who "apparently want to avoid the hardness of realism." Men who visit the Reception Centres (public shelters) are viewed as fugitives from their wives and families, or simply men who have found life easier by using Reception Centre facilities than by fending for themselves.

O'Connor summarized and evaluated the rehabilitation formula of the Salvation Army: "Social delinquency and failure are a lapse from grace which, found again, brings social security; the formula is pure magic and, as we know, in the long run ineffectual."[32] He also quotes from a discussion with a Brahman and a Jesuit who contrast the tramp ethic with Christian and Calvinist ideas about work and poverty. The tramp is seen as a symbol of escape from the futile, competitive, dehumanizing effects of "existing social arrangements."[33]

O'Connor concludes his chapter with a discussion of statements by "dedicated persons" who run private charitable missions. One of them, said to exemplify "perhaps the most advanced human virtue" (permissiveness), defined his role as making his clients as comfortable as possible, recognizing their crises and deprivation, and trying to provide friendship as well as modest material aid. It was the friendship his clients needed most:

They are not quite sure whether we are really sincere, and whether we can stand anything, and so they will try one thing after another, until at last they begin to see that nothing that they can do can really stop our friendship.[34]

The essence of the pastors' approach is an absence of condemnation.

But the type of man who comes to us not only needs justice, he needs charity.

. . .

The thing is that they value their freedom more than any kind of regimentation or kindness they may receive from hospital nurses and doctors.

. . .

I don't think they should be condemned out of hand for being in fact what they are . . . it's not sufficient to say simply that these men are lazy, and write them off as good-for-nothings.

. . .

If a man has itchy feet and can't settle down, there is nothing immoral in that. In other forms of society, nomadic societies, it's the chap who wants to settle down who's the misfit. I don't think we ought to blame the men therefore who move from town to town and job to job, almost by instinct.[35]

For O'Connor, it is not enough merely to adopt a permissive attitude toward the tramp. For him, the vagrant represents a man living sensibly; it is society that is out of step, and society as presently established will ultimately give way to the society that the vagrant represents. "Vagrants in cooperation with other authentic outsiders could well become a small nucleus of the kind of society that must, one day, cover the earth. . . . What has made them fail in our society might well make them succeed in a foretaste of the one to come."[36]

The idea that the staff of the Rehabilitation Centres might be able to reform the vagrant is repugnant to O'Connor.

In terms of "spiritual wisdom," . . . they are inferior to the vagrant; it is an eye-witness's experience that the staff are "spiritually" inferior to the trainees. . . . The congenital assumption of the staffs on these establishments is that the vagrant status is senseless, and even a little insane, whereas . . . it is profoundly reflective of the poverty of our society . . . The "self" of the vagrant, which is so much advanced beyond the "self" that the world "respects" and asks us to "respect," is completely unattended or overtly condemned.[37]

Laymen's views of the homeless and alcoholic

The public's view of homeless persons seems to derive mainly from family and community socialization, and is sustained and modified by the communications media. Our attempt to sketch the dimensions of popular attitudes about homeless men will draw upon newspaper accounts, responses of community leaders and private citizens, portrayals of skid row men by writers and cartoonists, and surveys of public attitudes toward alcoholism.

Portrayals in the press. One of the dominant responses to skid row people is fear, and fear prompts avoidance. A naive observer from a rural community embodies these elements in her reactions to homeless men in Chicago.

We went through "skid row" and saw a "gutter" man which was to be picked up by the paddy wagon when the police see him. There are supposed to be a lot of those men on the street who have passed out from drunkenness. I'm glad we only saw one. I wouldn't dare walk down that street because I was scared just looking at the people.[38]

This observer's fear should not be attributed to her naiveté. More experienced citizens, long-term metropolitan residents, frequently expressed the same emotions. Newspaper accounts call a place derelicts inhabit a "house of horrors," their approach in panhandling "the touch of terror," their presence an "infection" or "a blot on the city." Officials warn, "Don't give money to street beggars, not even when they are blind or lame or appear to be wretched or pitiable."[39] Common terms for homeless men, either "bum" or "derelict," are linked with other negative labels. When the New York City Transit Authority decided to wall off a Times Square subway arcade because "they could no longer cope with the crime and immorality there," one of the reasons given was that the arcade was a "breeding place of crime": "pickpockets, thugs, derelicts, and homosexuals use it as a meeting-place."[40]

Imagine the negative consequences for the public image of homelessness deriving from an article entitled "Wave of Bums Sweeps over Parks, Streets." Subtitled "The Touch of Terror," the article included the following information about the homeless.

Dirty, disheveled, sometimes dangerous and often traveling in packs, an unprecedented number of panhandlers and bums drift daily around New York City.

. . .

Bus Terminal at night: ". . . Junkies, panhandlers, homosexuals, drunks, drifters trying to sleep. . . . By midnight it was a gallery of disagreeable figures, a study in depravities."

Many of the new breed are in their 20's—though most of the young ones appear much older because of the deadly effects of a steady diet of cheap wine and little food.

A team of World-Telegram reporters has ranged through New York day and night for the past six weeks, seeking out the beggars and homeless drifters with neither the will nor energy to work.

They found that many of the young alcoholic drifters are potentially violent and will threaten passersby who turn down their touch.

They came across case after case involving hostile derelicts—a passerby threatened by a bum with a broken beer bottle on W. 44th Street in midafternoon; a couple dining at a sidewalk cafe near Gramercy Park menaced by a pair of derelicts armed with a hammer.

. . .

One Greenwich Village mother—typical of mothers all over town—said she no longer dares take her 12-year-old daughter into Washington Square Park because of the noisy bums who gather there in packs, drink from common bottles of cheap, sweet wine and harass passersby.[41]*

The use of words usually applied to animals rather than humans is remarkable. Note in the above quotation that the "noisy bums" gather in "packs," not bands or groups, and that the term is applied both by the reporter in the first paragraph of his article and in his quotation from the typical mother. Later in the same article a verb usually applied to insects was used: vagrants were said to have "swarmed" to the city.

The professional rehabilitation agents seem to share the view that skid row men are less than human. A journalist quotes the director of a relocation center for alcoholics as saying: "We are trying to make them social beings again after skid row has dehumanized them."[42]

It is a short step from the dehumanized to the demonic. Derelicts are compared to ghosts or evil spirits; their influx into a bus terminal turns it "into a kind of haunted house."[43] Again, they are linked with other deviant types: "junkies, panhandlers, homosexuals, drunks, drifters trying to sleep, and small bands of roving

* From *New York World Telegram and Sun,* November 1, 1961. Reprinted by permission.

youths" are said to gather and increase, and "as it gets later, it gets gamier." (An adjective for *human* gatherings? Permissible, perhaps, but full of antiderelict connotation.) At midnight the terminal becomes "a gathering of disagreeable figures, a study in depravities." A citizen describes the terminal as "seething with degenerates of all types."[44] The disagreeables are there to beg, leer, lurk, skulk, or strut, but most are characterized as desolate strangers, nuisances not menaces, who "sought nothing more than to be left alone."

In addition to alarm over violence and depravity, and the possibility of confrontations with animals and fiends in human form, there is a very real sense of competition for urban space. Skid row men are seen as "polluting" an area, so that it is not fit for other urbanites. The usual response to this "pollution" is to call for police action to "throw the bums out." The competition with the homeless for space extends even to condemned buildings. The destruction of an abandoned tenement building was the occasion for a neighborhood celebration because "bums and addicts" had slept in the house. As demolition workmen attacked the walls with crowbars and sledgehammers, onlooking children, shopkeepers, and parents helped "with encouraging shouts." Before the demolition the neighborhood was described as "helplessly awaiting a tragedy—either from the frequent fires (apparently caused by the irresponsibility of the homeless residents) or the degenerates who took up residence in the empty building." As the "House of Horrors" was demolished, a resident who had "feared new violence" approved. "Thank heaven. Now we can sleep soundly."[45]

The real competition is for space in public parks. An example is the battle for Washington Square Park in Greenwich Village. Village residents are described as "being driven from their favorite benches . . . by alcoholic derelicts, narcotic addicts, and sexual perverts." A legislator remarked, "Today you're just not safe from the scum that infests the Park." The president of New York University, which adjoins the park, commented that it was not possible "to run a university surrounded by degradation." Questioned about the rights of "the degenerates in the park," a resident remarked,

"Sure they have civil rights . . . but so do we family people. The problem of Washington Square has nothing to do with civil rights or racial discrimination. . . . The park has been defiled by the worst crumbs of both races, Negro and white."[46] Other writers have described derelicts as "overrunning" many small parks. Sometimes officials have recognized that the parks are homes for the derelicts. Proposed solutions to the competition are that the homeless be "kept out of the city or put somewhere." Otherwise, local residents may be unable to use a park "because of the quality of the people who do use it."[47]

One solution practiced in New York City is increased police action. "Village Assured of Added Police," reads one headline; "Park Patrols to get Plain Clothes Details and More Scooters," says another. Plain clothes details are described as especially effective "because undesirables would have no warning of their arrival."[48] A final solution practiced by a Brazilian police officer was to kill derelicts and beggars. He was sentenced to 136 years in prison for murdering 14 of them.[49]

In the past decade several events have enhanced the image of skid row as a place where depraved, violent men hide and plot. Richard Speck, convicted murderer of eight Chicago nurses, was living in a skid row lodging house when arrested. James Earl Ray, assassin of Martin Luther King, lived in a lodging house before the crime and was identified as a sometime skid row resident. Michael Natale, armed with a loaded revolver and a hunting knife, attempted to enter the Soviet Mission while Russian premier Kosygin was there. He was apprehended and identified as a resident of a Bowery hotel.[50] Joseph Grimaldi, the cryptic "Mister Z" of a plot to extort $100,000 from Trans World Airlines and who threatened to destroy "not less than one airliner" was identified in a national news magazine as a Bowery man.[51] Thus, labeled as misfits, degenerates, scum, subhumans who "swarm" and run in "packs," linked with mass murder, political assassinations, violence, and theft, described as vandals and polluters, eyesores and health hazards, imposing terrors on honest citizens, homeless men are a national problem crying for a "solution" of some kind. They are to be kept out, chased away, locked up, segregated in some place with "others of their kind." They even pollute the libraries.

At almost any hour it is impossible to enter (the New York Public Library at 42nd Street and Fifth Avenue) without being assailed in the third floor reference and reading rooms by smells horrific enough to make any normal person ill.

. . .

Then there are the derelicts, usually aged men, ragged and shattered by drink and poverty, who have come in from the outside cold to huddle together on the marble benches adjacent to the reading room entrance. It is embarrassing to describe what all of these individuals, young and old, smell like, and what they smell from. They *smell,* and one cannot get away from it or them, no matter how far to the rear of the North and South wings one hastens for relief. I am now taking a course in sprinting.

The reeking adolescents are one thing. But how can anyone have anything but pity for the poor old souls who have no other place to go and in the warmth of a public building are simply trying to find surcease from the nasty sting of a bitter day? At the same time, how can one be grateful that such refuge is available for others and still go about his research without having his nostrils assaulted by a reastiness awful enough to make him retch?

Certainly the subject is not a nice one. But shouldn't it be discussed? Because what is offensive in the main library must be no less prevalent in the branches, and in our many public museums. Is it unreasonable to hope something may be done about it?[52]

Characteristics of homeless men perceived by Manhattan civic and church leaders. In May 1964, a brief questionnaire was mailed to 205 representatives of Manhattan's Catholic parishes, public libraries, and civic and neighborhood social service associations in an attempt to locate the homeless men in New York City and to help characterize neighborhood reactions to their presence.[53] Recipients of the questionnaire were chosen from listings in the Manhattan classified telephone directory under "Churches—Roman Catholic," "New York Public Library," and from a list of more than 100 city and private agencies. The survey was intended to produce some "leads" for exploratory fieldwork, and sufficient information for project purposes was obtained from the 57 questionnaires returned. There were no attempts to increase the response rate via follow-up mailings. The low rate of return did not justify a detailed statistical analysis. However, responses to several questions illustrated the beliefs of agency administrators and other community influentials.

Almost all respondents were aware of some homeless men in their neighborhood. Most said that the men were more in evidence during the warm weather. However, awareness of homeless men did not seem to provoke interest in providing "solutions" to homelessness at the neighborhood level. Responses of agents of social service societies and neighborhood associations indicated that their clientele was well and narrowly defined, and contact with the homeless man was limited and unsympathetic. The agencies generally focused their attention on specific groups or problems in the neighborhood, thus excluding the drifters and transients. A few officials mentioned that they did offer occasional material or counseling help to homeless men; other responses ranged from "organization does not deal with this problem" and "they are usually ignored" to the active hostility of chasing the men or calling the police. The homeless man was not *their* problem.

Most of the clergymen said that they provided some assistance to transient and homeless men. Some offered money, food, clothing, and spiritual counsel. Meal tickets, generally reserved for use at Bowery Catholic Missions, were the most common offering, and referrals to Bowery lodgings or shelters the usual guidance. Several clergymen explained that their resources and facilities were designed for parish use, were hardly adequate to do justice in their limited province, and that resources must be appropriately allocated. Thus, the men were directed for food, lodging, and other needs to the location deemed most appropriate—the Bowery. There, it was thought, was the responsibility. Only there did the men belong, only there were they defined as members of the community. In fact, several clerics expressed negative feelings about the men: One referred to their proximity and then to thefts in the area; another mentioned that the men were chased away when they "panhandle in our Church." Other comments:

The situation is rather disgraceful and to me it appears as though the city and the various social agencies are simply too lenient with them. Why can't they work on farms in the country, if necessary financed by the city and state? They would be doing themselves well as well as helping others.

I think the city or borough should provide a home where strict rules of cleanliness are enforced for those who want to be rehabilitated, where they may go to take care of their personal needs.

One official mentioned the work of Operation Bowery; a clergyman referred to two sanatoriums for alcoholics.

Thus, it seemed that neighborhood interest in and concern about the homeless men in New York was neither widespread nor serious. The homeless man was not seen as a pressing problem in the local neighborhoods. When he did appear he was thought "in transit," not indigenous and not a matter of neighborhood responsibility. The homeless man did not find fellowship at the branch library; nor was he usually welcome at the local social service agency. Even Christian brotherhood seemed to have its limits.

Judging from this brief survey, it was apparent that the Bowery, a collection of special institutions and services in a distinct geographic location, performed important functions in the New York community. Among other things, its presence allowed local authorities to shift the responsibility for homeless people in their neighborhoods to some other area "where they belonged."

Reasons for losing in life. Related to both alcoholism and to homelessness is a survey of non-professional personnel in a mental hospital which aimed to determine opinions about important determinants of success or failure.[54] Respondents were asked to list "five personal characteristics or conditions that you feel are the most important causes of people defeating themselves and failing to get what they really want in life." Causes of "losing" most frequently mentioned were lack of initiative and goals, deficient education, low self-respect, and poor character, especially irresponsibility and selfishness. The various causes for losing were grouped into major categories, namely "motivational variables," "effective coping abilities," and "personality traits." Interpersonal relations, environmental conditions, and acquired knowledge and skills were also seen as important. "Winning" was seen as simply a matter of acquiring enough positive resources, having "traits and abilities that as an aggregate amount to competence." Losing was attributed not to mere aggregation, but rather to the combination of both deficits in "good" traits and excesses of undesirable traits. Deficiencies in motivations and abilities were particularly important in producing failure, as were excesses of negative, undesirable behaviors such as hate, egotism, arrogance, self-pity, fear, irresponsibility, indecision, and self-indulgence. Slightly less than half of the characteristics identified with losing were undesirable attributes and slightly more than half were reasons denoting a lack of desirable characteristics. The implications are that effective treatment requires not only the extinction or correction of undesirable characteristics but also the creation of desirable motivations and abilities. The failure is perceived as doubly deficient, doubly defective: He has undesirable attributes, he lacks desirable characteristics.[55]

Homeless men as viewed by the cartoonist

Hoboes, tramps, and skid row denizens are stock characters in American humor, and public attitudes toward the "bum" and the "derelict" are illustrated and, in part, formed by essays, jokes, and "human interest" accounts published in newspapers and magazines. While doing primary research on the life histories of homeless men, I began collecting cartoons about them. The collection was, at first, entirely unsystematic. A staff member might bring a relevant cartoon to the office; cartoons noticed in my own reading were clipped and saved. Later, the collection was increased by a systematic perusal of back issues of *The New Yorker, Saturday Review,* and the *Saturday Evening Post.*

Sometimes it was difficult to tell whether a drunken man in a cartoon represented a homeless man. The most common identifying characteristics were wrinkled, shabby clothes and an unshaven face. The most frequent situations were dialogues (or other activity) at a park bench and panhandling.

With respect to theme or "message," the cartoons were grouped into four classes: causes of homelessness, problems of homelessness, virtues of homelessness, and the effects of rapid social change on the life of skid row men. A summary of the major ideas portrayed in cartoons of each class is given below, along with illustrative statements from selected cartoons. No statistics on the proportion of cartoons in each type are given because of the ad hoc nature of the collection itself. What is reported here is not the result of a carefully designed content analysis aimed at describing the incidence of various types of messages in selected media about homeless persons. Instead, I merely wish to illustrate the kinds of messages about homelessness being sent to readers of a few wide-circulation American magazines. In keeping with sociological tradition, call it "sensitizing" or "exploratory" work.

Causes of homelessness. Cartoons reflecting notions about the causes of homelessness were sorted into types according to the etiological assumptions they contained. The types, or theories, involved were labeled "genetic," "untapped potential," "social environmental," and "motivational."

Genetic theory treats the homeless man as one marked from birth or early childhood. In physical or emotional makeup, he is different from other men, and there is little anyone can do about it. That such a man should live on skid row is not surprising, but rather a logical consequence of a life of deviance, failure, or isolation. He has always been a "black sheep." In one captionless cartoon four hobos playing craps are watched by a black sheep while the herd of white sheep grazes on the nearby hill.[56] Another cartoon illustrating the genetic perspective has a homeless man speaking to a companion: "Actually, I am a success. In school, I was voted least likely to succeed."[57]

The untapped potential view reveals the homeless man as a normal person whose abilities have yet to be harnessed or challenged. Only the proper circumstances are necessary to convert these "reservists" into active citizens. If they decide to give themselves up to responsibility and conformity, there is hope for them. Thus, a homeless man tells an employment agency worker, "I've decided to give myself up."[58] However, if the surrender is postponed too long, the chances for rehabilitation are progressively reduced.

Sometimes the avoidance of responsibilities is voluntary and part of a larger life plan. In one depiction, a disaffiliate tells an acquaintance, "I'm saving myself for the challenge of the Seventies."[59] In other cases disaffiliation merely represents an inability to adapt to a new stage of existence. A homeless man explains to a middle-class businessman, "I graduated from college with honors, but my second stage failed to ignite."[60]

In the social-environmental perspective, homelessness is caused by elements or people beyond the homeless man's control. We understand that the man had normal abilities and potentials, but that some external force or person intervened and upset a life history that otherwise would have been, if not successful, at least mediocre. The factors precipitating the skid to homelessness include alcohol, enemies, and misfortunes in love or business. The cartoon on page 74 illustrates the impact of alcoholism and at the same time takes a clever swipe at those who hold a one-factor (alcohol abuse) explanation for skid row.

The influence of enemies as a possible element in a man's downfall to skid row is portrayed in the cartoon reproduced on page 72.

Misfortunes in love occupy two beach bums lying sadly on the sand: "You're trying to forget *one* woman. I'm trying to forget an entire all-girl orchestra."[61] As for business reverses, we return to the omnipresent park bench, and one derelict explains to another,

"I never quite got the hang of it. I wheeled when I should have
been dealing and dealt when I should have been wheeling."[62]

A fourth orientation to the origin of homelessness is the "motivational hypothesis." In other words, homelessness is a voluntary
way of life, and its incumbents are motivated to be homeless men
and have few regrets. For them, the condition of homelessness is
not a manifestation of failure but rather a step into a better world.
It is possible that men who profess to be homeless by choice are
really offering rationalizations, reducing their dissonance by saying
that they are still "in control," and are doing what they want to do.
Nevertheless, for some skid row men the claim of voluntary homelessness is an honest one. Cartoonists have found claims about voluntary homelessness fertile sources of humor. Seated in an alley beside a garbage can, one homeless man says to another: "There are
the dreamers and the doers. I'm a dreamer."[63] Since their way of
life is voluntary, apparently they would choose no other even if
supernatural resources were available to them. Two derelicts are
sprawled in an alley; a sweet old lady with a wand hovers in the air
above them; one asks the other, "Hey, did I ever introduce you to
my fairy godmother?"[64] Secure and at peace with themselves, the
voluntary homeless men have no regrets about their avoidance of
the rat race for money and prestige. Having renounced the goals of
Western society, they see no reason why they should conform to its
means or expectations, nor do they expect it to reward them. One
homeless man puts it this way: "I've never done any sowing, so I
really don't expect to do any reaping."[65]

Earlier in this chapter we outlined some of Philip O'Connor's
ideas about the purity of the vagrant and his essential Christianity.
Modern society, judging man by what he possesses rather than what
he is, rejects him. Yet the man of possessions is corrupted by them
and by the ideology he must construct to protect them. The "motivational" view of homelessness portrayed by the cartoonists is in
line with O'Connor's position. There is nothing pathological in the
genetic structure or social experience of the homeless; they merely
have chosen a different way of life. Since they are not playing the

game, they cannot be judged by its rules. A homeless man explains to a businessman: "I started up life's ladder, then I said 'Ah, the hell with it!' and came back down again."[66]

The life of the homeless man, according to the cartoonists portraying the voluntarily homeless, is not unsatisfying, and there is every indication that if they were to begin all over again, many of them would not change much. This point is dramatized in the cartoon on page 73. The chilled homeless man would change only one thing: the climate.

The man who has voluntarily chosen his retreat is not the only one who rationalizes it or mentions its selling points. Homeless men of all types may find positive values in their way of life and may stress the fact that in it they avoid the problems, worries, and ulcerating responsibilities of businessmen, politicians, and commuters. An example: two homeless men on a park bench watch a grumpy businessman walk by: "Do you know what he's carrying in that briefcase? He's carrying worries and problems and troubles, that's what he's carrying."[67] A classic case is the comment of the ragged, unshaven man who shouts to the well-dressed gentleman reading a newspaper at the other end of the bench: "Hey, tycoon! Jumped out of any windows lately?"[68] One final depiction: the homeless man reads a newspaper, puts it down and walks away, saying, "Pollution, civil rights, DeGaulle, inflation, Russia, Cambodia, China . . . Hoo-Boy! They'd never get me to be president."[69]

Problems of homelessness. The adaptations necessary as homeless men interact with members of general society, and their difficulties and ingenuities in maintaining themselves without abandoning their homelessness have been frequently treated by cartoonists. In fact, much of the humor from "bum" cartoons comes from the juxtaposition of the "straight" world and the world of skid row, and the resulting insights. While they may be happy about avoiding the whips and scorns of status and the responsibilities that go with it, many homeless men appreciate and are envious of the perquisites

*"You honestly don't remember me, Mr. Dunlop?
I'm Grogan, number two man on your black list."*

*"If I had my life to live over again, I'd be
a bum in a warmer climate."*

"*My parents taught me to fear God and respect my fellow-man. I was president of my class at colle* *and was voted most likely to succeed. After graduation, I joined the staff of a large corporation a* *devoted all my energy to my work. I neither drank nor smoked nor let pleasure deflect me fr* *my objective. As the years passed, my devotion was rewarded with increasing responsibilities un* *finally I was elected Chairman of the Board. I was given an honorary degree by Columbia, and* *President of the United States bestowed on me the Medal of Merit for services in my country's beha* *At the height of my career, I was invited to pose for an advertisement featuring men of outstand* *accomplishment. I accepted this honor. The photographer posed me before his camera and placed* *my hand a glass of liquid. Out of curiosity, I took a sip—and then another sip—and another . . .*"

of power. A case in point: homeless men on a park bench watch a jet liner fly by. One says, "Just look at them up there, swilling champagne and shovelling in paté de foie gras at seven miles a minute."[70]

It takes a strong ego and firm purpose to avoid psychological damage when in contact with representatives of society. One of the few cartoons demonstrating the psychological costs of homelessness has a skid row man consoling a dejected companion whose attempt to beg from a businessman has failed: "Just because he didn't give you a dime doesn't mean he found you unlovable."[71] In fact, remaining inert in the face of continuous and not always subtle social pressures is fairly difficult. Even marginal membership in a society involves a certain amount of worry and responsibility, and the modern man's retreat may be more difficult because he lives within reach of the newspapers, television, and radio. Witness the uncaptioned cartoon showing a tired skid row man approaching a park bench in sleepy anticipation. He covers himself with a newspaper left on the bench, and settles to rest. Before sleep can come his eye catches a headline in the newspaper on his face, he suddenly sits up and reads the item, and then, worried and sleepless, sits discouraged on the bench.[72]

Some of the problems of skid row men are not very different from those facing more affiliated citizens, and the skid row men resort to familiar strategies in attempts to solve them. According to the cartoonist, the problems of the skid row entrepreneur are like those of other businessmen, although perhaps smaller in scale. The grizzled, shabby pencil salesman stands on the street corner with a sign "Please do not ask for credit" attached to his pencil box.[73]

Somehow it is incongruous for a homeless man to try to use the economic institutions which serve the more settled population. The humor in such cartoons seems to come from the brazenness of the homeless man or from the dilemma faced by an official who must "deal with the situation" the homeless man has created by entering an institution "where he doesn't belong."

The homeless man has extensive contact with employment institutions. Yet somehow it becomes funny when the cartoonist portrays an unkempt and unshaven tramp, toes sticking out of his shoes, smoking a cigar and proclaiming to a stuffy representative of the Ace Employment Agency, "Actually, I'm seeking a position where I can better myself."[74] The homeless man's attempt to use other economic institutions is similarly ludicrous. In the cartoonist's version of the Bowery Savings Bank, skid row men are unceremoniously ejected.[75]

There is little that is humorous in the homeless man's dealings with the law. For years the well-known "revolving door" has harrassed and stigmatized the homeless, wasting their lives, society's money, and legal professionals' time. When cartoonists have dealt with relationships between policemen and skid row men, the "game" of police–tramp relations has been emphasized, with—unrealistically—the tramp "winning." Thus, the homeless man affirms his independence by violating a "Do Not Litter" sign when the policeman beside the sign turns his back.[76] The issue of status criminality receives a wry comment in the instance of a drunken man (not clearly identifiable as a skid row resident) who shouts at the booking sergeant, "There's your justice! One law for the sober, another for the drunk."[77]

Virtues of homelessness. Many of the cartoons show "virtues" of disaffiliates either by contrasting them with people of other classes or by demonstrating that the homeless are not much different after all. Part of the attraction of skid row seems to be that it is viewed as a place where a man can find congenial company regardless of his past or his personal appearance. Consider two more park bench situations. One derelict compliments another, "I enjoy talking to a man like you."[78] Conversation between another pair of homeless men includes the line "So what if we are a couple of no-good lazy bums—nobody's perfect."[79]

The homeless man's non-conformity cannot be attributed to lack of opportunity. In making this point, cartoonists demonstrate that some of the men are reasonably well-informed about customs and fads in other strata of society. Long-haired and bedraggled, they stare into the barbershop, but respond "Just looking, thanks," when a barber approaches them.[80] Or, stretched out in an alley, one comments to another, "I hear the big change uptown is from Martinis to Scotch-on-the-rocks."[81] There are constant reminders that persons of higher status, above the skid row man by society's reckoning, are not very different from them. A hobo and a well-dressed businessman pass in the street—both are wearing the same kind of patterned vest[82]; a businessman skids on the ice and falls, the homeless man, observing from the park bench, says "I'm sorry, but somehow that's terribly funny."[83]

Cartoonists also have shown the skid row man's generosity. He may have few worldly goods, but what he has, he is willing to share. Lying in the gutter, he offers a swig from his bottle to a little boy walking with his mother. "No thank you. I don't drink," the lad responds, as his mother glances disapprovingly at the generous man in the gutter.[84] Perhaps because he is constrained to do so, the homeless man looks to the inward man, not the external appearance. Commenting on the world scene, one of them points to his heart as he complains: "Missiles, missiles—it's what's in here that counts."[85] His misfortunes may give him keen insight into the problems of others. One cartoon sequence portrays him as a zealous and helpful counselor to others with personal problems, and at the same time cognizant of his own needs and interests. A discouraged, middle-class man stands on a city bridge. He is approached by a panhandler, who stands in amazement as he is given wallet and watch. Then the discouraged man climbs to the edge of the bridge and prepares to jump. The panhandler pleads with the would-be suicide, and finally convinces him that things are not so bad. Stepping down with a new hold on life, the man warmly thanks the beggar, then asks for his watch and wallet back. The panhandler refuses, and the last frame shows the irate citizen chasing a fleeing panhandler.[86] Another cartoon demonstrates that the disaffiliate understands the virtues of charity and can be quick to point out selfishness in high places. The panhandler shouts after a portly gentleman who has refused—or worse, ignored—him, "You better start casting some bread upon the waters, Jack!"[87]

Effects of social change. The disaffiliate's reactions to social and technological change are the subject of numerous cartoons. Some portray the passing of an era. A cluster of hobos stand perplexed before a new train whose sleek design offers no place for them to climb aboard and ride.[88] A beggar solicits aid from a man carrying a bagful of groceries and is given trading stamps rather than money.[89]

Social change may provide new opportunities for homeless men. "Progress" for society may provide benefits for them. For example, we noted above that ready access to the news media might make retreat more difficult. At the same time, other aspects of the information explosion have beneficial effects. Two tramps stretch out on park benches and cover themselves with newspapers. One comments, "This is the time of year when you begin to appreciate the *Time*'s fuller coverage."[90]

The homeless man is the ultimate adapter, and often displays great ingenuity in utilizing the trappings of modern urban life. Changes in electrical and automotive technology have increased his options. In a beauty shop, a homeless man sits under the hair dryer, the only male in a row of women. "I just came in to get warm," he explains.[91] Automobiles with electric razors present a new opportunity. A skid row man leans against a signpost as a car is parked, waits until the driver leaves, makes sure he is unobserved, then steps into the car, shaves himself, and walks away.[92]

The adaptive skill of the homeless man is most apparent in the arts of panhandling. He is quick to note political innovations that may improve his life. Unshaven but hopeful, he appears at an Internal Revenue Service office and tries. Unfortunately, he is told, "I'm sorry, but the Guaranteed Annual Wage is still at the verbal level."[93] Aware that vast sums of money are being spent in social science grants, some to study problems of poverty and alcoholism, he seeks to tap the resources of the Ford Foundation in his own

variety of grantsmanship. In one case, two skid row men approach
the Foundation offices; one advises, "Now, remember—try to get it
in small bills."[94]

His skill at adaptation turns apparently irrelevant social innovations into economic opportunities. "Could you give me a dime for
Dial-a-Prayer?" he politely asks a middle-aged woman.[95] Or, just
outside the Berlitz School of Languages, he panhandles students:
"Vous n'avez pas un sou pour une tasse de café?"[96] Holding a
wilted plant, he pleads, "Lady, could you spare half a buck for
some plant food?"[97] A calculated appeal to human kindness often
is successful. The panhandler scores, and as his "live one" drops a
coin into his hat he points to the skid row man standing against the
wall and says, "Thank you, sir, and how about a little something
for my friend, who has too much pride to beg?"[98] Operating alone,
he may stand near an outdoor cafe, watching others eat, until someone guiltily responds, "Oh, for Pete's sake, pull up a chair."[99] As a
last resort, the homeless man may retain his integrity in non-
demanding minimal affiliation of some kind. He may work one day
a week or maintain contact with relatives when it is in his interest.
This adaptation is aptly put in a cartoon showing the cagey, con-
tented, cigar-smoking, easy-living hobo lying under a tree while his
wife cooks a meal at the campfire. "You're sweet, Sammy. Most
men, when they go on the bum, want to get *away* from their
wives."[100]

In the cartoonists' portrayals, the vagrants and skid row men
tend to be in control. The role of alcohol abuse is not overplayed,
perhaps because panhandlers and voluntary retreatists can be
funny, but chronic alcoholics, as alcoholics, are not. Voluntary
homelessness is emphasized, cleverness is applauded. The stock
situations are panhandling and bench-sitting, living off society and
observing it from the sidelines. The thrill of "the hunt" are dramatized. "Ha! Trailed you to your lair!," says the enterprising skid
row man when the wealthy old man answers his door.[101]

If Wallace is correct when he writes, "No one will dispute the
fact that skid row is the lowest point in the status order of so-

ciety,"[102] then there is need for inputs which emphasize the intelligence and adaptibility of the disaffiliates. Certainly the dominant theme of the cartoonists that skid row men are recognizably "human" and not basically different from other men is a positive contribution.

Public attitudes toward alcoholism

Let us emphasize again that there is no necessary congruence between public attitudes about alcoholism and opinions about skid row men. Admittedly, one component of the homeless man's identity is his imputed chronic alcoholism. But one tactic in the long battle by rehabilitation professionals to have alcoholism accepted as a disease has been to stress the difference between the typical alcoholic and the skid row derelict. It has been emphasized consistently that "alcoholic" and "skid row man" are very different concepts. Hence, the traditional negative connotations of alcoholism remained linked to the public image of skid row, while the more positive image created by the purveyors of the disease concept was tied to the concept "alcoholic." A comment in a 1966 editorial of the *American Journal of Psychiatry* clearly made a distinction between the "skid row derelict" and the "alcoholic," identifying the latter as "a worthwhile person suffering from an illness which can be successfully arrested."[103] The unspoken inference, perhaps unintended, was that the skid row derelict was not necessarily a worthwhile person, and that his defects were not capable of successful treatment.

Large-scale studies, including some national surveys, have demonstrated that well over half and perhaps as much as two-thirds of the public accepts the notion that alcoholism is a disease.[104] There are ethnic differentials in the extent of acceptance of the concept, with populations more vulnerable to alcoholism, such as the Irish, Negroes, and Puerto Ricans, less likely to accept the disease concept than Protestants and Jews. Even in the ethnic groups least favorable to the concept, the rates of acceptance are well over half. There are also clear educational differentials; the greater the education, the greater the likelihood that the disease concept is accepted.[105] However, a belief that alcoholism in the abstract is a disease does not mean that drinkers' behavior will be viewed as symptomatic of illness. Haberman and Sheinberg have shown that people who defined alcoholism as an illness sometimes did not recognize the gross behavior of the spree-drinker as an indication of illness. People who did recognize spree-drinking as "sick" behavior were likely to regard it as mental or emotional sickness, and to identify the psychiatrist as the most appropriate helping resource. Those who did not recognize alcoholism as an illness tended to favor clergymen, social workers, nurses, and psychologists as outside helpers, and one-fourth of them indicated that the drinker must help himself and rejected the use of outside helpers.[106] Taken as a whole, Haberman and Sheinberg's study of New Yorkers' attitudes toward drinking clearly shows that most people see the alcoholic as a problem for the professional experts.

Another measure of public attitudes about alcoholics is the negative treatment accorded recovered alcoholics. In one study, adults in two Mississippi communities were asked to agree or disagree with five statements reflecting their acceptance of a recovered alcoholic. Each respondent was asked if he would sponsor him for membership in a favorite club, share an office with him, room with him, discourage his child from marrying him, and to imagine falling in love with him (or her). Nearly one-fourth of the respondents were unwilling to associate with a recovered alcoholic under any of the named conditions. There was an inverse relationship between projected degree of intimacy and willingness to associate with the recovered alcoholic. Sixty-three per cent could not imagine themselves falling in love with a recovered alcoholic. The researcher concluded,

. . . individuals suffering from emotional or mental disorders form a subcultural group with some of the characteristics of a disadvantaged minority. . . . despite the widespread acceptance of alcoholism as an illness, the recovered alcoholic is still viewed by some as possessing a blemished character, and . . . he pays a penalty for being "different."

This penalty is often avoidance and segregation from full and meaningful interaction with others. . . . the rehabilitated alcoholic is likely to
meet resistance from certain quarters in his attempts to reestablish himself in the community, and as a result, may be forced into social positions of a lower status.[107]

Arnold Linsky has tried to document changes in the public image
of alcoholism by comparing the attitudes of people in different
age groups. His data, based on interviews with 305 residents of
Vancouver, Washington, indicate that acceptance of social drinking
is directly related to contact with the communications media, and
inversely related to age. He also found that acceptance of alcoholism and of alcoholics varied directly with years of education and
inversely with age. Acceptance of public responsibility for alcoholics and optimism about the efficacy of treatment followed similar
patterns.[108]

Linsky asked his respondents about their views on successful
treatment of alcoholism. Two-thirds preferred a "modern therapeutic orientation," embodying medical or psychological treatment.
The other third of the respondents preferred the use of will power,
religious help, or legal control, in that order. Linsky interpreted
these findings to mean that "the trend toward acceptance of professional and therapeutic treatment for alcoholism has come at the expense of public faith in the efficacy of will power, religious help,
and legal controls for getting alcoholics to stop drinking."[109]

A content analysis of an open-ended question about probable
causes of alcoholism produced five major causal theories: 1. physical, chemical, or genetic breakdown, 2. defective moral character,
3. personality disorders, 4. psychological reactions to stress, and 5.
the habit-forming nature of alcohol itself. Over half of the respondents attributed alcoholism to personality disorders or psychological
reactions to stress. Biological and moral defectiveness and the habit-
forming nature of alcohol had the most supporters among respondents aged fifty and over, and the personality and psychological
reaction theories were most popular among the youngest respondents, aged eighteen to twenty-nine.

The popularity of the personality and psychological reaction theories of alcoholism among the young was interpreted to mean that these theories are growing in popularity, and that there is a general trend toward "sympathetic understanding for the alcoholic." Also of interest is Linsky's attribution of the popularity of the psychological and personality disorder explanations to the effects of the mass media, not the demonstrated validity or efficacy of these modes of treatment. The perceptions of young people about the treatment and nature of alcoholism are seen as a consequence of ideological change and effective information campaigns rather than a triumph to scientific evidence and its acceptance. Linsky's survey findings are supported by content analysis of popular magazine articles on alcoholism which demonstrates "a dramatic shift . . . in the image of the alcoholics, from a delinquent to a sick person, during the last seven decades."[110] These findings suggest that personal contact with alcoholics is not nearly as important a determinant of attitudes about alcoholism as is "contact with cultural norms pertaining to alcoholism." The mass media and formal education support and to some degree extend the changing attitudes, but a more basic cause is a cultural trend toward increased approval of alcohol use as a "social instrument" and, stemming from this, a more sympathetic approach to people who "cannot handle it."[111]

It may be that growing acceptance of the "disease concept" of alcohol and increased sympathy for alcoholics will have some positive spin-offs for homeless men. But they are a tiny minority within the alcoholic population, and the strenuous efforts of professional spokesmen to disassociate the skid row image from that of the alcoholic, combined with a recognition of the powerlessness of the homeless man means that no great expenditure of energy or funds is likely to be dedicated to convincing the public that he, like other alcoholics, is "a worthwhile person." Add to this the antiderelict public sentiment we have already noted, the desire to achieve a solution to the problem posed by the existence of "misfits" and "scum," and it becomes apparent that there may be serious negative ramifications of the widespread acceptance of the disease concept of alcoholism. For the homeless, the vaunted benefits of the disease concept may be outweighed by the increased medical "control" implicit in the concept. In fact, some current practices and statements portend greater difficulty, or at least greater loss of freedom, than would the continued revolutions of the infamous revolving door.

We are indebted to Thomas Szasz for his careful assessment of some of the moral aspects and potential costs of the adoption of the disease concept of alcoholism.[112] Szasz does not doubt the well-intentioned motives of those who would "medicalize" human problems. The form that medicalization has taken, however, is to label a diversity of human behaviors, including alcoholism, as forms of mental illness. People who exhibit these "diseases" are thus vulnerable to the established societal machinery for treating mental illness, and this may be far more corrosive of the liberties of the chronic alcoholic than his being adjudged criminal has been. The good intentions of the medicalizers do not forestall the disastrous moral consequences of their definitions of the situation, their transmutation of one form of social deviance into another, *more* stigmatizing type.

Szasz rejects the disease concept of alcoholism on several grounds. He argues that although excessive drinking may predispose one toward other physical disorders, it is not synonymous with those disorders. True, it is a state of poisoning, but it is a self-induced state. The alcoholic may have genetic deficiencies—a medical disability—but this does not decrease his responsibility for behaving in a way that minimizes the social costs of his disability. If alcoholism is seen as a defect of personality which causes one to drink excessively, to call that defect a disease is simply an exercise in labeling. Szasz, in good sociological form, argues:

This view of alcoholism aptly illustrates my contention that mental illness is a myth and a metaphor. What we call "mental illness" is a type of action or conduct: we call a person "mentally ill" when he behaves in certain "abnormal" ways. Thus the term "mental illness" is but a new name for certain types of social performances or roles.[113]

Szasz stresses the difference between alcoholism and other diseases. Patients may choose whether or not to accept treatment for a physical disease. The sick role, he insists, must be chosen by the patients. A man with cancer has a right to refuse treatment. If alcoholism is a disease, the patient has a right to decide whether or not he wishes to be treated; many alcoholics do not want treatment. However, if alcoholism is defined as mental illness, there is precedent for involuntary treatment, for denial of a patient's civil rights for his own and society's "good." Szasz insists ". . . it is quite clear that the fundamental purpose of defining alcoholism as a disease is to bring it under the umbrella of mental illness and so justify the involuntary hospitalization and treatment of the so-called patient."[114] He makes a telling comparison between the penalties in New York for a tuberculous patient willfully endangering the public with his tubercular sputum (one so charged is entitled to a trial and, if guilty, may be fined ten dollars) and for alcoholism (a New York law allows an alcoholic to be committed for as much as six months' involuntary hospitalization at the behest of his relatives or friends, and with court approval, he can be committed for a longer period). If we are really serious about the notion that alcoholism is a disease, there is no need for involuntary treatment. People with other organic disabilities are not exempt from responsibility for their deviant acts, nor should the alcoholic be. "In our time, one of the most insidious dangers to individual liberty in America lies in the steadily increasing use of medical rhetoric and the ostensibly therapeutic actions justified by it."[115] It seems probable that this encroachment on individual liberties will fall most heavily upon those least able to protect themselves: the homeless men on skid row. So we will postpone judgment as to whether the growing "sympathetic concern" for alcoholics will make them, and skid row men with them, beneficiaries of the "widening compassion" Linsky sees as a probable consequence of public acceptance of the view that alcoholism is a disease.[116]

Our approach to the question "What do people think about homeless men" has been indirect, and most of the basis for our answer is "soft" data, but there is no mistaking the distressing shape of that answer. The catalogue of separate but related labels, which in their overlapping approximate the perceived essence of skid row men includes disaffiliate, poor man, beggar man, thief. The homeless man is seen as dirty, defective, and morally inferior; he is diseased, hopeless, and non-redeemable. He tends to be treated by agents of society with intolerance and disrespect, avoidance and fearfulness, disgust and apprehension. In the public press, people are warned against him, and terms like depraved, degenerate, derelict, and degraded are frequently used. The dangerous misfits—and a skid row address is enough to mark a man as misfit—are best shut away, shut out, avoided, or contained. Even representatives of helping professions or charitable organizations are more apt to refer homeless men elsewhere, to "where they belong," than to treat them as people with soluble problems. The lepers may be fed and clothed, but only at special stations for the unclean in the colonies set aside for them.

A review of selected cartoons about homeless men revealed several sympathetic portrayals, tributes to the integrity and creativeness of the homeless man, and some hopeful signs in surveys which reveal a growing public acceptance of the disease concept of alcoholism. But alcoholics, even reformed ones, are still stigmatized, and the equating of alcoholism with illness, especially mental illness, raises the possibility of involuntary hospitalization for the most powerless alcoholics, those who reside on skid row.

4 | Who's on skid row

Having examined attitudes toward skid row men, let us turn to the men themselves. We shall study the question, who is on skid row, from two perspectives. First, there is a discussion of the homeless man's characteristics, such as age, marital status, ethnicity, occupation, income, and disability status. Certain of these characteristics seem to go together, and some writers have distinguished apparent patterns as representing "types" of skid row men. The concluding section of this chapter is a discussion of these typologies and their underlying dimensions.

Characteristics of skid row men

According to Donald Bogue the three dominant characteristics which distinguish skid row men from other citizens are their homelessness (defined narrowly as life outside private households), poverty, and acute personal problems. Not all the skid row men share these conditions, but their simultaneous incidence is more common on skid row than anywhere else in the city.[1] Much of the uniqueness of the skid row social milieu is attributable to its high concentration of people with these kinds of problems. In addition to these three dominant characteristics, we will also consider briefly the age, race, nativity, residential stability, and education of skid row men.

The family life of skid row men. Although the family ties of skid row men are often non-existent or attenuated, it is an exaggeration to say that they lack contact with their families. On the contrary, some of them see their relatives fairly often. A 1960 survey showed that one out of thirteen Philadelphia skid row men had lived a week or more of the preceding year with a relative, and almost half said that they had seen or talked to relatives during that year. One-fourth of the men had some contact with a relative at least monthly.[2] Reports from other skid rows provide additional evidence that a substantial number of skid row residents maintain kinship ties. Thirty-five per cent of a random sample of Bowery men had seen at least one family member during the past year.[3]

Surveys of skid row men typically have not been "anchored" to comparable studies of residents in more settled neighborhoods, and consequently investigators have had to guess about whether an observed rate was high, low, or unexceptional. However, the study of Bowery men referred to above also included interviews with a "normal" sample of low-income men living in a more settled neighborhood. Two-thirds of them claimed that they had seen a relative within the past year. It would seem that when age, urban residence, and socio-economic status are taken into account skid row men are about half as likely as other men to see their relatives at least annually.

Homeless men in Britain seem to maintain approximately the same frequency of contact with kin. The National Assistance Board's 1965 census of users of four types of facilities for the homeless revealed that 29 per cent of the residents of lodging houses and hostels had been "in touch" with relatives within the month. The meaning of "in touch" was not explicitly defined, but "it was made clear that it involved more than sending or receiving an odd Christmas card or postcard." Of the 711 men found sleeping outside ("sleeping rough"), 38 per cent had been in touch with relatives during the past year. Comparable proportions for residents of Reception Centres and applicants for National Assistance, were, respectively, 32 per cent and 50 per cent.[4]

Another dimension of family life in which skid row men are atypical is frequency of marriage. In contrast to questions about contact with kin, which have been asked fairly infrequently, questions about marital status have been a part of almost all studies of skid row populations. Findings have consistently shown that about half of the men on skid row have never married, and between 30 and 40 per cent of the remainder are divorced or separated from their wives. About one in ten are widowers.[5]

Proportions of the never-married in comparison populations (e.g., males aged 14 and over in Philadelphia, 1950; residents of the Park Slope neighborhood in Brooklyn, 1966) are between 25 and 30 per cent. Moreover, when controls are imposed for the age of skid row men—since the population is an aged one, the men have averaged more years of opportunity to marry than, for example, a population made up of males 14 years of age and over—the atypicality of skid row marital histories is even more striking. Bogue shows that if the population of skid row had the same age composition as the national population of adult males, the never-married proportion would be 64 per cent, almost four times the national rate.[6]

Caplow *et al.* identified the atypical marital history of skid row men as presumably the principle factor besides low income which accounted for their presence on skid row. In the general population, the older the person the higher the probability that he has been married. But among the skid row men this seems not to be so. Instead, some studies show that the older homeless men are less likely to have been married than the younger men. Thus, among men 30 and over on Philadelphia's skid row, the highest rates of lifetime "single blessedness" were among the men 75 and over. Among homeless men in Minneapolis, two-thirds of those over 70 had always been single, compared to two-fifths of those under 50.[7]

Marital composition varies with the nature and historical period of the homeless population studied. The figures cited above all derive from random samples of skid row residents in the United States. There used to be more single homeless men than there are now. Seventy-four per cent of the Chicago shelter clients studied by Solenberger had their "conjugal condition" recorded as "single," and another six per cent were divorced or separated.[8]

Homeless men in England, Scotland, and Wales are even less likely to have married than their American counterparts. Two-thirds of the users of lodging houses and hostels have never married, and comparable or higher proportions characterized men who sought financial aid from local offices of the National Assistance Board or who were living in Reception Centres.[9]

Skid row men who do marry have extraordinarily unstable marriages. Despite the high proportion of skid row men who have never married, divorced men are ten to fourteen times as common on skid row as in the general population of adult males.[10] In fact, marital instability is an important antecedent of homelessness, and many men "flee to the skid row environment in confusion and disorganization as a rather direct result of the failure of their marriages."[11] Moreover, stressful family interaction may lead to or exacerbate personality disorganization and problem drinking. The men then drift to skid row as their drinking becomes uncontrollable.

Bogue's study of the marital histories of the separated and divorced men on skid row highlighted incompatibility as the leading cause of marital dissolution, followed by the skid row man's drinking (a major cause in at least 27 per cent of the breakups) and infidelity (one-fourth of the men identified their wife's infidelity as a major cause, and one man in twenty said that his own infidelity was a major factor). When formerly married Bowery men were asked to identify sources of conflict in their marriages, 45 per cent said that their own drinking was often a problem, and 37 per cent admitted that their absences from home strained the marriage. Marital infidelity and financial problems were not on the standard list of problems presented by interviewers, but many men commented that money problems plagued the marriages, and the frequency of reported sexual infidelity by one or both partners suggested that it was almost as serious a problem as drinking.[12]

The marriages of skid row men tend to be multiproblem marriages. For example, a former lathe operator interviewed on the Bowery told how his marriage disintegrated at the same time he lost his sight and his job. "My eyes were going bad," he stated. "I couldn't work and bring money home"; and at age twenty-four his first wife divorced him. A year later he remarried. The second marriage lasted only a year. Again there were financial problems, and he accepted a six-month job in a California aircraft plant. When he returned to the East, his wife asked for a divorce. She wanted to marry a neighbor.

Another Bowery man said his wife's expensive tastes created problems. "My wife liked expensive clothes. If she couldn't afford expensive things she would wear rags; and I liked to see her look nice, but could not afford it." However, money was not the only problem. His wife thought he was gone too much, and they fought about in-laws, his drinking, and each other's friends. Despite these problems, the marriage lasted for sixteen years. It ended this way:

Jealousy; something was going on. She had other men. When we separated I went to New York. When I came back a few years later, she had two more kids. So we got a divorce.

That was 1942. He began living on the Bowery in 1943, and when interviewed had lived there twenty-three years.[13]

The poverty of skid row men. In 1958 the median income of skid row men in Minneapolis was $80 per month. Actual living costs in the skid row area were estimated by the county welfare board at $74.50 per month. In other words, the typical skid row man had an economic margin of $5.50 per month beyond bare necessities. Furthermore, comparisons with figures for previous years left no doubt that the lot of the homeless man was not improving. Their wages had not kept pace with rising prices.[14] Five years later Bogue published statistics based on the 1950 census contrasting the income distribution for skid row census tracts and that for the forty-one American cities where the skid row census tracts were found. Forty-nine per cent of the population in the skid row tracts earned less than $1,500 in 1949, compared to only 27 per cent of the residents in the cities as a whole.[15]

The 1960 Philadelphia skid row survey found that more than one-third of the skid row residents had no earned income in the previous year. Adding controls for age revealed that it was not merely the aged individuals who were not earning wages. Over one-fourth of the residents between 45 and 54 years of age did not have any earned income, and for the men aged 55 to 59 the figure was 35 per cent. Fully 55 per cent of the men reported an annual income of less than $1,000. In estimating the extent of "rock bottom" dependency on skid row, the authors estimated that if the men had to pay their own way, lodging costing fifty cents a night would be too expensive for half of them.[16]

The Philadelphia investigators also obtained information about non-wage income. Four-fifths of the respondents said they did not have any retirement benefits, public assistance, gifts, or social security benefits. One man in eleven admitted stealing, begging, or gambling as a source of income. Thus, non-wage income was, at best, merely supplemental.[17]

In 1966 29 per cent of a sample of Bowery men reported an annual income of $500 or less. This proportion of low-income men was larger than had been reported in several surveys conducted seven to nine years earlier in other skid rows. In other words, Bowery men in 1966 had *lower* incomes than skid row men in other cities had had several years earlier. Given the intervening inflation, it follows that the differential in actual buying power was even greater than the difference in dollars would indicate. Thus, the Bowery had more destitute men than the skid rows of Philadelphia, Sacramento, Chicago, and Minneapolis.

Although the Bowery had the highest proportions of men at the extremely low end of the income scale, Minneapolis had the lowest median income. The Minneapolis sample median income was under $1,000; the Chicago, Philadelphia, and Bowery samples were between $1,000 and $1,500. One of the "richest" skid rows was Sacramento where the median income in 1957 was between $1,500

and $2,500 and almost one-fifth of the residents reported incomes
of more than $3,500 a year. Less than 10 per cent of men on the
other skid rows had incomes that high.[18]

The poverty of skid row men is placed in even greater relief by
contrasting their incomes with those of more "normal" citizens. In
Pittsburgh's Federal Anderson Project Area, which included "the
principal collection grounds for skid row characters in Pittsburgh,"
and "a conglomeration of business and residential uses unacceptable elsewhere," one-third of the "families" (including unrelated
individuals) had incomes of under $2,000 in 1960. In the rest of
the city, the incidence of such low income was only one in nine. The
1957 median income of skid row men in Chicago was less than
one-third the median income of the United States males aged fourteen and over ($1,083 as compared to $3,684).[19]

The low income of the homeless man does not mean that he is
lazy or that he has not done his share of hard work. In fact, he has
made a substantial economic contribution as an unskilled worker
in the agriculture, transportation, and construction industries. Wallace has summarized his contributions and rewards.

Isolated from the community, exploited by employer and employment
agency alike, the homeless man has always done the hardest work under the worst possible conditions and at the lowest wage. He has cleared
the frontier, extended and maintained the railroads, built dams and
levees on the rivers, and helped to harvest the crops.

This contribution has earned him nothing. The homeless man is only
remembered for his loafing, his wandering, and his drinking. In the
past he was sometimes cursed, at other times feared. Today he is simply
ignored.[20]

Poverty and the stigmatization which accompanies it are major
determinants of almost every aspect of the skid row way of life. The
indigence of the homeless dominates their interaction with representatives of society.

They work at spot jobs, make the harvest for a few months, or live off
meager pension checks. Their poverty is often increased by bailing out
of jail or paying off fines. When arrested they are especially vulnerable

to being robbed, rolled, or clipped. Because they are bums they do not deserve property receipts. These men not only *lose* their money when they make the bucket, but their poverty becomes the major reason for doing time in jail. With each arrest their sentences are lengthened while those with money pay the same amount. . . . When a tramp repeatedly compares $20 bail with the months he does in jail he comes to realize the deep significance of his poverty. As he goes to court and sees others, who are earning money from steady jobs, released because they have steady jobs, he is again reminded that monetary considerations are primary in our system of justice.[21]

Employment. There are three major linkages between the world of skid row and that of the wider society. All involve forms of exchange between homeless men and other citizens. The dominant linkage, in terms of the amount of literature it has spawned, is the bond between the skid row man and the social control agent. The latter, employed by one of the "helping institutions" such as a welfare center, a public shelter, or a gospel mission, provides services for a skid row clientele, but is paid for those services by some segment of the wider society. The skid row man is client, target, or recipient, but is not an equal partner in the exchange which determines the nature and extent of help available.

The other two major linkages between skid row and the rest of society are employment and commerce. In the first case, the skid row man is employee; in the second, he is customer. The latter role defines his relationship to skid row facilities such as restaurants, lodging houses, bars, and secondhand stores. The owners and many of the staff members of these institutions are outsiders, and their economic interaction with homeless men forges a link between skid row and the local and national economy.

It is in the role of employee that the skid row man makes his most important contribution to other subsystems of society. As customer and client he is at a disadvantage; he does not have much money to spend, and he does not pay for—and hence does not exert much influence upon—his relationships with rehabilitation agents. But as employee he makes a real input: he fells trees, picks crops, repairs railroad tracks, washes dishes, cooks in resort kitchens, sails in merchant vessels, and loads merchandise.

Finding adequate employment for homeless men has usually been viewed as one of the most important priorities of skid row programs, and the occupations and occupational capabilities of skid row men have received much attention. Information about the skid row man's relationship to the world of work is readily available. For general purposes, Wallace's chapter on "Jobs," Bogue's account of "The Workingman on Skid Row," and Anderson's "Work" are recommended. Anderson's *Men on the Move* and Allsop's *Hard Travellin'* provide more detailed coverage.[22]

Studies conducted between 1958 and 1966 found that at any given time between one-third and one-half of the skid row men were gainfully employed. Of course, unemployment figures vary with business cycles, and it is probable that during recessions employment rates for skid row men are somewhat lower than at other times. In some ways skid row areas are inverse barometers of local economic conditions. When unemployment rates are down, many of the marginally employable men on skid row get jobs and occupancy rates in skid row hotels fall off. One hotel manager summed it up: "The lodging houses are barometers of business; business down, you're up."[23]

The nature of skid row employment varies from place to place. It tends to be low-status work, poorly paid, and the specific duties change with the economic structure of the community. In the coastal cities there are many seamen who live on the row between voyages. The 1957 survey of Sacramento's skid row revealed that more than half of the men were unskilled laborers, and almost two-thirds of the laborers were farm laborers.[24] By contrast, the Chicago survey in 1963 indicated that only one-third of the skid row men were laborers, and a majority of those were railroad workers. One of every five Chicago skid row men were restaurant workers, either waiters, countermen, dishwashers, or cooks. Another 20 per cent were transportation workers, with railroad work being the dominant subcategory. Heavy drinkers and alcoholic derelicts were overrepresented among the skid row railroad workers, so much so that Bogue theorized that either the railroad was a major benefactor of chronic alocholics, employing them when no one else would, or else the drinking culture of the railroad maintenance gang perpetuated heavy drinking as a substitute for normal family life. The Chicago survey showed the proportion of farm workers to be extremely small; less than 4 per cent of the men interviewed had held farm jobs during the previous year.[25]

Finally, Bogue found that while white collar and skilled jobs were not the usual jobs of skid row men, when all steady jobs held during the past year were taken into account, one-tenth of the skid row men had worked as craftsmen, another tenth as clerical workers, and one-fifth as operatives. Thus, a substantial number of skid row men had contact with "better jobs" which they did not or could not keep.[26]

As for duration of jobs, 12 per cent of the Chicago skid row men who worked during 1967 held the same job for an entire year. About one-third of the men changed jobs every day or so or changed regular jobs at least every two months. Being physically handicapped or being a heavy drinker increased the probabilities that a man would change jobs frequently.[27]

In England, 47 per cent of the men staying in lodging houses and hostels were employed at the time of the 1965 survey, and about two-thirds of these had been employed six months or more. Of the unemployed, a slightly higher proportion had been unemployed six months or more. In fact, there seemed to be three stable populations: the usually employed, the usually unemployed, and the marginal employed who worked part of the time. Thirty-one per cent had been employed six months or more, 32 per cent had been employed within the past six months (precisely half of these were employed at the time of the survey), and 37 per cent had been unemployed six months or more.

As in the United States, the unemployment rates of lodging-house residents varied by location, ranging from 76 per cent in Scotland to a low of 37 per cent in the eastern region of England.

Other samples of homeless men manifested the following unemployment rates: persons sleeping rough, 60 per cent; persons using government Reception Centres, 80 per cent; persons applying for national assistance, 93 per cent.[28]

Bogue said that the high proportion of skid row men who did not work was understandable in the light of five major factors: (1) some of the men work in seasonal occupations; (2) many are disabled, handicapped, or sick; (3) many of the men are old and cannot work, and the old men who can work have difficulty competing with younger men for jobs; (4) many are chronic alcoholics or heavy drinkers who work only enough to get by; and (5) some are "ambitionless 'bums'" who work as little as possible. Too often public attitudes toward skid row take into account only the last two factors. They are important, but they are involved in less than half of the unemployment on skid row. According to Bogue the chronic alcoholic is only a special case in the general process which has caused certain "unemployables" to drift to skid row. The real problem is that there are flaws in the social legislation designed to prevent the impersonal competition of our economic institutions from "brutalizing" the powerless:

Almost any American citizen, if denied work opportunities for a prolonged span of time would end up in the Skid Row soup line unless saved from this fate by a family or by some program of social legislation—irrespective of his drinking habits.[29]

Personal problems: disabilities, disease, and drinking. Physical disabilities are very common among homeless men, and most students of homelessness have remarked about the high incidence of impairments and disfigurements among them. Explanations for the high incidence of mutilation and disfigurement vary, but most observers have noted the stark evidence of violence, accidental or intentional, on the bodies of the homeless. Not only defective bodies, but also mental illness or impairments are greatly overrepresented among skid row men.

Among the earliest statistics on the physical condition of homeless men is Solenberger's finding that two-thirds of her 1,000 cases were diseased or defective. Two-hundred and fifty-four men were "either temporarily or permanently crippled or maimed." At least one man in eleven was suffering from tuberculosis, and 17 per cent were "crippled, maimed, or deformed" either from birth or by accidents.[30] Mental problems also were frequent.[31] Using conservative diagnostic criteria under which only men whose mental defects were "self-evident" or "definitely ascertained" were included, eighty-one of her thousand men were mentally defective or unfit in some way. Since "border-line cases" were not included, it seems safe to say that at least one out of ten of Solenberger's cases were suffering from mental illness or were mentally defective.[32]

One of the earlier field experiences which produced an observation of widespread impairment among the homeless was Eric Hoffer's stay in a federal transient camp in California in 1934. Hoffer, working as a migrant agricultural worker, was referred to the camp by a policeman and spent about a month there. While he lived in and observed the camp, he wondered why his campmates were living in such a place, and whether their difficulties would be solved by jobs. "Were we indeed like the people outside?" he asked. In attempting to answer that question he noticed that 30 of the 200 inmates had crippled arms or legs. Then he counted other types of human damage. There were 78 men without teeth, 60 confirmed drunkards, 50 aged men, at least a dozen with chronic diseases, four mildly insane, four fugitives from justice, and six who were "constitutionally lazy." Only about one-third of the residents were "apparently normal." To Hoffer, these statistics meant that "we in the camp were a human junk pile."[33]

He also looked at faces:

There were some good faces. . . . But the damaged and decayed faces were in the majority. I saw faces that were wrinkled, or bloated, or raw as the surface of a peeled plum. Some of the noses were purple and swollen, some broken, some pitted with enlarged pores.[34]

Even the characters of the men in the camp were defective:

. . . on the whole, one would hardly say that these men were possessed of strong characters. Resistance, whether to one's appetites or to the ways of the world, is a chief factor in the shaping of character; and the average tramp is, more or less, a slave of his few appetites. He generally takes the easiest way out. . . .

The majority of us were incapable of holding onto a steady job. We lacked self-discipline and the ability to endure monotonous, leaden hours. We were probably misfits from the very beginning. Our contact with a steady job was not unlike a collision. Some of us were maimed, some got frightened and ran away, and some took to drink. We inevitably drifted in the direction of least resistance—the open road. The life of a migrant worker is varied and demands only a minimum of self-discipline. We were now in one of the drainage ditches of ordered society.[35]

In assessing "The Role of the Undesirables," Hoffer compares the migrant workers in the federal transient camp to the pioneers who had settled the west, and argues that individuals such as the homeless men may play a major role in shaping a society.

The importance of these inferior elements as formative factors lies in the readiness with which they are swayed in any direction. This peculiarity is due to the inclination to take risks ("not giving a damn") and their propensity for united action. They crave to merge their drab, wasted lives into something grand and complete. Thus they are the first and most fervent adherents of new religions, political upheavals, patriotic hysteria, gangs, and mass rushes to new lands.[36]

Observers of the passive skid rows of the 1950's and 1960's may question Hoffer's description of the homeless as having a "propensity for united action" or as "first and most fervent adherents" of anything. The ranks of the homeless have changed, and today passiveness is the rule among the skid row men. Rooney has outlined the details of the change from protest activity to passive acquiescence among the homeless, unattached males and concluded that

. . . there have been marked changes in the attitudes and behavior of skid-row men. They are no longer an aggregate of aggressive working men with a great sense of pride, self-reliance, and independence, but rather a concentration of passive, inept men largely dependent on public institutions and bearing a very diminished sense of self-worth. Formerly, skid-row residents actively confronted and challenged the social order, but now they passively seek to avoid the demands of society and have withdrawn from all major responsibilities.[37]

But if the activism and sense of untapped potential which Hoffer observed among the transients in California no longer characterize the homeless man, the physical and mental disabilities are still there. Rooney comments on the function of skid row in the 1960's and thereafter:

. . . skid row has largely lost the function of an employment center for either migratory or resident casual workers. Its continued existence appears to depend upon one important remaining function: providing a refuge for drop-outs from the working class who have psychic disabilities, a significant proportion of which involve alcoholism. If present trends continue, the population of skid row will continue to decline, and the proportion of psychically disabled skid-row men will increase. Consequently skid row may come to function primarily as an open asylum.[38]

In 1952 Feeney et al. compared skid row alcoholics who had been sentenced to the workhouse in Washington, D.C., with voluntary patients at the alcoholism clinic in that same city. In comparison with the clinic patients, the random sample of male workhouse inmates was shown to be seriously disabled both physically and mentally. Half of the workhouse inmates had suffered severe head trauma leading to unconsciousness (46 per cent of these head injuries had occurred before drinking became a problem), but none of the patients in the comparison group had suffered such injuries. Four of the fifty workhouse men were epileptics; none of the clinic patients were. Twenty of the workhouse men had physical deformities, compared to only eight of the clinic patients. But the clinic patients were more likely to have histories of "internal" disorders of the heart, lungs, kidneys, liver, and other organs, and were much more likely to report severe alcoholic reactions such as delirium tremens or "black outs." Thus, the obvious, most stigmatizing faults were most common among the skid row alcoholics.[39]

Psychiatric evaluations showed that the skid row men were more likely to manifest overt psychoses (30 per cent versus 8 per cent), while neuroses and borderline psychoses were more frequent among the clinic patients. The researchers linked the arrests of the workhouse inmates to their psychoses.

Ambulatory patients in the Workhouse group may be subject to arrest for their bizarre behavior rather than for severe intoxication. Small amounts of alcohol might release controls and cause more exaggerated peculiarities of behavior. It is also possible that the same peculiarities might be ignored by the police officer when the individual cannot be charged with intoxication.[40]

Feeney et al. concluded that the deformities and injuries in the histories of the skid row men reflected accident proneness, possibly linked to factors such as "impulsiveness, lack of adequate supervision during childhood, more hazardous occupation in later life, or poor judgment because of low intellectual functioning."[41]

Sutherland and Locke's statistics on homeless unemployed men living in Chicago shelters in 1935 show that approximately one-third of the men were "incapacitated for hard labor" by "organic handicaps and difficulties, such as loss of limb, partial blindness or deafness, and hernia." One of every twenty men gave indications of psychoses serious enough that psychiatrists recommended their transfer to the Psychopathic Hospital. About one-fifth of the men manifested some problem of psychopathy. Sutherland and Locke noted that both physical and mental health estimates underestimated actual prevalence of sickness because men who were chronically or temporarily sick were in infirmaries or state hospitals and were unavailable for interview.[42]

Donald Bogue's extensive survey of residents of Chicago's skid row in 1958 also revealed extremely high rates of disability and illness.[43] Four-fifths of the men interviewed reported at least one *current* disease or sickness. One out of every eleven men manifested mental illness, and the same proportion had other chronic mental or nervous trouble. Six per cent were missing a foot or an arm. One-sixth of the men had lost all their teeth, and over 40 per cent had ten or more teeth missing. Forty-nine per cent of the men who had some of their own teeth had not seen a dentist in at least five years. Bogue commented that "probably it would be difficult to find a segment of the population with worse average dental condition."[44]

Approximately three-fourths of the respondents in the Philadelphia study reported specific medical conditions. Over one-third of the men had disabilities which limited their work capacity, the most common being deformity or stiffness in foot or leg, followed by defective vision, tuberculosis, arthritis or rheumatism, heart trouble, hernia, general rundown condition, asthma, arms or legs missing, back trouble, and paralysis.[45]

Caplow *et al.* termed the health conditions on Minneapolis' skid row "catastrophically bad." Among the reasons for the high morbidity rates were low income and substandard housing. More important for our present discussion of the stigmatization of homeless men, however, was the observation that many of the residents of the skid row area were there in the first place because of their chronic diseases or handicaps acquired earlier in life. Even the transients attracted to skid row by its entertainment facilities were described as manifesting a great variety of physical and mental health problems.[46]

Tuberculosis is one of the diseases which manifest startlingly high rates among skid row men. In Feeney *et al.*'s sample of skid row men who had been sent to the workhouse, 20 per cent had histories of tuberculosis.[47] One of every thirty men *reported* tuberculosis to Bogue's interviewers.[48] Seven per cent of the Philadelphia skid row men had histories of tuberculosis. On skid row in Minneapolis in 1957 the rate was lower (about 1 per cent), but that 1 per cent represented 320 times the rate for the rest of the Minneapolis citizenry at that time.[49]

The pervasive role of tuberculosis as a part of the skid row milieu is aptly illustrated in the fictional account of "Herb," an arrested inebriate who when brought before a Chicago judge explained that he was "okay" but had to go back to the TB sanitarium:

In any other courtroom in the city this admission would bring startled gasps from those in attendance, but nobody in this courtroom was concerned enough to murmur. Tuberculosis is an ever present part of the way of life of these men.

The conversation between Herb and the referee was not lost on Tim. He suspected that he frequently had been only a step or two ahead of the TB germ, and that in his rundown condition it could hit him any time. Looking around he saw other men who were TB victims, former TB victims, and future TB victims.[50]

Closely related to the health and disability status of homeless men is another major personal problem, excessive drinking. The alleged alcoholism of its men is the dominant element in the public stereotype of skid row. Extensive discussion of the drinking patterns of homeless men are readily available and will not be reviewed here.[51] Group drinking patterns among skid row men are discussed in the section in Chapter 5, "Informal Relationships."

Several studies of the extent of drinking among skid row men have found that approximately one-third are heavy drinkers, another third drink moderately, and the remainder drink very little or are abstainers. Between one-third and one-fourth of the drinkers claim to be spree drinkers or periodic drinkers, but it is probable that many of them are merely heavy drinkers whose consumption is periodic because of financial or other factors. The proportion of abstainers ranges from 15 to 28 per cent. If residents who have been heavy drinkers in the past are counted along with the current problem drinkers, the resulting total includes at least half of the skid row population.[52]

Although perhaps one man out of every three skid row men is a problem drinker for whom drinking is the dominant activity of life rather than an avocation, most skid row men are not problem drinkers, and they are not on skid row because of their drinking. Nevertheless, the proportion of problem drinkers in the skid row population is higher than in any other urban neighborhood. Merited or not, the stigma of alcoholism is apt to be imputed to the possessor of a skid row address.

Age. Skid row men are old men, and they look older than they are.

A forty-year-old man may look fifty or even sixty. Sometimes they exaggerate their age to legitimate their retired status. It is not uncommon to hear a statement such as "I'm an old-timer now. Do you know how old I am? I'll soon be 58."[53] They are also old in orientation to the future; they seem to anticipate death more than other men. Young and middle-aged Bowery men answering a question about their status a year hence were more than six times as likely to mention the possibility of dying as were men of comparable ages who lived in a more settled neighborhood.[54] But apart from the self-perceptions of retirement and the feelings of imminence of death, even disregarding the dried-up old men whose appearances reflect suffering and exposure rather than a multitude of years, skid row remains a community of the aged.

In census tracts containing skid rows one person in nine is 65 or older; on the rows themselves, the proportion is much higher. There are no children, few young men, and many middle-aged and old men. The median age generally falls between 50 and 54. The proportion of men under 35 ranges from 5 to 15 per cent; there are from two to seven times as many men over 65. Institutions for the aged have higher proportions of old people, but there are few "open" communities with age distributions so highly skewed.

Thus, his chronological age, and more important, his bearing and attitude, mark the skid row man as "over the hill." Regardless of chronological age, he looks old and thinks old. "Up the tile stairways of the flophouses sit the most retired men in the world."[55]

Racial background. Most skid row men are white men. The extent of racial mixture varies from city to city. The most visible minority on Seattle's First Avenue are American Indians, although expert estimates suggest that the proportion of Indians and blacks are about the same. The largest non-white minority in the "Pacific City" skid row was the blacks who accounted for one of every eight residents. There were also 4 per cent chicanos. The racial structure of homeless populations in the Southwest is more complex because there are three minorities present in substantial numbers: Indians, blacks, and chicanos. In Sacramento, the chicano minority outnumbered the blacks slightly; the proportions there were 15 per cent and 14 per cent, respectively. Most of the other residents were white.[56]

The Chicago skid rows were described by Bogue as "Caucasian islands in a sea of Negroes, Puerto Ricans, and Mexicans who have settled in the oldest and most deteriorated slum areas around the central business district." But despite the multiracial context, between 86 and 89 per cent of the men were whites. About 2 per cent were American Indians, and the remaining 9 per cent were blacks.[57]

A comparison of the racial composition of seven different skid row populations revealed proportions of blacks ranging from 3 per cent in Minneapolis (95 per cent of the men were white) to a high of 29 per cent in New York City's Bowery area.[58] In most skid rows the proportion of blacks is less than the proportionate size of the black population of the city as a whole. Given the fact that skid row men are drawn disproportionately from the lower socioeconomic strata and that blacks are overrepresented among low-income populations in American metropolitan areas, the shortage of blacks on skid row is even more striking. James Rooney has addressed this problem in an unpublished paper in which he hypothesizes that the underrepresentation of blacks may stem from the existence of racial discrimination which renders skid row facilities less accessible and desirable to blacks, and the structure of lower-class black communities which allows homeless men to find a niche within the community boundaries.[59]

Nativity. Skid row is not an assemblage of marginal immigrants whose language problems or other conflicts between the culture of their native land and the norms of metropolitan America have forced them to the status of homeless outsiders. All of the large-scale studies of homeless men conducted during the past twenty years have demonstrated that at least three-fourths of the skid row inhabitants are native born, and usually the proportion is higher than that.

A comparison of the nativity statistics for skid row samples in Chicago, Minneapolis, Philadelphia, the Bowery, Camp LaGuardia, and chronic police case inebriates in the Monroe County Penitentiary disclosed that foreign-born homeless men were most common in Minneapolis and New York City, where they made up about one-fourth of the skid row population. The dominant country of origin varied. In New York and Philadelphia the Irishmen were the most frequently encountered skid row immigrants, accounting for about one of every five of the foreign-born homeless men. But in Minneapolis half of the immigrants on skid row were Scandinavians.[60]

Further information about national origins may be gleaned from responses about the nationality of skid row men's parents. The 1966 Bowery survey included a question, "What countries did your parents' families come from? The answers revealed that most Bowery men belonged to one of three distinct ethnic populations, American blacks, Irishmen, and Northern Europeans (men of British, German, and Scandinavian ancestry).[61]

The skid rows of the past two decades have proved much more "local" than was anticipated. Consider the Bowery. One-fourth of its native born men (and one-fifth of all Bowery men) were born in New York City. Almost 60 per cent of the native-born Bowery men were born in the Northeastern states, with Massachusetts and Pennsylvania making the most substantial contributions after New York State. Thus, the "clientele" of the Bowery seems to be largely local and regional, and only secondarily national or international. The only sizable flow of migration to the Bowery from outside the Northeastern states is the stream from the South, where almost one-third of the native-born Bowery men originated.[62]

The data from Chicago tell a similar story. About one-fourth of the men interviewed by Bogue were born in Illinois, and the same proportion were native to other states in the North Central United States. Another group of about the same size came from the Southern states.

Adequate comparison data are difficult to obtain. Using rates he acknowledged as deficient, Bogue estimated that the skid row man was perhaps twice as likely as the average resident of Chicago to have been born in Illinois. Bogue also commented that the impression of observers of the Chicago skid row scene that skid row had been invaded by Southerners was based on fact. The proportion of residents born or reared in the South was twice as high on skid row as for the Chicago citizenry as a whole.[63]

For a final example, let us consider Rochester, New York. Pittman and Gordon discovered that four of every ten chronic inebriates in the Monroe County Penitentiary were natives of New York State. Apparently citizens of Rochester had been blaming public drunkenness on outsiders and transient elements, for the authors found it necessary to emphasize their finding that many of the arrested inebriates were hometown or homestate men: "The popular stereotype of the inebriate offender as a Negro from the South, an Irishman from Boston, or an immigrant is by no means the complete picture." They also attributed part of the "push" to skid row to the adjustment problems of men from non-metropolitan settings, noting that even their white offenders of English background tended to be men raised in small towns and rural areas who were in the process of adapting to urban culture.[64]

The nativity patterns of skid row men have not been carefully analyzed, and the available evidence stems from only a few cities. Taken as a whole, it suggests that the major skid rows in the nation are, first and foremost, centers for disaffiliates drawn from a local and regional hinterland. Beyond that, they seem to receive some spin-off from the major migratory streams of the day. Thus, among the older men, there are noticeable segments representing the waves of European immigration to the major eastern and central cities, as well as many Southerners, who represent the massive migration of rural and small-town Southerners to the cities.

Residential mobility. We noted above that a very substantial proportion of skid row men—between 40 and 60 per cent—are natives of the city or region where their skid row is located. But using proportion of natives as an indicator minimizes the extent to which skid row men are local products. If we define men who have lived in a city for extended periods of time as local residents, the predominantly local nature of men of skid row is even more evident.

Over 90 per cent of the men interviewed in the 1960 Philadelphia study had lived there for more than a year; over half had either been born in Philadelphia or lived there at least twenty years. The men were also long-term residents of skid row. Over half had lived in the Philadelphia skid row neighborhood for five years or more.

The major flow of new residents to skid row is from other neighborhoods in the city where the row is located. Within the skid row itself there tends to be considerable residential mobility; almost two-thirds of the residents reported last moving to their present address during the year preceding the interview. To summarize, then, it seems that most skid row men move to the row from other neighborhoods in the city, are relatively long-term residents of the city, and once located on skid row, tend to become long-term residents there. The only significant present-day migrations are seasonal movements away and back to the home base (36 per cent of the Philadelphia respondents said they moved out of the neighborhood during the summer) and fairly frequent changes of residence within the skid row neighborhood itself.[65]

Caplow and his associates found considerable residential stability in Minneapolis, also. One out of every six skid row residents had lived at the same address for at least ten years; two-thirds of the men had lived on skid row continuously for at least the year preceding the interview; and 97 per cent could be considered old residents, in that they had first established residence in Minneapolis at least a year before the interview. There were even three elderly men who had lived in the same lodging house for more than forty years.[66]

Education. The skid row man has less education than the average American male, but that can be explained largely in terms of his age and social-class background. Nowadays, average levels of education attainment are higher than they used to be. Other things being equal, the older the man, the less formal education he has.

Access to education is also a function of socioeconomic status; the poorer one's parents, the less education he is likely to have. The combination of these two factors—age and socioeconomic status—is sufficient to account for the apparent deficiencies in the educational attainment of skid row men. In fact, given the atypicality of the age and social-class background distributions of skid row men, it is surprising that the differentials in education are not larger than they are.

Both the Chicago and New York studies demonstrated that when the educational distribution of skid row men was compared with that of appropriate comparison groups, there were no significant differentials. Bogue contrasted the educational experience of his skid row sample with a "composite" profile of educational attainment computed from national statistics on low-income workers (operatives, service workers, and non-farm laborers) and found that 19 per cent of the skid row men and 18 per cent of the composite comparison group had completed high school. Incidence of total absence of formal education was 3 per cent for both groups. Bogue drew two implications from these findings: 1. skid row was not populated by any substantial group of the highly educated who had skidded to homelessness because of excessive drinking, and 2. the educational preparation of skid row men was far above the level necessary for their current employment. Clearly, "Skid Row is neither the 'last stop' for alcoholic business and professional men, nor is it a collecting place for the semi-illiterates and uneducable men of the nation."[67]

In the New York study, a comparison of the educational achievement of Bowery men and of a control sample of "normal" men in a low-income neighborhood revealed the same pattern. Twenty-seven per cent of the Bowery men had completed high school and 15 per cent of them had fewer than five years of schooling. For the control sample, the comparable proportions were, respectively, 25 per cent and 11 per cent.[68] As in the Chicago data, it was apparent that inferior formal education was not an important antecedent of skid row living.

We have discussed nine attributes of skid row men, and for each have summarized the findings of several empirical studies. Having presented so many facts and figures from so many sources, let us recapitulate. Skid row men are most unique in their marital histories: only about half have married and most of these marriages were short-lived and stressful. Nevertheless, the skid row men maintain some kinship ties, and perhaps one-third of them see a relative at least annually. They are extremely poor, their dominant ties to outside society are apt to be short-term, low-status jobs, and at a given time, as many as half of them may be unemployed. Disability or chronic illness characterize a majority of the men, and at least one-third are problem drinkers; they are old and seem older, are mostly white and native born, and are not particularly disadvantaged educationally. At least half are native to that section of the country where their skid row is located, and most are long-term residents of their city and often of skid row itself.

Types of the homeless

Preparing classifications of the homeless is an art at least half a millennium old. *Liber Vagatorium,* edited by Martin Luther and published in 1528, had a classification of beggars and advised the reader how to deal with each type.[69] More than 400 years later Nels Anderson devoted four chapters of *The Hobo* to "types of hobos." Anderson's typology has been most influential and has formed the basis for numerous classifications by later investigators. He began with an informant's assertion that "There are three types of the genus vagrant: the hobo, the tramp, and the bum. The hobo works and wanders, the tramp dreams and wanders, and the bum drinks and wanders."

Influential sociological typologies. Anderson expanded these three types into five: the seasonal worker, the occasional worker, the wandering tramp who worked only when convenient, the bum who neither worked nor wandered, and the home guard who lived in Hobohemia and did not leave town.[70]

The seasonal workers were men who had definite occupations somewhere during part of the year. They might winter on Chicago's West Madison Street and pick fruit in the summer, or perhaps have both a summer and a winter job. They were distinguished from the hobos or occasional workers chiefly by the fairly definite schedules they followed. In contrast, the hobo worked at whatever was convenient without regard to the seasons. He lived by his labor, traveling and working without a set pattern. There were many types of hobos, including harvest hands, lumberjacks, and gandy dancers. Usually the classifications reflected the type of work the hobo happened to be doing. There were picturesque names for the hobo vocations. The "mucker" was a construction laborer, the "dino" worked with dynamite, the "apple knocker" picked apples, and the "beach comber" was "a plain sailor, of all the men most transient." The tramp's distinguishing characteristic was getting by without work wherever possible. He wandered for the joy of it; work was an evil to be avoided. Typically he was "neither a drunkard nor a bum, but an easy-going individual who lives from hand to mouth for the mere joy of living."[71]

The seasonal worker, the hobo, and the tramp were migratory types. There were also two stationary types, the home guard and the bum. Often the home guards were tramps or hobos who had settled down. Their wandering over, they worked at casual labor, lived on skid row, and stayed put. Anderson estimated that almost half of the residents of Hobohemia were home guards. The other stationary type was the bum, a man partially or totally dependent, sometimes unemployable, criminal, or addicted to alcohol or drugs. The bums were "the most pitiable and the most repulsive types of the down-and-outs."[72]

Beyond these five types, there were numerous subclassifications: the able-bodied and the non-able-bodied, the employables and unemployables, the peddlers, beggars, and moochers. Finally, there were predatory individuals in the tramp class, including "the gun" (robber or burglar), "the jackroller" (robbed fellow tramps while they were drunk or asleep), "the mission stiff" (lived on handouts from missions), "the grafter" (exploited charity organizations), "the bad actor" (troublemaker or nuisance whose family paid him to stay away from home), "the jungle buzzard" (begged from tramps in hobo jungles), "the punk" (youth who traveled with a jocker), and "the jocker" (exploited boys either sexually or by having them beg and steal for him).[73]

Basic to Anderson's fivefold typology were two underlying dimensions—the nature of a man's employment and his propensity to travel about. These dimensions reflected the professional and public attitudes toward homelessness characteristic of the early 1900's. It was felt that providing employment and stifling wanderlust and laziness would solve most of the problems of homelessness.

In the 1940's and 1950's, however, the stereotype of the skid row man's uncontrollable alcoholism gained currency and to some extent replaced uncontrollable wanderlust and congenital laziness as the primary characteristic of the homeless man. Therefore, when Donald Bogue wrote about skid row men in Chicago forty years after the publication of Anderson's work, he added one more dimension—the presence or absence of chronic alcoholism—to the two which were the basis of Anderson's typology. Of the resulting six categories, five were directly related to work status. They were 1. the aged and physically disabled (by definition out of the labor force), 2. the resident workingmen, 3. the migratory workers, 4. the bums, beggars, and panhandlers who could work but chose not to, 5. the criminals and workers in illegal enterprises (not unemployed, merely employed in unusual and unacceptable occupations), and 6. the chronic alcoholics. Like Anderson, Bogue found it necessary to describe other types of skid row residents which, taken together, account for the residue of inhabitants not clearly classifiable in the six major categories. These included runaways and adventurers, vacationers, young veterans and unstable young men, sex perverts, the mentally unsound, and "normal residents."[74]

Bogue's sixfold typology appeared in a chapter entitled "Who Lives on Skid Row, and Why—Views of Resource Persons." The data for that chapter came from interviews with 161 "resource persons," and the typology proved useful as an organizing device. The bulk of Bogue's book, however, was a report of findings from interviews with 613 residents of Chicago's skid row areas. The classification scheme used in organizing and interpreting those findings was not the six-category system rooted in Anderson's work, but a new twelve-category model whose basic dimensions were the three factors Bogue singled out as more important than all others as determinants of the extent to which skid row men could be rehabilitated. These three factors were disability status, drinking classification, and age. There were six categories of severely and moderately handicapped persons, and six of slightly handicapped or less handicapped men. The six categories under each of the handicap classifications were:

—elderly (65 and over) teetotalers and light drinkers
—elderly moderate and heavy drinkers
—young and middle-aged (20 to 64) teetotalers and light drinkers
—young and middle-aged moderate drinkers
—young (20 to 44) heavy drinkers and derelicts
—middle-aged (45 to 64) heavy drinkers and derelicts

When Bogue distributed his respondents among the twelve categories he found that most elderly men on skid row did not have a drinking problem, but about 80 per cent of them were seriously handicapped. One-fifth of the skid row men seemed to need no rehabilitation of any kind. Ten per cent were young heavy drinkers who were not handicapped, and this group seemed the "most promising" for rehabilitation efforts; the "least promising" group contained the 9 per cent of the men who were over forty-five and had both a drinking problem and a serious physical disability. One-eighth of the men fell into an "intermediate group" with modest potential for rehabilitation, because they were either aged and unhandicapped or young and handicapped.[75]

Another influential typology of skid row men has a single underlying dimension, drinking behavior. The typology grew out of exploratory fieldwork among skid row men in Seattle. The investigators used non-directed interviews with hospitalized alcoholics supplemented by sessions with members of Alcoholics Anonymous who had formerly lived on skid row. Informants were told that the researchers were "interested in the extent and nature of groupings on Skid Road." Eight distinct groupings were recognized. There were two categories of non-alcoholics: 1. the permanent residents, who had pensions or other dependable incomes and maintained fairly stable friendship cliques, and 2. transients. The alcoholics were more complex, and six types were observed: 1. the older alcoholics, frequently pensioners who were looked after by their landlords, 2. the "bums" who did not adhere to skid row standards and were avoided, 3. the "characters" who behaved erratically and were often arrested, 4. the "winos," unpredictable, run down, and rejected by higher-status alcoholics, 5. the "rubby-dubs," typically isolates who drank non-beverage alcohol, and 6. the "lushes," the prestige group of skid row alcoholics who had reasonably good physical and mental health, adhered to skid row norms, and usually were only temporary residents of skid row.[76]

A psychological perspective. Levinson has proposed that the skid row population may be divided into two major classes: the "true homeless" and a residual category of all others who happen to live in the neighborhood. The "true homeless" are men who live on skid row but are neither mentally ill, chronic alcoholics, criminals, nor too poor to live elsewhere. All those who reside on skid row and do not "belong" in accordance with Levinson's definition he would remove via "appropriate social policies." Those men left would be the "true" homeless men who had learned a fundamental detachment from life and who did not accept societal values.[77]

Neither the rewards nor the punishments of society are relevant to the true homeless man. He has removed himself from most sanctions and does not accept the norms. He has little esteem for others, and he does not care what they say about him. Nor does he seek higher status; rejection does not bother him. Instead, he lives by the principles of least effort and of self-sufficiency. As Levinson depicts him, he has little thought for the past or the future. He is not introspective and impartially ignores both the inner and the outer world. He denies his need for affection and responds to demands or stress by withdrawal. He does not seek security, he passionately avoids responsibility and involvement, he values his leisure. By common standards he is a deviant. By his own, he is a professional, and his status is hard won, requiring a period of socialization perhaps as long as that necessary to become a physician. In summary, all homeless men have one thing in common:

They implicitly reject our life and its values and are content merely to exist, vegetate with least effort, watching the world and their lives pass by. In a word, their orientation is on *being* rather than *becoming*.[78]

Skid row men are worthy of study because that core of common characteristics which are the distinguishing marks of the homeless is not limited to skid row.

. . . the homeless man can be found throughout society. . . . There are many men in every strata of society whose learning experiences have been of such a nature that they reinforced their desire to withdraw from their social groups, companions, and jobs. The unattached man who perpetually moves from one furnished room to another, the playboy who somehow never manages to hold on to a job, the unattached businessman who retires from life at a very early age and then roams around the country on a minimum budget—all these men and many others are component parts of the invisible mountain of homelessness.[79]

Many of the characteristics Levinson ascribes to the homeless also apply to the young adults who are "dropping out" of accepted channels for achievement in our own times. His statement that the homeless man is a symbol of what is wrong with society, made in 1963, now seems almost prophetic:

. . . the homeless man is a symbol of what's wrong with our society, an indication of man's brutality to man. He is the beacon light warning us of the reefs ahead. It may be noted that when social conditions become worse, the number of homeless men increases. Finally, he is the Rosetta stone of social pathology and psychopathology. When the homeless man passes from the scene, it will be one of the major indices pointing out that a key to our major sociopsychopathological disorders has been found.[80]

In a paper published five years before the one discussed above, Levinson was much less attuned to the homeless man as an indicator of societal imbalances and more inclined to blame a sick personality rather than a sick society. Personality problems had propelled the homeless man to skid row. After all, he was able to tolerate life in an "usually intolerable state of devaluation" on skid row, and the mere fact that he was able to live there, rather than seeking withdrawal through suicide, mental illness, or other forms of adaptation meant that he was unique. By not seeking a healthy solution, by being capable of tolerating life in the gutter or in a shelter, he manifested a defective personality.

Levinson's analysis of the homeless man's personality was based, in part, on an assessment of Rorschach protocols from forty native-born white homeless men at the men's shelter in New York City. His analysis of these protocols showed that the men were depressed and emotionally immature, were not adaptable, lacked drive and goals in life, experienced difficulty adjusting to society, and felt worthless and full of despair. In addition to these negative characteristics, the men had few interests, were apathetic, indifferent, passive, insecure, lacked the ability to empathize and understand others or themselves, were intellectually inefficient and had thinking disorders.

An anthropological approach. Perhaps the most extensive taxonomic endeavor is James Spradley's application of componential analysis to the world of skid row. His overview of previous attempts to understand skid row men led him to isolate four identity models, each held by a distinctive public.

The popular identity of the skid row man, the view accepted by the man in the street, was that he was a bum, immoral, irresponsible, and unpredictable. The medical identity attributed to the skid row man was "alcoholic," the legal identity of "common drunkards" focused on their vagrancy or chronic public drunkenness, and their sociological identity was "homeless men."

These four models may be useful in helping people relate to the

skid row men, but because they derive from the perceptions of outsiders, they are not accurate representations of skid row subculture
but instead are reflections of the dominant American culture.
Spradley wanted to discover the conceptual frameworks by which
the inhabitants of skid row organized reality. He described his work
as an "ethnographic study of identity," and applied field techniques
developed by anthropologists in the study of kinship systems. The
method "seeks to find out how people in alien societies organize
their knowledge about themselves, but it does not prescribe which
criteria should be significant, allowing these to arise from the empirical situation."[81]

In Spradley's case the "alien society" was skid row, its citizens
were urban nomads, and among the significant landmarks he dis-
cerned was that "tramp" was the primary identity of the urban
nomads, followed in importance by the "inmate" identity.

His "taxonomic definition of the tramp domain" included fifteen
kinds of tramps, which were reduced to eight significant "core
terms." These eight were "working stiff," "mission stiff," "bindle
stiff," "airedale" (one who travels by walking and has no social
anchorage except the pack he carries), "rubber tramp" (he has a
car), "home guard tramp," "box car tramp," and "ding" (begs for
a livelihood, no social anchorage). Major dimensions underlying
these eight types were amount of mobility, mode of travel, whether
their home base was anchored socially and psychologically, and
means of earning a livelihood. All but the home guards are mobile;
the box car tramp and the ding are most devoid of social ties and
responsibilities.[82]

Even greater richness appeared in the "inmate" identity. The
"cover term," inmate included four distinct dimensions ("drunk,"
"lockup," "trusty," and "kickout"). There were at least sixty different kinds of trusties, reducible to sixteen core terms.[83]

Underlying continua: disaffiliation and defectiveness. One of the
most distinctive typologies of skid row residents is Samuel Wallace's
catalogue of "careers on skid row." Each of the categories is a way

station, a stage in a man's "progress" along the inverted status hierarchy of skid row. First is the *aficionado,* the partially socialized outsider who continues to define himself as a member of the outside world, perhaps as a welfare client, casual laborer, artist, or tourist. At the other end of the hierarchy is the completely acculturated member of skid row subculture, the drunk, who "lives his life totally within the deviant community" and represents the end product of a long and expensive education. "It has taken years of socialization en route to homelessness and a complex process of career commitment to produce this totally deviant individual."[84]

Other positions are the alcoholic, the hobo, the professional beggar, the mission stiff, and the tour director. Mission stiffs or "reliefers" are men supported by missions or public agencies. Tour directors are "the wanderers, the dreamers, the disenchanted, the self-styled artists who have landed on skid row for a variety of personal reasons" and who spin fanciful stories to journalists, tourists, and researchers who come to look at skid row and its men. "The tour directors are often the first persons that the skid row visitors meet, and probably more than one book on skid row has been based on tales dreamed up by these grass-roots, skid row folklorists.[85]

Wallace linked his six primary skid row statuses to career patterns. The drunks, hobos, and beggars were likely to be recruited from mobile workers who had become laborers living on skid row before adopting a "respectable" skid row status. A second typical career pattern was for welfare clients to become reliefers or pensioners, eventually winding up as mission stiffs, beggars, or drunks. Finally, the *aficionados* who continued to participate in skid row life were likely to end their careers as alcoholics or tour directors.[86]

In a more recent work Wallace reviewed many of the definitions of skid row and homelessness used by researchers and discovered five basic variables incorporated in them, namely, place of residence, amount of residential mobility, degree of participation in skid row institutions, strength of family ties, and extent of poverty.[87] He combined these five characteristics in an attribute space and subsumed them under the general term "skid-rower." As I have written elsewhere,[88] the choice of "skid-rower" as the overarching, inclusive concept is unfortunate and perhaps even misleading because half of the cells in his typology apply to persons who do not reside on skid row. Wallace is correct in maintaining that the disparate populations examined by students of the isolated and unattached had a common, unifying element. But use of the term "disaffiliation" or one of its synonyms would be preferable to designating those who manifest that element as "skid-rowers," and thereby diverting attention from the majority of the unattached:

What the five characteristics have in common is that they all are related to "detachment from society characterized by the absence or attenuation of the affiliative bonds that link settled persons to a network of interconnected social structures. . . ." Thus, transience tends to prevent one from establishing stable social bonds, residence on skid row and involvement in its institutions places one in a stigmatized minority of outcasts without providing the bonds of solidarity and interpersonal responsibility common to many other out-groups, chronic inebriety disrupts social bonds as well as physiological balance, extreme poverty prevents one from performing customary roles in society, and living without kin removes one from the social context described as most intense and supportive as well as from those roles to which the interpersonal responsibility of greatest scope tends to be attached. In short, these elements utilized by various writers to describe the homeless or skid-row population all have to do with the weakening or absence of affiliations.[89]

We are proposing, then, that a single continuum—that of disaffiliation—might serve as an organizing principle to bring theoretical order to the conceptual heterogeneity of skid row research.

There is, however, a major flaw with the use of disaffiliation as the characteristic trait of the homeless, and that is that it is hard to explain the animosity of settled society toward skid row men in terms of their lack of affiliations. From a theoretical point of view we can argue that the disaffiliate is the ultimate stranger, that he is dangerous because he does not participate in our organizations and hence is beyond the power of most of our sanctions. But the virulence of the negative attitudes toward the homeless illustrated in Chapter 3 is not explained by the skid row man's disaffiliation. Besides, in an urbanized society a total disaffiliate can "pass"—the symbols of his disaffiliation need not be visible. If there is a common denominator to the antipathies toward the homeless, it seems related to the epithets such as "degenerate" and "derelict." It derives not from his disaffiliation, per se, but from his stigmatization as worthless, diseased, worn out, used up, and somehow sub- or post-human. In a word, it has to do with his perceived defectiveness as a human being.

The defectiveness of the skid row man stems from his occupying several stigmatized statuses at once. On almost all of the characteristics discussed in the first part of this chapter, the homeless man occupies a stigmatized or inferior position. To begin with, there is a physical, visible basis for antipathy toward the skid row man. He is defective physically: the ruined, scarred face, the toothless mouth, the missing limbs, the strange actions of the psychotic or mental incompetent; all of these are highly visible signs that the man is strange and that interaction with him is not likely to be rewarding.

Then there are the stigmatizing aspects of his character: the past of drunkenness, arrests, and prison, and the long periods of institutional living. In addition, he is old, and chronological age is itself a stigmatizing characteristic in our youth-centered society. He is deviant because he has no apparent family, no typical ties which bind him to a posterity and an ancestry.

He is poor, and in an achievement-oriented society obvious poverty is stigmatizing. He is frequently unemployed, and he is defined as a welfare recipient or a beggar. He has a bad address. Over everything else is the imputed alcoholism, the addiction which makes him a man out of control, perhaps not a man at all.

All of these images and positions—all of these kinds of defectiveness—combine to make the skid row resident a most persecuted man, and to make him the victim of a long series of psychological assaults, many of them self-directed. To summarize: the skid row man is, or is perceived as being, defective physically (scarred, handicapped, aged, and diseased), mentally (psychotic, senile, or manifesting bizarre symptoms), morally (a pervert, criminal, or addict), psychologically (low self-esteem, high self-aggression), socially (disaffiliated), legally (treated by the police and courts as a resident of an occupied country rather than as a free man), economically (impoverished, unemployed), and ecologically (he resides in a neighborhood in which no "decent" person would live).

The self-hate generated by the dissonance between internalized values and skid row status would seem to be such that life would be intolerable without accepting the inverted values of the skid row. To understand skid row men, and more importantly, to treat them, the effects of the imputed defectiveness must be known and neutralized. A conceptualization of the "basic" nature of skid row men as men to whom massive defectiveness is imputed would seem a useful starting point.

5 | The social organization of skid row

Formal organizations on skid row are colonial in nature. They are directed, and for the most part staffed, by people from respectable society. The skid row man does have an impact on these organizations, but the nature of that impact is more reaction than independent action. He is acted upon, not actor. In the realm of informal relationships, however, the homeless man plays a more directive role. The drinking patterns, friendship relations, and much of the racial discrimination on the row are his to shape and control.

This chapter is divided into two major sections, reflecting the distinction between formal skid row institutions and informal patterns of interaction. In practice the distinctions between these categories are not entirely clear. Consequently, there is material subsumed under the heading "Formal Organizations" which might as appropriately have been placed later as part of the discussion headed "Informal Relationships." Also, it should be noted that some aspects of the social organization of skid row are treated in other chapters. For example, much of Chapter 7 ("Social Control") is about the formal organizations on skid row, and sections of Chapter 6 ("Homeless Women") are relevant to the discussion in this chapter. Thus the present division is somewhat arbitrary, a matter of convenience, and not of empirical reality.

The formal organizations of skid row

Three institutions dominate the skid row scene. They are distinctive, necessary elements which, when they appear in close proximity, indelibly mark a neighborhood as a skid row. In descending order of importance, they are the cheap hotels and lodging houses, the gospel missions, and the bars. The structure of these institutions reflects the disaffiliation and the problems of the homeless men whom they serve. Most of our discussion of formal organizations of skid row will pertain to these three institutions.

Hotels and lodging houses. The cubicle hotel or lodging house is the most important skid row facility. There are other sleeping facilities available—public shelters, gospel missions, rooming houses, and hotels with rooms—but most skid row men live in the lodging house. On the Bowery four out of five men are lodging house residents; in Chicago the proportion is two out of three. In contrast, relatively few men live at the missions. Most skid row censuses have shown that at any one time fewer than 10 per cent of the men sleep in missions, although occasionally, as in Philadelphia, mission dormitories may sleep as high as one-fourth of the men.[1]

The cubicles in skid row hotels are very small, perhaps five by seven feet. The partitions between them reach only part way to the ceiling. The tops are covered with wire netting to discourage thieves from crawling over. The cubicles are open at the top, and sounds from other men on the floor are clearly audible. Inside the cubicle there is a stand of some kind—sometimes merely an apple box—and a cabinet attached to the wall. The other furnishings are a metal cot, a chair, and some hooks or nails in the wall.

Good housing on skid row provides security for possessions, protection against fire and other lodgers, cleanliness, and silence. One of the marks of a "quality" hotel is the lengths to which the management will go to minimize noise, usually by carefully screening potential lodgers. The men recognize fine gradations in quality of hotels. The hierarchy of distinct "levels" of housing set down by

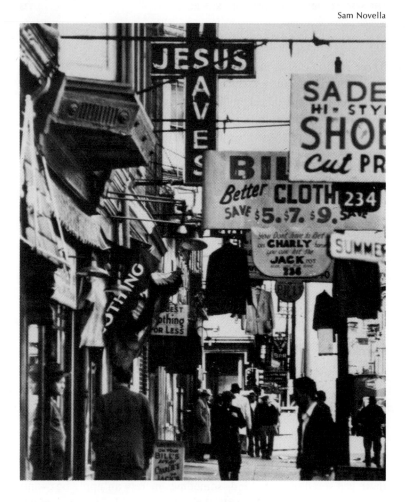

Skid Row establishments in Philadelphia, about 1963.

Hotel cubicle in which the body of a seventy-five-year-old man was found. "Canned heat" is stacked under the bed.

Wallace includes, in order of acceptability, tourist hotels ("in skid row but not of it"), single-room hotels, cage or cubicle hotels, missions, and public and private dormitories as well as less desirable places to sleep like transportation depots, public shelters, and boxcars.[2]

Sometimes the lodging house occupies the upper stories of a building; the ground floor may have a bar, restaurant, or other business establishment. Up the stairs there is a main doorway and a clerk's cage. Beyond the cage, with windows fronting on the street, is the center of lodging house activity, the lobby. Life in the lobby is usually placid; the men smoke, lounge around, read newspapers or paperbacks, talk, or sit and stare. In many houses the dominant activity is watching television. Occasionally there is a game of cards. Some lodging houses enforce a "no drinking" policy in the lobby, others allow it. Some of the better lodging houses have soda, candy, and ice cream machines.

There is a great variety in the cleanliness and general atmosphere of lodging houses. Some cater to a specific clientele, such as old men or welfare clients. The houses also vary in size. On the Bowery in 1966 they ranged in capacity from 79 beds to 566 beds.

A skid row lodging house provides services other than lodging, especially to long-term residents. A clerk or manager may help an inebriated man to his room, cash his checks, and hold his mail and property for him. In fact, when asked who took a personal interest in them, lodgers were more apt to mention a clerk or proprietor of a lodging house than anyone else except relatives. And 60 per cent of the lodgers interviewed in Nash's study of Bowery lodging houses said they thought the manager of the house where they lived would be willing to extend them credit if necessary.[3]

The importance of the lodging house extends beyond the fact that most skid row men sleep there. They spend many of their waking hours there also. The Minneapolis survey showed that half of the respondents spent over five hours a day either sitting in the hotel lobby or in their rooms.[4] So both in terms of proportion of men serviced and the amount of time spent there by the men, the lodging house dominates the skid row scene.

By normal standards the residential facilities of skid row are very inadequate. Even in the best lodging houses a man is cramped for space, and in the worst he is assaulted by noise and foul smells, attacked by vermin, and constantly exposed to filth, disease, and the depredations of other men. He may be sexually assaulted, mugged, or robbed. But the "best" facilities have their partisans, and many skid row men are satisfied with their housing.

When Chicago men were asked what they liked or disliked about life on skid row, 11 per cent said that they liked their hotels and living accommodations. Dissatisfaction was more prevalent, however; one-fourth of the respondents singled out skid row hotels as specific targets for their dissatisfaction. A question about their feelings for the hotel in which they were living elicited positive statements from about half of the men. One in three expressed strong dissatisfaction; the rest of the men who had an opinion said they thought that their lodging was better than other places on skid row, but disliked it anyway. Five major factors contributed to their unhappiness about housing. Most frequently mentioned was the dirt, then the noise, the small size of rooms or cubicles, the prevalence of drinking and rowdiness, and the nature of the other residents in the hotel. Each of these factors was mentioned by between 16 and 19 per cent of the men.

The men were also asked about things they liked, and the responses were mostly the positive counterparts of the things disliked. Thus, one-third of the men liked the cleanliness of their hotel, and about one-fifth mentioned their satisfaction with other residents, the management and clerks, and the quiet.

The great variation in facilities was manifest in the finding that in one-third of the skid row hotels between 90 and 100 per cent of the residents were satisfied. But the bad hotels outnumbered the good. In almost one-half of the hotels, only a few of the men said they liked their residence. "It is unmistakably clear that the managements of some hotels have only happy customers, while in other hotels almost everybody dislikes living there."[5]

When Philadelphia men were asked a general question about what they liked about living on skid row, only 4 per cent mentioned housing. When interviews probed specifically for the men's attitudes about housing, over half said they liked the place where they lived. Thirty-six per cent responded negatively to this question, a somewhat smaller proportion than among Chicago men (45 per cent). The major complaints of the dissatisfied Philadelphia lodgers were the lack of cleanliness, excessive drinking and other negative attributes of other men, and poor management. The rank order of things liked reflected the positive aspects of these same dimensions: cleanliness, low rental, other residents, quietness, and management.[6]

These responses do suggest that many of the lodging houses are inadequate and, in Bogue's phrase, "candidates for demolition," but surprisingly, they are nonetheless acceptable to the men. However, the judgment of acceptability seems to be linked with low aspirations dictated by the skid row man's financial situation. In an exploratory study of residents in Bowery lodging houses, the men were asked if they liked the lodging house in which they were living. Four out of five said yes. The same study showed that long-term Bowery residents were more apt to like lodging houses than more recent arrivals. Reasons given for liking the most preferred lodging houses on the row (not necessarily the one where the man was living at the time of interview) were the type of people who lived there (mentioned by 22 per cent of the men), cleanliness (17 per cent), management policies (13 per cent), a resident's freedom to come and go (10 per cent), and the quiet (9 per cent). Reasons for disliking the "least favored" lodging house were the type of people living there, the fact that residents there got robbed (24 per cent), management policies (16 per cent), and that the place was dirty (8 per cent).[7]

Perhaps the most meaningful way to explain the nature and functions of the lodging house is to take a closer look at some of them. The hotels discussed below are located on the Bowery. Each represents a distinctive "level" of lodging house.

The "Dakota Hotel" was a high-class Bowery lodging house located at the edge of the Bowery proper. The building was old but well kept. The owner took pride in providing a decent place for his men to live; periodically he remodeled a stairway or repainted a section of cubicles. He also recruited lodgers actively. When an old customer dropped in, he would launch into a sales pitch about how conditions had improved in an attempt to get the old friend to move in again.

The owner's interest in the men seemed sincere. He provided cola, candy, and ice cream machines, cashed their checks, and sometimes wrote letters for them. At times he would hold back a portion of a man's check when he saw that the man was likely to "blow it all" and face a couple of weeks with no cash. He seemed completely honest in this. The money was always returned when the man's condition improved.

Only white men stayed at the Dakota. The owner insisted that if a black appeared who qualified, i.e., who was dressed neatly, not scarred up from a lot of fighting, and not drunk, he would admit the man. In practice, the black stayed away. No men with "muni tickets"—lodging tickets issued by the Men's Shelter—were admitted either, but several residents received welfare checks from the city.

The authority of the law was never far from the Dakota, and the men who lived there behaved or were not readmitted. One man played his radio so loudly that he disturbed other lodgers. When he refused to open his door or turn down the volume, a police officer helped the clerks break down his door, bundle up his possessions, and evict him.

Occasionally a man was evicted from the lobby without being allowed to go to his room and gather up his personal belongings. When such a man sobered up he usually came back and demanded his property. There may have been times when a man did not retrieve his belongings, but in all cases observed by our field workers, the management returned the property, although often the man had to plead, wait, and plead some more before the management yielded to his importunity.

Despite the owner's steady campaign for new customers, men evicted from his house were usually not readmitted. Several men returned and begged to have their old rooms back, promising that if they were given "just one more chance" they would be model lodgers. With one exception, these petitions were refused. The men knew that the owner would carry out his threats, and as a result of his consistent discipline, the Dakota remained a "tight," orderly establishment in a milieu of transiency and drunkenness. The owner was proud that he housed the better class of homeless men, and was willing to overlook some of their minor faults, including drunkenness, provided they were quiet and caused no trouble.

All of the clerks at the Dakota were long-time employees. They liked to talk about the history of the place and the famous and infamous persons who had lived there. The present status and whereabouts of some of their old customers was a frequent topic of conversation. There was a lot of kidding among the clerks, and between clerks and lodgers.

All but one of the clerks lived off-Bowery, and most of them felt superior to the lodgers. Their long experience had taught them how to handle Bowery men; they could be domineering and tough when the situation demanded it, particularly if they felt someone was making unreasonable demands. But sometimes the endurance of the homeless men prevailed.

On one occasion, when the owner was absent, a man approached one of the clerks and asked for a "loan." The clerk refused at once, but the man continued his pleas for almost an hour, punctuating his repetitive "please, Mr. Jones, please!" with long periods when he stared at the clerk in silent reproach. At last the clerk could stand no more. He slammed down the window to his office, shouting at the suppliant "Go away! No! No! Get out of here!" and stalked up and down in the little office loudly complaining at such impertinence. The man shuffled a few steps away, pretended to be leaving, and a few minutes later appeared at the window again. After a few minutes the clerk wordlessly handed the man a quarter and waved him out.

Most of the lodgers at the Dakota were long-term residents. Many had lived in the same cubicle for several years. There were established groups of men who drank, gambled, or talked and watched television together.

Very few men stayed around the Dakota in the mornings and early afternoons. Technically they were supposed to be out by 10 A.M., but this rule was waived for a few. Nevertheless, most lodgers left in the morning to work, walk, sit in parks, or loiter on the Bowery sidewalks. At night the television room was full. Sometimes there were gatherings in the foyer or on the sidewalk in front of the house. On weekends especially there was a lot of commotion and boisterous activity, but in general the Dakota was a quiet place.

A second hotel, "Victor House," was in many respects the opposite of the Dakota. Located in one of the worst sections of the Bowery, it was dark, dingy, noisy, and rundown. Most of its lodgers were blacks, many of them on "muni" tickets.

There was less racial discrimination at Victor House than in most skid row hotels. In fact, there was little discrimination of any sort. In contrast to the Dakota and its high-class clientele, the management of the Victor prided itself in taking anybody, and few men were ever evicted.

The house rules were enforced informally by the clerks and the owner, who sometimes punished a man by insisting that he abide by the written rules. Referrals from the Men's Shelter were granted the same privileges as paying customers, except that there was a higher probability of the revocation of these privileges if a man were troublesome. It should be stressed that "troublesome" is a relative term. Behavior that would have been intolerable at the Dakota was overlooked at Victor House. The owner spent little time in the hotel. Most of the actual power was in the hands of the manager and his assistants.

The owner had a medical orientation to the troublemaker, viewing him as a sick person who needed understanding. One morning he rushed downstairs to quell a major disturbance, and addressed one of the men involved: "I know you're not a troublemaker, you're a sick guy, you should be in a rest home, but I don't know how you can find one." Returning to the office, he explained, "It's a disease, and you got to understand these guys."

The clerks at the Victor mixed freely with the lodgers. They often spent their off-duty time in the lobby, talking and joking with the men. On evenings and weekends the lobby was crowded and noisy, often so noisy that one had to shout to be heard. The loud laughter, shouting, and swearing seemed to suggest that lodgers at Victor House had more fun than the "elite" cloistered away at the Dakota, but it may be that the resident of the Victor simply expressed himself more freely. The Victor also had its long days of quiet apathy.

"India House" was similar in some respects to each of the lodging houses described above. Like the Dakota, it had a sizable population of white old-timers. It also had "muni" men, some of whom were black. But the reception given "muni" men at India House was quite different from that at the Victor. At India House men on "muni" were made uncomfortable. They were not allowed to loiter in the lobby or to watch television, but had to go directly to their rooms. In the mornings, they had to be out of the building by 7 A.M. Thus, they formed a transient group separate from the house's more permanent residents. Clerks and "permanent" lodgers united in despising the "muni" men and usually called them "winos" and "bums."

As in other houses, clerks exerted a great deal of control via informal "favors" which they might do for the men. In other words, a lodger was often allowed special privileges which the clerk could revoke if the men misbehaved. Some of the discrimination against men on "muni" tickets was accounted for by the wider range of privileges which clerks allowed the old-timers and paying customers.

Missions. Next to the lodging houses, the most distinctive institutions which set skid row apart from other sections of the city are the gospel missions. Most missions offer something to eat, a place to sleep and clean up, and some kind of "salvation." Some of the missions make attendance at religious services a prerequisite to meals and lodging. Others offer temporary sustenance to all who pass a preliminary screening and do not insist that their clients hear a sermon or receive spiritual counseling sessions, although they are encouraged to do so.

The soft sell—with food and shelter available irrespective of a man's attitude about God and heaven—is atypical. Usually the mission requires some show of contrition by the supplicant before he is considered worthy to share the scarce resources of the private charity. The enforced exposure to religious exhortation is not necessarily demeaning.

If your religion has a hell-fire-and-damnation fundamentalist theme, you will not object that first the Mission feeds your soul and only afterward the rest of you. If you are not religious, you may look upon the hour-and-a-half service as a performance in which you must sing for your supper. In fact, though, you are required to do no more than sit in the pew and expose yourself to the mission's ministrations.[8]

The proportion of skid row men actually participating in mission rehabilitation programs is much lower than the one-tenth who are housed in missions. The rehabilitation programs tend to be resident programs, and ideally a man makes a commitment to stay for several weeks or months. Most of the missions operate on the philosophy that their limited resources are best used to help men acquire a religious anchoring to life along with the more prosaic necessities. (The existence of public welfare helps the missions to justify these priorities: the indigent who is not interested in "improving himself" can get public aid.) Any long-term aid from a mission is for men willing to work within the mission's program, adopt its goals, and live by its rules.

In most cities several types of missions serve the homeless.[9] An extensive treatment of their clientele, programs, and problems is beyond the scope of this book. We will outline a few programs, and illustrate homeless men's attitudes toward the missions. More extensive accounts of their activities and relationships to disaffiliated men are found in the works of Wallace, Bendiner, Wiseman, Anderson, and others.[10]

One of the largest mission-type enterprises is the Salvation

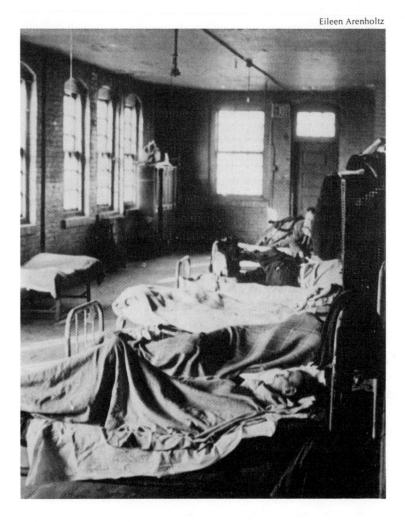

A gospel mission dormitory.

The Galilee Mission, Philadelphia.

Army's international network. One of their rehabilitation programs is described at length in Wiseman's *Stations of the Lost,* under the label Christian Missionaries. Criteria for admission are having a treatable handicap and manifesting a sincere desire for self-improvement. Another important and sometimes critical variable is whether the man's occupational skill fits him to work in the Missionaries' salvage operation. The Christian Missionaries provide all the necessities of life to homeless men admitted to their centers. The regimen includes compulsory religious services twice a week and daily meditation periods; "work therapy" for weekly "gratuities" ranging from four to fifteen dollars per week, "companionship therapy" (enforced group living), living in a "structured milieu" with numerous regulations, and the possibility of group therapy and vocational counseling. There are also informal pressures for audience participation in religious services; the standard formula for these testimonials is that "the original condition of the alcoholic on arrival to the Center was one of atheistic helplessness and that he found inner strength at the Center."[11]

Clients said the program provided adequate living facilities, good clothing, and good food, but "much of the good feeling engendered by the physical plant is lost because the men living at the Center feel that they are treated like children who cannot be trusted." Because the Christian Missionaries combine spiritual salvation and a thriving salvage business with the dispensing of Christian charity, the men they serve view them as exploitative and hypocritical. Many aspects of the rehabilitation program and similar practices at other missions are viewed negatively. The men resent having religion "shoved at" them, "being worked," "being used," and being stuck in "social stagnation." They also complain that there is little psychological aid for the drinking problem or help in finding jobs.[12]

At the McAuley Mission six blocks from the Bowery, men who come for assistance are placed in a transient men's dormitory. According to the superintendent, all but the noisiest drunks are fed and housed for at least one night. Medical aid, fresh clothing, food, and a place to rest are available even if the man decides not to accept the mission's residency program. Those who do accept it must agree to stay at least three weeks, and to do simple housekeeping chores or repair work. They are not permitted to drink, nor even to smoke, inside the mission building. They must attend gospel services and participate in Bible study and religious counseling. The graduated course in Bible study is an attempt to "overcome the shortcomings, or perhaps absolute blank, in a man's religious training." Generally men stay only a few weeks. The counselors try to keep them there long enough that the unaccustomed religious ideals will have time to take root.

The attrition rate is high. The mission could easily keep a man longer by putting less of an emphasis on religion or by relaxing some of its other rules. It could also serve a far larger number of men by limiting itself to transients and serving free food to all comers several times a day. This could be justified as elemental Christian charity. It would result in impressive statistics regarding the number of men served and perhaps make it easier to raise funds. But few, if any, men would be rehabilitated either socially or spiritually.

The mission now says there are rules a man must live by. If he agrees to live by these rules he will be offered love, friendship, and guidance so that he can discover a new life. No matter what he has been in the past, here all is forgiven and he can make a fresh start. If he does not want to live by the rules, if he does not want to take the first step, if he does not want to search for a solution to his problems, he can leave.[13]

In Chicago the Olive Branch Mission offers nightly religious services for the homeless, along with food, clothing, lodging, and employment counseling. First aid is available from a registered nurse. There is also a resident program for about thirty men at a time. Residents receive free meals and lodging until they get jobs. After that they pay part of their own expenses.[14]

In Seattle the Jericho Inn Mission furnishes beds for all who enter on a first-come, first-serve basis, provided the men are sober and behave themselves. The men are required to attend services. The Puget Sound Christian Indian Mission serves a more specialized clientele. Men come in mainly for clothing, counseling, and referral services. Alcoholics are escorted or sent to a detoxification center; men who need food or lodging are directed to other agencies. The mission holds religious services but attendance is voluntary. Clients do not have to be Indians, but about three-fourths of them are.

Some skid row men speak well of the missions. Many receive emergency help from them. But most speak disparagingly of them, reaffirming the negative image of the "mission stiff," the man who has prostituted himself to the missions. More than anything else, the "strings attached" charity which demands the facade of penitence, interest in religion, and repudiation of the values of homelessness seems to rankle. The typical skid row man knows his heart has not changed, merely the level of his blood sugar. He seeks not eternal salvation but immediate surcease of hunger. The message of the missions is "we will help you, but you must be what we want you to be." The kind of help the independent homeless man seeks, but rarely finds, is summarized: "we will help you, because you are you, because you are a man."

The homeless man expects compassion and charity, but he receives little of either. From state bureaucracies he might expect inconsistency and inefficiency. But from the gospel mission, with its continual harping on Christian ethics and the unworthiness of the unregenerate skid row man, inconsistency and violated expectations spell hypocrisy and bad faith. An ex-client of the Christian Missionaries says,

I'll tell you why most of us go there. Because we're desperate. We need a roof over our heads. But I'll tell you something else. Next time I'm that bad off, I'll jump off the bridge instead of going there again.[15]

Even more hostile is Tom Kromer's description of death in a skid row mission:

I am in this mission. I lie up on top of this bunk. It is a high bunk. It is a three-decker. If I should turn over on my stomach in my sleep, I would fall out and break my neck. This is a big room. There are a thousand here besides myself. I lie up here and listen to the snores of a thousand men. . . . I look at the rafters overhead and the shadows that play across them. I think of vultures hovering in the sky, waiting. They dart across the rafters and onto the walls. I see them swooping down on their prey that lie sweating in the lice-filled bunks. Their prey is a thousand men that lie and groan and toss. . . .

"There is no God," I say. "If there is a God, why is such as this? What have these men done that they live like rats in a garbage heap? Why does He make them live like rats in a garbage heap?"

It is all dark in here. Dark save for the light and the shadows that come from the electric sign outside. It is a big sign. It hangs from wires in front of this mission. "Jesus Saves," it says. I can hear the shuffle of stiffs as they slouch in front of the door outside. They lean up against the sides and sprawl on the curb. They are waiting for nothing. They are too late. There are plenty of beds left in here, but they are too late. You have to come early and listen to the sermon if you want a flop in this joint. They are too late. I lie here and wonder since when did Jesus Christ start keeping office hours?

. . .

I turn my eyes to the stiff in the bunk next to mine. Through the shadows I can see him lying there. His face is pasty white. The bones almost stick out of his skin. All you can see is the whites of his eyes as he rolls them back and forth. . . . I turn my head away from him, but I still can hear him groan. . . . I cannot help looking at him. . . . He does not breathe. He only rattles. Why doesn't someone do something for this poor bastard? Do something! That is a good joke. When he rattles to death on top of this lousy bunk, it will only be one less to swill down their lousy carrot slop. God damn them. Some day they will pay for this.

. . .

I lie up here and think. Here is a stiff who has lived his life, and now he is dying under these lousy blankets in a mission. Who is there to care whether he lives or dies? If all this stiff needed was a glass of water to save his life, he would croak anyway. Nobody in this mission would give him a drink of water. This stiff is dying, and this other stiff in the next bunk is raising hell because the rattles from his hollow chest keep him from sleeping. This stiff has not always been a stiff. Somewhere, sometime, this stiff has had a home. Maybe he had a family. Where are they now? I do not know. The chances are he does not know himself. He is alone. The fritz has made him alone. He will die alone. He will die cooped up in a mission with a thousand stiffs who snore through the night, but he will die alone. The electric light outside will go on and off in the dark, "Jesus Saves," but that will not help this stiff. He will die alone.

I yell to this mission stiff who is the night man.

"What the hell are you yellin' about?" he says. . . . "There is a man dying up here in this lousy bunk, and you ask me why am I yelling?" I say. . . .

"What do you think I am goin' to do with him?" he says. "I am no wet-nurse for a bunch of lousy stiffs."

"You are a God-damn mission stiff," I say, "and mission stiffs are sons of bitches."

"You can't talk like that to me," he says. "I'll have you kicked out of the mission. Tomorrow I'll have you kicked out of the mission."

"You call an ambulance for this stiff," I say, "or I will call it myself, and beat the hell out of you besides."

"I will call the ambulance," he says, "but you will not be here tomorrow. I'll see that you are not here tomorrow."

. . .

Pretty soon the doctor is here. There are two guys with him. . . . They carry a stretcher between them.

. . .

This croaker climbs down off the bunk.

"This guy has not got a chance," he says. "I can't do anything for this guy. He is starved to death. He is skin and bones. He will be dead in an hour."

"What'll we do with him?" this mission stiff says.

This bastardly mission stiff does not want to be bothered with an old stiff who will be dead in an hour. He is afraid he might have to help carry him downstairs. All mission stiffs are the same. They are all bastards.

"Load him up," this croaker says to the guys with the stretcher, "we'll take him with us."

They load him on the stretcher and take him out. . . .

There are not a thousand snores through the night now. There are none. These stiffs in the bunks raise up on their elbows and watch these two guys in white carry this stiff out. These stiffs know what they are watching. They are watching a funeral. This stiff is not dead yet, but they are watching a funeral. He will not come back. You will see them carry out plenty of stiffs in a mission on these stretchers. You will never see them again after they carry them out. We know that we are watching a funeral. When they carry you out of a mission, you are dead.[16]*

The bars. The bars, together with the lodging houses and missions, comprise the essential institutions of skid row. The bars must be close, preferably scattered among the lodging houses and the missions. Places to drink, sleep, and to put you up when you are out of money—these are the heart of skid row. The other facilities—the "horsemarkets" or cheap restaurants, the barber colleges and public parks, the pawn shops and secondhand stores—are frill, and can be located elsewhere. Bendiner describes Bowery bars:

> The bars of the Bowery are its life—sources of its nourishment, meeting ground, forum—miraculous with the power of creating a world without sharp edges, a rounded, hazy, ludicrous, unimportant world.
> To attain that level, men are willing to panhandle, occasionally to do worse. It is ordinarily quiet in the bars, with only the eternal conflict of the haves and the have-nots, the drinkers and the cadgers.[17]

For many skid row men, the bars are "home," and the lodging house is merely a place to spend the night until the bars open the next day. In most skid row bars, the homeless men predominate until 5:00 or 6:00 P.M., then the clientele changes; the working men having a drink on the way home take over for a few hours, to be replaced by people out for entertainment later in the evening. A few skid row bars, such as Sammy's Bowery Follies in New York, are tourist attractions.

One of the few intensive studies of the skid row bar is an unpublished memorandum by George Nash completed for Columbia University's Bowery Project in 1964. At that time there were twenty-nine bars in the Bowery area, twenty-seven of which catered to the homeless clientele. Nash visited all of these bars, and made an extensive participant observation study of one of them, the Happy Hour Bar. Many of his observations about the nature and functions of the skid row bar were corroborated in a subsequent paper about tavern culture by Matthew P. Dumont.[18]

---

* From *Waiting for Nothing* by Tom Kromer. Copyright 1935 by Alfred A. Knopf, Inc. Reprinted by permission of the publisher.

"Sleeping it off": Skid Row sidewalks, doorways, and alleys are beds for homeless alcoholics. Sleepers are easy prey for thieves. (Bowery, New York City, 1963.)

Manhattan's Bowery District as portrayed in Reginald Marsh's "White Tower Hamburger" (1945).

Many of the "regulars" who spend their days in one or two favorite bars are on hand when the bar opens in the morning. Some Bowery bars open at 7:30 A.M. although they cannot begin serving alcoholic beverages until 8:00. The half-hour before the "eye opener" can be purchased is one of the most animated times of the day. At one Bowery bar Nash observed that there were more customers when the bar opened than any other time of the day.

The major activity of the "Happy Hour" was the coming and going as men went outside, sat on the sidewalk or wandered away, and then returned. Some of them slept beside the building. There was some conversation; according to Nash the most frequent topics were cigarettes, money for wine, and a man's "Bowery background" (where he was from, what his nationality was, how long he had been on the Bowery). Other frequent topics were military service, police and police activity, drinking, jobs, facets of windshield-wiping (one of the principal occupations of many of the regulars), what the nearby missions were serving for lunch, and finally, the matter of "the colored," whom many of the whites blamed for increasing violence on the Bowery. Not discussed were sports, death, illness or injury, the men's personal lives, the current addresses of the men, sex, or other cities. Some of these omissions may have been atypical; some may reflect the unique characteristics of the men who were regulars in the Happy Hour Bar.

Dumont noticed the narrow range of conversation topics in the tavern he studied, but said that within that range were reports of personal loss, illness, isolation, and death. Dumont reported fragments of conversations he overheard. They had to do with cancer, cirrhosis of the liver, a friend's death, hospital facilities, and financial losses. Part of the difference between the Bowery bar and the urban tavern studied by Dumont may lie in the greater solidarity among Dumont's "regulars," several of whom lived in the same rooming house a couple of doors away from the tavern.[19]

Among chronic alcoholics who live on skid row, wine is the predominant beverage. In the Happy Hour Bar none of the regulars bought anything but muscatel wine. Beer is also popular in some skid row bars. Among Bogue's respondents beer was the most popular beverage; 42 per cent of the men claimed to drink beer and almost nothing else. However, it was the light and moderate drinkers who usually drank beer. Among the heavy drinkers and alcoholic derelicts wine was more important. Three-fourths of the derelicts drank either wine or wine in combination with other drinks, the latter pattern depending upon the drinkers' financial resources.

Sixty per cent of the skid row drinkers interviewed in Chicago said that they usually bought their drinks at the bar, and another 10 per cent said they bought their drinks there about half the time. The importance of the bar to skid row drinking behavior is thus evident.[20] But skid row bars do much more than serve drinks. They furnish a variety of peripheral services for their patrons. Some of them serve food and coffee as well as drinks. The bartender will occasionally loan a man money, or make up the difference between the change the man can raise and the cost of a drink. They also provide check-cashing services, serve as a mailing address for some of the regulars, and provide refuge when the paddy wagon comes by. Sometimes people needing workers come into the bars seeking help; Nash was offered a job as a circus worker while observing in the bar, and when he turned it down another Bowery man was approached and took the job.

A very important function is that of public rest room and water fountain. According to Nash, "no one who comes into the "Happy Hour Bar" is ever asked a question or refused admittance," and there is quite a bit of traffic through the side door into the men's room and out again. Dumont's study of the urban tavern also noted that "the unrestricted opportunity to urinate" was a major provision of the bar.

When they are not in their rooms these men, who often have urinary frequency from the combination of alcohol intake, prostatism and urinary tract infections, have little opportunity to empty their bladders. They do not have the license that more respectable-looking people have to use gas station or restaurant washrooms. The old-timers are occasionally arrested for exposing themselves while attempting to urinate.[21]

The role of the bar as a "windshield-wiping headquarters" is interesting. The three main intersections on the Bowery where homeless men step into the traffic and wipe windshields of cars stopped at traffic lights were all close to the Happy Hour Bar. Nash estimated that about one-third of the bar's regular customers wipe windshields and regard it as an honorable way of making enough money to pay for their drinks.

Frank, the good-looking Chippewa Indian who gets $180.00 a month pension for having been injured as a Marine Lieutenant in the Second World War, goes out in his suit and wipes windshields. He was proud that it took him only ten minutes to get up a dollar for a bottle. Cal, a handsome regular in his mid-thirties who wore dirty khaki trousers and shirt, explained that windshield wiping was his regular profession. He had hopes of building enough of a stake at windshield wiping to buy some wine which he would be able to sell bootleg on Sunday. With the proceeds of that, he then hoped to open a whorehouse.[22]

The bar is also a place for homosexuals to pick up some of the men. Nash himself was propositioned, and one of the regulars explained "how these homosexuals work":

They're good for getting you cleaned up. They sure have nice rooms; they live by themselves. They will never give you no money but they'll give you a good meal and it's a good place to get cleaned up.[23]

Finally, the bar is a place to sleep. In his survey of Bowery bars Nash checked nineteen of them at about midnight. In eight of them, men were sleeping with their heads on the table. Bars in other parts of the city do not allow men to sleep, but on the Bowery, at any time of the day or night, you can find men sleeping in the bars.

Nash's summary of what went on in the Happy Hour was that

The best description of the activity at the Happy Hour Bar during the entire day that I spent there would be to say that nothing happened. Inactivity was the rule, and there was no entertainment or joviality to break the monotony.[24]

Most skid row bars are not as "dead" as those on the Bowery. More often, the homeless men's "dominance" of the bar ends at about 6:00 P.M., and the "action" starts. Younger patrons arrive, and there are some female customers. The variety of deviant behavior represented broadens: prostitutes and B-girls ply their trade, and jackrollers work on men with more money than the homeless alcoholics who drink there during the day.

We concluded the section on missions with an account of death in the mission. Death also occurs in the bars, and the sense of community and concern for one's fellows is no more evident there than in the missions. The incident described below was presented as one of a series of incidents illustrating the absence of a sense of "community" on skid row.

I entered the Sunshine Bar at 6 o'clock on a mild spring afternoon because I noticed an ambulance pull up on the sidewalk in front of it. The ambulance driver, nurse, and two policemen walked in and went to the corner near the front door where X lay on his back. The nurse took a look at him and felt his pulse. "Sure he's dead," she said to the policeman. The bartender came up and spoke quietly to the policeman. Three or four men in the bar came forward to look. The policeman got the needed information and the bartender went back to work. The people went back to their places inside the bar. There were 56 men in the bar at the same time that X lay dead in the front corner. Almost all were shabby Bowery men. Most of the men had not moved even when the police came in. If they realized X had died, they showed no emotion.

There was some delay in removing X as the ambulance driver and the policeman debated the procedures that should be followed. There was a hat over X's face, otherwise his body was not covered. He wore dingy work clothes.

The bulk of the tables were in the back of the bar at some distance from X. There were two small tables between the bar and the front door, one of which was beside X. Two men with glasses of wine walked over and sat down at the table, about six feet from where X lay dead in the corner. Someone yelled, "See what happens when you drink?" The man sitting next to the corpse answered, "I'm no bum, I pay for my drinks!" He and his companion laughed and drank their wine.

Tom, a small man who spent a lot of time in the Sunshine, gave me details as best he knew them. X had been a friend of his for six or eight months, but Tom didn't know X's name. Tom did know that X had a sister in Pennsylvania. X had just gotten out of jail that day after serving 60 days at Riker's Island. He came into the Sunshine Bar without money and he needed a drink. The bartender had him sweep the floor and clean the toilets in exchange for drinks.

After X finished working he stood in the corner. He had what appeared to be an epileptic fit and fell down in the corner writhing. Then something happened—perhaps a heart attack—and X didn't move anymore. The bartender noticed him and called the police who called an ambulance. Presently X would be gone and forgotten, but in the meantime the Bowery men sat at their tables, apparently unaffected or unknowing.[25]

Employment offices. There are many private agencies which cater to the casual laborer. Some, like Labor-Aides in New York City, do not charge a man for a job, pay him for half-a-day's work even if he finds the job impossible for some reason, and pay him daily. No one bothers to check on his background or identification. Manpower, Inc., is another private agency which serves the homeless, but it withholds part of a man's pay until the end of a week and therefore is less attractive to many homeless men. Then there are the agencies which have to be paid before they will find a man a job. A one-day job may cost a man over a dollar. Sometimes the agency will agree to have the fee deducted from the man's pay, but often it requires the fee in advance.[26] Finally, there are the "slave markets," street corners where workers are picked up for jobs by men in trucks, occasionally without a word being exchanged between employer and potential employee. Later the trucks return to the corner and the workers get off. Some observers report that more men are hired in the streets than through the employment agencies.[27]

Other formal organizations on skid row. Other institutions which may serve skid row men are restaurants, liquor stores, secondhand stores and thrift shops, pawnshops, junk yards, public parks, barber colleges, all-night movies, public libraries, banks, and hospitals. Wallace calls these facilities "Skid Row's Etcetera."[28] In addition, there may be small grocery stores adjoining a skid row area where the man can purchase wine, beer, and food.

Public transportation systems and their stations also are used by the homeless. The subway may serve as an all-night lodging. In fact, one of Barnard Collier's informants recommended it above the Bowery lodging houses:

"There's the flophouses," he said. "Down in the Bowery. Don't stay in a flophouse. They stole my shoes once. You got to sleep with your shoes under your head. Then you can't sleep because they let you smuggle liquor in and they vomit all night and you can hear every noise. They give you little cells. . . . Better to sleep in the subway."[29]

For those interested in the fine art of subway sleeping, a chapter of Edmund Love's *Subways Are for Sleeping* is recommended.[30]

The blood banks are located away from skid row, but they are an important resource for the skid row man. One reporter estimated that almost 10 per cent of the 300,000 pints of blood annually used by New Yorkers was the blood of Bowery derelicts.[31] Nash interviewed a homeless man who had gotten around the health department regulation that donors should not give blood more often than every ninety days. The man was encountered outside a blood bank. He said,

I usually never give blood more than once a month but one day I needed ten dollars. I went in here and gave a pint and got my five dollars. Then I wiped my arm clean—you know, so they wouldn't see nothing. I went up to midtown and gave another pint. It didn't hurt me at all.[32]

Another type of businessman patronized by homeless men is the junk dealer. In New York City some junk dealers furnish large wooden-wheeled carts for homeless men who work for them. Other men use baby carriages or burlap bags. They collect paper, cardboard, rags, and metal. Some of them dig through trash barrels, others have regular routes and pick up boxes and other trash from small retailers. An average working day may net a man somewhere around two dollars, but occasionally he will get lucky and find some scrap copper, lead, or aluminum and then he makes more.

The poor amidst prosperity: Homeless man in Manhattan, 1964.

A toothless Negro homeless man wheels his baby carriage into a junk dealer's modern fireproof building. . . . "You've got thirty pounds of paper there and the ten pounds of magazines—we'll count the same as the paper—that's fifteen cents, and for the aluminum it'll be another ten cents," says the swarthy, healthy-looking young man of Italian descent who has followed his father into the business. The homeless man says nothing and walks slowly over to the father and stands silently near him. Five minutes later, the father says, "What's wrong?" The homeless man still says nothing. The father reaches into his pocket and pulls out a dime, "Oh, alright!" The homeless man walks off, still a nickel short of the forty cents needed for the pint of wine.[33]

Nash saw homeless men trying to remove copper gutters from an empty school building to sell them for scrap, and another time saw them taking radiators and batteries from abandoned cars.[34]

The Men's Shelter is another formal organization of skid row. The following account is chosen not only because it applies to the Shelter, particularly, but because the general sense of perpetual waiting—almost "waiting for nothing"—which pervades it accurately portrays the tone of most encounters between homeless men and representatives of formal organizations. The homeless man waits for services at shelters, hospitals, missions, and employment offices. He waits silently to turn in his junk to the junkman. He waits in the drunk tank to come before the judge, he waits in the jail for his sentence to end, and when he is not waiting for some respectable citizen to get around to noticing him, he waits in the bars and on the streets and in the lodging-house lobbies. In these last instances, he is not waiting *for* anyone. He probably is not sure why he waits. Kromer's title *Waiting for Nothing* is perhaps the most appropriate three words ever uttered about skid row men. The following article catches the spirit not only of the New York City Municipal Men's Shelter but of the life of all the men at the bottom:

Somewhere between the first drink that gives them the courage to panhandle and the last drink that sees them through their nightmares, the men on the Bowery make it to the Muni, the Municipal Shelter in the grimy brick building on East 3rd Street.

Late at night they flop on the concrete floor of the big room. During

Life is waiting: In line for a health check at the Men's Shelter (New York City, 1963).

the day they get two meals served up with only a tablespoon to make sure no one gets killed—at least on the premises. Most of the time they just wait in line.

There are lines for patients. Lines for men who have a gripe. Lines to get meal tickets from clerks protected behind metal screening. Lines for bed tickets in the hotel cubicles topped with chicken wire to keep the man on the other side of the partition from stealing. Lines for a recreation room where men sit staring silently with their arms folded. Lines stretch endlessly through the brick limbo and lead back to oblivion.

The men shuffling beneath a fading pastoral mural cringe inside their layers of rags and rarely speak. They never take their coats off. Many have crutches and skins knit together around the ragged edges of knife wounds, bottle wounds, and wounds unremembered.

There are old men whose life has been waiting and young men who have learned to patiently lean or sit against the wall. Most are sober. A few reel. Clutch at a pillar. Throw a few wild and powerless punches before sinking back into quiet swearing.

Only the staccato commands of the shelter employees puncture the stillness.

"Hey, you, get over there," the guards shout as they herd the men into the elevators. "Move, Mac. On your feet, fella. Hurry up, Pops."

The contempt echoes off the dirty green walls and produces flashes of resentment in the faces on the line.

Pride never completely dies.

Men turn their heads away when a photographer wanders through. One man gets up from his dinner and, until shoved back into his chair by an official, stands screaming at the man with the camera. "I don't want my kid to see me here."

Pride refuses to die in the shabby peajacketed man explaining his panhandling technique. "I don't wipe windows," he said. "When you're out in traffic stopping cars everybody knows what you're really doing. I just go up to a man and ask if I can talk to him for a minute. That way, maybe people going by will think I'm just asking for directions."

Sometimes if enough pride survives the street and the Shelter, a man convinces one of the rehabilitators that he is worth trying to salvage. Then there is a chance that he will get out of the endless lines. Or at least part of the way.[35]*

---

* Reprinted by permission of *The Village Voice*. Copyrighted by The Village Voice, Inc. 1968.

Informal relationships

The informal organizations of skid row tend to be transitory, with limited capacity for providing stable social bonds or "roots" for the men of skid row. This is not to say that certain of the institutions of skid row are not fairly durable *as institutions*. The thieves market, for example, manifest considerable stability over time, its location is generally fixed, and the modes of offering and obtaining merchandise are fairly constant; but it is not a device for binding individuals into ongoing social relationships. The celebrated bottle gang is another example of a fleeting informal relationship which is normatively structured. However, the nature of that structure dictates that the bottle gang has little effect in creating the stable ties which in combination are the components of a community.

In the remainder of this chapter, we shall consider several distinct facets of informal social relationships on skid row, including bottle gangs, the thieves market, racial discrimination, and friendship.

The bottle gang. One of the best accounts of group processes among skid row men comes from James Rooney's observations as a participant in skid row life in Stockton, Sacramento, and Fresno, California.[36] According to Rooney, the bottle gang fulfills both socio-group (external goal-directed) and psyche-group (emotional and interpersonal) functions for skid row men. Usually members of the bottle gang cannot afford to buy their own wine nor drink in bars, but by pooling their resources they can come up with enough for a bottle of cheap wine which all "stockholders" in the group may share. Sometimes after a group is formed the members still do not have enough money for a bottle. If that happens, then the first activity of the group is to find more stockholders or raise cash in other ways, frequently by panhandling. Rooney's comparison of the bottle gang and corporate enterprise follows:

The wino bottle group or "bottle gang" is similar to a corporate group in that a number of individuals pool their capital for a common goal.

The management of the capital is handled by a leader who acts as general chairman. Each member is a stockholder and maintains rights to consumption of the communally purchased bottle of wine. . . .

If the solicited person has sufficient money and is willing to participate, he gives his contribution to the leader. The handing over of money toward the purchase of a "jug" of wine establishes a contractual relation by which a contributor becomes a member of the group. The contract forms a corporation in which the members hold certain rights to the consumption of the proposed bottle of wine, and the leader has the obligation to purchase and share the wine with the members.[37]

Usually there are from three to five members in the bottle gang. It may include long-time acquaintances or strangers. Membership in the group is determined only by one's availability and willingness to "go in on a bottle." Its members are interchangeable. "Almost any individual is substitutable for another"—and whatever continuity of personnel does exist comes about merely because the same men may live in the same location for long periods of time. Rooney distinguishes between "permanent" bottle gangs ("a core of regular associates with one or two strangers recruited expediently") and "temporary" groups ("men who most likely never met before but are brought together for an occasion of wine drinking and social interaction").[38]

Among the psyche-group functions of the bottle gang are the opportunity to play the role of leader (his duties include providing the initial capital and leading in the supplementation of that capital, if necessary), selecting the type of wine and purchasing the bottle, and acting as host. After the wine is purchased, the group finds a fairly secluded place, safe from moochers as well as the police, and the leader opens the bottle and passes it to his left. Each man takes two swallows, the leader drinks last, caps the bottle, and then there is talk for a time before the second round. The talk usually centers on the good qualities of the participants and the negative characteristics of other persons or skid row institutions.

Rooney emphasized the psyche-group functions of the bottle gang by noting that "The group drinking experience is the only situation in the Skid Row social system in which a man receives personal recognition and affectional response."[39] On skid row these commodities are in short supply, and the ease at which one gains acceptance and esteem in the bottle gang makes it an important psychological bulwark for many of the men.

This contractual relationship serves as a structure for meeting the winos' emotional needs for interpersonal contacts. The contract forms a small intimate group in which individuals seek acceptance and personal affirmation. That such a bottle gang is formed more for the sake of personal interaction than for economic necessity is indicated by the case of individuals with sufficient money to purchase their own wine who prefer to participate in a series of groups successively throughout the day.[40]

It does not matter that the participants do not know each other's names, or that the group will dissolve when the wine is gone. For a time, one becomes a respected insider and is fully accepted, and the price is right. The fact that the participants consume equal proportions despite their unequal contributions toward the price of the bottle suggests that the psyche-group functions of the group outweigh the socio-group functions.[41]

Rooney did not discuss social control mechanisms at length, except to note that "chiselers"—men who pay off former benefactors by offering drinks to persons outside the group at the expense of legitimate "stockholders"—may be excluded from future groups, but the "may" here is a very large one. The most important thing about a member of a bottle gang is that he "belongs" because he has bought his way in: ". . . the social relationships of each individual are determined solely by his pecuniary condition."[42] This emphasis on expediency operates to prohibit the formation of close personal bonds, and it also prohibits the mounting of effective sanctioning procedures against chiselers. Because participation in the bottle gang does not involve "mutual adjustment of personalities," there is minimal investment of self. The pseudosolidarity and identity affirmation bought via participation in the bottle gang may serve as a substitute for more stable relations, and the existence of bottle gangs may inhibit the formation of more enduring ties among skid row men.[43]

In describing the bottle gang, we must be careful not to ascribe a structure to it beyond that which exists. Gleason has noted the usual absence of preliminaries in the formation of "a corporation" by skid row men,[44] and Peterson, to whom we are indebted for one of the classic accounts of the bottle gang, cautioned that the drinking groups tend to be of short duration and that usually they are relatively unstructured and lack even a nominal leader. Jackson and Connor corroborated this point: "There seems to be little leadership in the group. Action may be initiated by almost any member. Whether or not the rest of the group follows him depends largely on their mood of the moment. No one ever tells the others to do anything."[45] Nevertheless, Peterson identified two roles critical to the success of a "wine-procuring organization," the promoter ("the outstanding man in the group when it comes to raising money") and the runner ("the individual in the group who is usually sent to buy the bottle").[46]

Life on skid row has been described as "group-oriented" and containing a "web of expectations and obligations which provide economic and emotional support" to skid row men.[47] Certainly there are expectations and obligations, but the solidarity or social integration which derives from them is very weak; the obligations are weak, the sanctions weak, and the web of community spun therefrom is fragile indeed. Drawing upon data collected in Seattle and Spokane, Peterson and Maxwell stated that the "most imperative" of the mores in wino culture was the obligation to share. They went on to note the sanctions imposed for violating this obligation: "Such a person is shunned by winos and such behavior is severely condemned, for sharing is a matter of survival."[48] Despite its label as a "survival" issue, the violation of the "most imperative" of mores creates no permanent exclusion. In fact, the ease with which one neutralizes the "severe" condemnation for refusing to share illustrates the extreme wispiness of the web of obligations covering skid row. The exclusion for non-sharing is not absolutely irreversible; in fact, it is so easily reversible as to raise questions about its utility as a sanction:

All it takes for a man suddenly to regain a host of "friends" and an elevated status is to come into some money and be willing to share it. His grievous faults suddenly evaporate. For anyone is a "good guy" if he has a dollar, and a prince of a fellow if he has five.[49]

Social control derives from the ability to exercise sanctions, and sanctions stem from organizations. The more impermanent a group, the less it is able to level sanctions effectively. Sanctions on skid row are imposed by outsiders, by the rehabilitation agents, policemen, hotel owners. The greatest sanction the men in a bottle gang can muster—exclusion—is quickly neutralized by the proceeds from a few minutes' panhandling.

One of the most systematic descriptions of the bottle gang is Rubington's account of the six stages in the cycle of a bottle gang, as observed in "Maple City."[50] First there is the "salutation," where potential participants meet. This phase quickly leads to "negotiation," in which a "promoter" or "initiator" announces that he has money he will give toward purchase of a bottle, and other interested parties report the amounts they are willing to chip in. It may be necessary to find someone else to contribute to raise the price of a bottle, but finally enough is secured and the promoter chooses someone to go buy the bottle. Thus the "procurement" phase arrives. When the "runner" returns with the bottle, the promoter opens it and takes two short drinks, and passes the bottle to the runner. The "consumption" phase has begun. After the first drink the group enters the "affirmation" phase, in which the skill of the runner, the generosity of the promoter, and various negative characteristics of outsiders are proclaimed. Under the direction of the leader, subsequent rounds take place until the bottle is emptied. Then the bag and bottle are surreptitiously disposed of, and the group breaks up ("dispersal" phase) unless another cycle is activated by any of the members. Rubington also outlines the rules for each stage of the cycle, and identifies functions of each stage.[51]

In contrasting bottle gangs in Maple City with those described by previous researchers, Rubington noted that Maple City did not have a well-defined skid row area, and that the bottle-gang drinkers were dispersed. Consequently, the probability of "getting in on a bottle" was less than in the more concentrated skid row areas. Moreover, the increased mobility needed to find potential bottle-gang participants increased the visibility of the drinker to citizens and police. The resources for obtaining a bottle, such as opportunity for panhandling with relative impunity, were less available in Maple City. Finally, the surveillance by police was less predictable in Maple City, and so constant vigilance was necessary, in contrast to the relaxation that can occur on a more concentrated skid row once the police have made their rounds.

All of the above factors operate to weaken the degree to which the bottle gang can control its members. Moreover, because the need for participants is greater in Maple City, the members can be less selective, and "blitz drinkers" who drink as much as they can as fast as they can are more likely to be included, to the detriment of the other gang members. Finally, because the sanctions available are weak, the more experience one has in East Coast bottle gangs of the type studied by Rubington, the more he breaks the rules.[52]

We should not pay too much attention to the minor inconsistencies in the descriptions of bottle gangs. Rooney says the promoter drinks last, Rubington says he drinks first. Rooney combines the promoter and runner into a single role, Rubington and others make them separate roles. There is no reason why the bottle gangs observed by Rubington on the East Coast should be exactly like those in which Rooney participated in Fresno or Sacramento. The important point is that on skid rows throughout the nation an impermanent but fairly predictable group structure exists which allows homeless men to maximize their alcoholic intake per penny and at the same time to experience interpersonal satisfactions and affirmations of their own self-worth.

Another excellent illustration of the formation and initial activities of a Chicago bottle gang appears in Gleason's *The Liquid Cross of Skid Row,* which describes both the formation of the "corporation" and the panhandling necessary to supplement the corporate assets. It is recognized that each of the participants "holds back" or does not declare part of his resources, and that each knows, or suspects, that the other is holding back. Thus,

Tim knew that Big Thunder and Combat were holding back on him just as he was doing on them. When he said he had only ten hundred [ten cents], he was conveniently overlooking the two thousand he had in his watch pocket. Almost everybody on The Street holds back a little for the next venture. Nobody invests everything he has in a corporation unless he has virtually nothing at all. If a man has twenty hundred, he declares only ten hundred. That's the financial law of The Street.[53]

In addition to "saving" something for the next venture, "holding back" may serve as a protective device against being "rolled."[54]

Another account of a bottle gang—a Minneapolis group described in one of the "Participant Observation Journals" of the University of Minnesota researchers—is published in Wallace's *Skid Row as a Way of Life.*[55] One of the participants in the gang declares "This is the second bottle I bought today. But when I'm with friends I don't care. I'll give you guys the shirt off my back." Wallace commented, "The way in which winos organize themselves illustrates the group control over drinking and the pattern of mutual sharing characteristic of skid row subculture."[56] But given the proportion of skid row men who drink alone and the lack of effective sanctions for violations of the "mutual sharing," we must conclude that the sharing supposedly characteristic of the "subculture" is manifested by relatively few of its residents. Or perhaps the sharing occurs only during the brief life of the bottle gang. Outside of the bottle gang, mutual exploitation seems to be the norm. The frequent petty thievery of shoes, wallets, and even eyeglassses from men sleeping or drunk illustrates the norm more tellingly than the mutually suspicious bargaining and careful watching of number and amount of drinks that are displayed in the bottle gang. The prevailing antipathy and distrust among skid row men is a more potent indicator of the norms of skid row life than the fact that homeless men emphasize their generosity and comaradie when drinking together.

It is probable that the extent of group drinking on skid row is somewhat exaggerated. "Practically all drinking on skid row takes place in groups," Wallace asserts, and "few men drink alone."[57] Some accounts of skid row bottle gangs seem to support this view, but there is evidence that the bottle gang is not the typical mode of skid row drinking. Large-scale surveys of representative samples of skid row residents have revealed that much solitary drinking occurs on skid row. For example, Bogue found that skid row men in Chicago usually drank in bars. He also observed that approximately one-third of the Chicago skid row drinkers bought bottles, and about half of these drinkers said they consumed these bottles alone. In other words, only one-sixth of the drinkers habitually bought bottles and drank their contents in company with others, i.e., participated in bottle gangs.[58]

Although drinking in the bar often (if not usually) takes place among strangers, the norms of "bar sociability" apply. This means that persons present, regardless of their backgrounds or former acquaintance, are "open" to conversational interaction with all others present.[59] Encounters in bars are short-lived, conversation tends to be tentative and superficial, and it is understood that along with the right to initiate interaction with all present is the right of any party to terminate the relationship at any time.[60]

It should be stressed, however that bar-drinking may be perceived by the drinker as either solitary or companionate. The mere physical presence of other bodies need not be defined as "company" (as persons who find their most solitary hours on the subway will attest). The presence of others is no guarantee against psychic isolation, and certainly much skid row drinking in bars is a very solitary type of drinking. In one exploratory survey of the Bowery, respondents were questioned about both the places where drinking occurred and their company while drinking. Half of the men who said that they usually drank in bars also asserted that they usually drank alone and only about one-third of the bar drinkers said that they usually drank with friends.

In the more extensive survey of Bowery residents which provided the basic data for the "Homelessness Project," interviewers inquired "do you usually drink alone or with others?" The majority of respondents said that they usually drank with others. One-third of the Bowery drinkers said they drank alone, about half said they drank with others, and one-fifth reported both patterns. The distribution for a comparison sample of lower-income, settled respondents was about the same. The conclusion was that Bowery men were not much more likely to drink alone than were men in the non-skid-row sample, and neither were they more likely to drink with others. It was plain that to view skid row as a place where almost all drinking occurred in a group context and bottles were usually shared was a false perception. If anything, there was less drinking with others on skid row than in other lower-class urban contexts.

Nor did a researcher's description of activities in a Bowery bar suggest much group behavior:

I observed where the men sat in order to see if friendship patterns could be determined on this basis. The regulars ordered their drinks at the bar but drank them at their tables. However, there was no pattern as to where the men would sit. The men would sit at one table in a group; one by one they would get up and go to other tables and re-group. There never seemed to be any pattern at all during the entire day. All of the regulars behaved in an individualistic fashion. Despite the fact that some seemed to have best friends, they did not sit with them exclusively. The groupings occurred more or less by chance and shifted constantly. No one person always sat at the same table with any other. All or most of the men were friendly to one another. There were no signs of any small groups. During the course of the day I spoke to at least 25 different men. Many of the other men spoke to as many as 15 or 25 other men. The men came and went on an individual basis.

Many of the men would go outside and sit on the sidewalk beside the building. Some of them lay down and slept beside the building. Again, there was no patterned grouping.[61]

Thus, it appears that most skid row men drink in bars, in a context of the skid row type of bar sociability. Much of the drinking occurs in the presence of others, but the associated behavior is not necessarily group behavior; more frequently it is aggregative behavior. Outside the bars, on the streets, in the parks, in the alleys, the bottle gangs are formed and pass through their stages of life as organizations, but the majority of skid row men do not participate in them.

Friendship. Caplow has described skid row social interaction as manifesting

> . . . the norm of non-interference, a certain placid acceptance of things as they are, and a good deal of gregariousness without the development of bonds of friendship. . . . The curious, callous indifference which surrounds acts of violence, assaults, robberies, and so on in the Bowery bars and on the Bowery streets is the product of a fundamental denial of the creation of casual responsibilities.
>   The Bowery man is, first and foremost not his brother's keeper, nor does he admit any keepership relationship on the part of anyone else. . . ."[62]

Part of the reason for the extremely limited effects of bottle gangs and other informal groups in producing a cohesive community is the antipathy skid row men feel for each other. When asked what they thought of other men living on skid row, 40 per cent of the Chicago respondents said that they did not like other homeless men, and an additional 25 per cent expressed noncommittal or ambivalent attitudes. Less than one-third of the men said that they liked other homeless men.[63] Moreover, despite Wallace's identification of the drunk as the highest skid row status, heavy drinkers on Chicago's skid row were just as alienated from their fellows as were the men who claimed to be teetotalers. This is not to say that the men had no good things to say about skid row: 85 per cent of the men could mention something they liked about the area.[64] But almost 40 per cent of the Chicago respondents said they had no close friends on skid row, and an additional 44 per cent had "only a few" close friends. Bogue reported that alcoholic derelicts seemed more willing than other homeless men to make friends with their neighbors on the row, but such men emphasized that they could not trust other skid row men.[65]

Bogue combined a number of items about attitudes toward skid row and its men into a summary measure of "acceptance of skid row" and found that the over-all results showed that approximately three-fourths of the men rejected skid row life. An index of "degree of integration and self-identification with skid row" showed that half of the skid row respondents were "aloof" or "withdrawn," compared to 22 per cent who were identified as "assimilated," and 28 per cent defined as "accommodated." Bogue concluded that:

Taken as a whole, the summary measures overwhelmingly support the contention that the answer to "What do homeless men think of Skid Row Living?" is that they hate it! This verdict is shared by controlled and uncontrolled drinkers alike. Moreover, these men have so little "we-feeling" that it seems almost a contradiction in terms to speak of a "Skid Row society."[66]

The findings from Chicago are corroborated by research from other cities. When residents of Sacramento's skid row were asked why they lived there, only 6 per cent mentioned the proximity of friends.[67] Men on the Philadelphia skid row also lack ties to their neighbors. Fifty-seven per cent of the Philadelphia men who answered a question on close friends reported none, and an additional 13 per cent reported only one or two friends. About 40 per cent of the men said they knew of no one who would lend them money if they were broke. Thus, "the majority of residents of Philadelphia's skid row are not only homeless, but apparently isolated as well from the support and warmth of any friendships."[68] Skid row men in New York City were even more isolated. Only one-third of them had a "close friend" anywhere in the city.

Another example of the weakness of informal ties among skid row men is Patricia Nash's finding in a pilot study of ninety-two Bowery men that two-thirds of the men said they had not and would not lend money to other Bowery men. In the same sample, only 16 per cent of the men said that they had a "best friend" living on the Bowery, and one-third of the men said that they had no "best friend" anywhere. Nash also asked "Who would you say takes a personal interest in you." Thirty-seven per cent of the men said that no one did, one-fourth mentioned a relative, and a substantial number mentioned a proprietor (that is, a manager, owner, bartender, *not* a skid row man).[69] Nash concluded that her findings supported a pattern of "general friendliness but little interdependence":

For the most part interactions are casual. The men are "free to come and go as they please," to put it in their own words. They do not casually lend money to one another. They do not have each other as best friends. They don't leave the Bowery with one another, and in a pinch they depend on either an outsider or no one at all.[70]

In the Homelessness Project major survey, Bowery men were asked about the number of men in the neighborhood that they knew by name. Then they were asked, "Would you like to know more?" Seventy-seven per cent said no, and their antipathy toward their neighbors was graphically illustrated in the comments that accompanied their answers. Remarks like "I'm sorry that I know the ones I do," and "I know too many now" were common. Other illustrative responses:

Why should I? I'm always alone. The less men you know, you always have a dollar in your pocket. I don't want to know them. I want to be alone.

They try to rob you; cause you trouble.

These are a low type of people. They're degrading. I don't want to know them.

If they are agreeable to me, yes. I'm a very choosey person. In the last two months I haven't spoken to anyone in this hotel.

They don't want to know me; when I got nothing, nobody wants to know me.

These guys are no good down here—they steal from each other. There's no helping these guys.

I'd be glad to if they were people you'd like to talk to. But there's no mutual understanding. I'm a different type of man.

Every time I see the ones I know, they always ask for a quarter. I see them, I turn the other way.

I'm not interested. Anyway, the less friends you have the better off you are.

Nash's comment about friendship, the "largely individualistic" nature of life on the Bowery, is revealing:

Although the men are frequently to be seen in groups, most of their behavior is actually individualistic. The men enter and leave the Bowery bar by themselves. Even at opening time, the majority of the men bought themselves drinks despite the fact that it would have been far more economical for them to have chipped in and bought bottles. The men walk to the Men's Shelter by themselves. The overwhelming majority of the men walk into the "horse markets" by themselves and sit down by themselves at tables and carry on no conversations while they are eating. There are friendships, some of which stretch over long years, but the men differentiate little between new friends and old friends on the behavioral level. Several of the men announced to their associates that I was a "best friend" despite the fact of less than an hour's acquaintance.[71]

Henshaw also has observed the individualism of skid row residents, noting that being robbed by drinking companions has made them "cynical about friendship and wary of casual acquaintances." The individualism of Bowery men carries over to more structured contexts such as rehabilitation camps. For example, at Camp La-Guardia, ex-Bowery men were observed:

. . . the residents scatter the lawn chairs individually around the grounds rather than arranging them in groups so that they can sit and talk. Residents usually eat their meals very quickly without talking to the other men sitting at the same table. One never sees an extra chair pulled up to a diningroom table to allow a man to join his friends. The factors determining the rate of interaction of the men are psychological —the men's defenses—rather than structural—the opportunities provided by the social structure of the camp.[72]

The basic untrustworthiness of the skid row man is summarized in the comment of a Pacific City homeless man:

The nicest guy in the world, who wouldn't be dishonest under, uh, non-drinking conditions, will take the shoes right off your feet if he needs a bottle and you're asleep.[73]

Wiseman has described the "general air of open conviviality" that characterizes skid row. She compares skid row and the college campus (e.g., "Both areas offer a great deal of acceptance and friendship; that is, by the very fact a man is *in* the area . . . he is extended some friendship."). She quotes several homeless men about this aspect of skid row. For example, one respondent said, "You don't have to worry, you can make friendships. People just walk up and make friends with you." And another said, "People on Skid Row are so open. It's a good place to drink."[74] But the college campus, by virtue of the predictability of its residents—the students are committed to at least a semester—provides a degree of predictability that skid row cannot match. One can demonstrate this by comparing the number of close friendships or organizational ties which characterize the usual college student and those of the homeless man. The unpredictability of skid row friendships was remarked by one of the respondents in The 1966 Bowery survey who said he would like to know more of his neighbors: "But a place like this, you get to know a guy and after a week he gets lost somewhere."

Wiseman has emphasized that the outsider's view of the attenuation of social relationships among skid row men is not entirely shared by the men themselves, and we agree that the skid row man almost always has some good things to say about the row. At the same time, however, the men's reports of the extent of their friendships, the frequency of their conversations with other men, and their typical drinking companions, if any, as revealed in numerous studies of the entire population of skid row, including Philadelphia, Chicago, and New York, indicate that the conviviality seen by some observers has little consequence for long-term friendships or even self-protection. Instead, a pseudoprimary group situation prevails; there is the appearance of comradeship, but the absence of loyalty and responsibility. As Jackson and Connor observed about apparent group relationships among skid row men is Seattle:

In many ways these seem to be primary groups but they are not characterized by intimacy or mutual trust and identification. Few alcoholics trust other group members and many stay with groups in which there is no one they like as a person.[75]

Racial discrimination. One of the few extensive discussions of race relations among skid row men is an unpublished paper by James Rooney which analyzes relationships between blacks and whites in Philadelphia's skid row.[76] In that work Rooney describes racial discrimination in streets and parks, housing, food, and drinking establishments, employment, public assistance, and other institutions. In assessing race relations as manifest in informal relationships among the men themselves rather than as imposed by lodging house owners, employers, and social workers, here we shall consider only two of the institutions of skid row, namely, streets and parks, and food and drinking establishments.

Rooney observed that although skid row men do a great deal of standing and walking, often in pairs or groups of three or more, usually such groups are racially homogeneous: "Continued observation has revealed that although whites and Negroes may nod or stop to speak for a few moments and even may engage briefly in friendly horseplay, long-term sustained conversations occur only within homogeneous racial groups."[77]

Such self-sorting extends to the lines in front of gospel missions or other institutions where men await free food or other services. For example:

Those men who arrive at the mission buildings with another are in racially homogeneous pairs and stay together through the service. Individuals who arrive alone stand behind the next person in line regardless of race. However, when the mission door is opened, Negroes and whites are very unlikely to take seats together. Rather, Negroes tend to group into a few voluntarily formed clusters scattered throughout the audience. Those Negroes who take a seat apart from the clusters will remain isolates for the duration of the service. This seating arrangement is a spontaneous occurrence in all missions [in Philadelphia] except one, which has a directed policy that Negroes be seated at the rear of the congregation.[78]

The same kind of self-sorting occurs in public parks. Persons sharing a bench rarely converse; yet the benches tend to be chosen via racial criteria. Only occasionally do whites and blacks share a bench. Gleason has suggested that the same kind of racial sorting occurs even in drunk court:

The Negroes began trooping in. This indicated that the procession soon would end. The Negroes always come last. In many ways Skid Row is the most democratic place on earth, but segregation is enforced there, by unspoken agreements, because of the violent tempers of some men who come to The Street from the hill regions of the South.[79]

Of the sixteen skid row bars studied by Rooney, one actively discouraged black customers, and another was patronized by blacks almost exclusively. Most of the blacks patronized a few selected bars; during one survey on a weekday afternoon four-fifths of all blacks drinking in bars were concentrated in only five bars. Not only were black skid row men concentrated in certain bars, but within those bars serving both black and white customers a further selection by race was observed. Seating arrangements and interaction patterns were along racial lines:

In most instances, whites and Negroes sit separately in small, self-selected clusters around the bar regardless of whether or not there is interaction between members of the clusters. Under these conditions, meaningful, sustained interaction occurs only within racial groups, paralleling the structure of interaction which occurs on the streets and in the parks.[80]

Sexual interaction, however, was frequently across color lines. Many of the homosexual liaisons occurred between blacks and whites. Heterosexual interaction also tended to be biracial because all of the regular prostitutes in the skid row area were blacks. It is probable that had there been white prostitutes as well as blacks, there would have been some racial selection. In Minneapolis, Lovald found that white women were preferred over blacks, and blacks were preferred to Indians.[81]

In contrast to the situation in the streets, parks, and barrooms, there was no evidence that racial factors structured interaction in restaurants. With the exception of one establishment owned and managed by blacks and patronized by them, the Philadelphia skid row restaurants served whites and blacks without imposing any special seating arrangements, and no self-selected seating pattern was observed. Rooney suggests that the absence of voluntary racial segregation in the restaurants is explained by the fact that, in contrast to interaction in streets, parks, and bars, interaction in the skid row restaurant tends not to include primary, or even pseudoprimary relationships.

. . . it is important to note that eating places are not used as a locus for establishing personal relationships or conversation of any sort. With little exception, all men eat in silence. Restaurants in skid row still operate as Anderson described them nearly fifty years ago. The food is served to the customer in less than two minutes after he orders by one of a crew of fast walking "hash slingers," who set out the food without ceremony or conversation. . . . The customer then gulps down his food, usually without looking at the customer next to him at the counter and gets out as rapidly as possible. Since the conduct of eating does not involve personal relationships or lowered social distance, physical distance imposed by separately seated groups is not necessary to maintain the skid-row norm of containing primary relationships within racial group.[82]

One factor related to the racial discrimination on skid row is the stereotype of the black jackroller. The jackroller assaults and robs his victim, almost always injuring him in the process. The aged and the inebriated are the preferred victims. Rooney reported that

All white persons encountered in barrooms and on the streets who mentioned jackrollers in casual conversation during the course of my participant observation reported these thieves to be Negroes. This was true regardless of whether the respondents themselves were the victims or observers of the attack or learned of such incidents only through hearsay. The association of Negroes with jackrolling is so well defined that folklore of the white majority on skid row scarcely recognizes the possibility of white jackrollers. Although I was the victim of a jackrolling attempt by two white men during prior research in a Chicago alley in 1958, nevertheless my own observations bear out the fact that the folklore truism is essentially correct, although slightly exaggerated.[83]

The same stereotypes were common on the Bowery in New York City. White Bowery men warned observers for the Homelessness Project to stay away from certain lodging houses because there were "lots of tough Negroes there." We were also warned to watch out for gangs of blacks on the streets. In one of the Bowery bars a white from Georgia told us that white men usually walked two or three together on the Bowery for protection. He said he had been rolled for eighty-two dollars recently; he was coming out of an employment office and was slugged in broad daylight by two blacks. Later another skid row man remarked that the thugs seemed to know when the checks arrive, and that after check days one saw the most bruised and battered men. He went on to say that most of the jackrollers were blacks, and then apologized for his apparent racial prejudice, still affirming that "that is just the way I've seen it."

The thieves' market. One of the unique institutions of skid row is the Thieves' Market, which provides a setting for economic exchange as well as entertainment. On the Bowery the traditional location for the Thieves' Market is in front of the Salvation Army Memorial Hotel. In the wintertime it may begin on the west side of the street to take advantage of the sunshine, then move across the street in the afternoon. On the Bowery the Thieves' Market is a daily affair; in Pacific City (California) it follows a weekly cycle, occupying a downtown parking lot which is empty on Sundays. A description of typical Market activity in Pacific City is:

Men sit on the raised wooden car abutments and barter, or they walk around peering into each other's sacks and making offers. Major bartering items are both standard and transistor radios, watches, sport coats, cameras, electric razors, and clocks. These items are sold in both good repair and unrepaired condition. Those persons buying an item that needs repairing will take it to their rooms, fix it, and return to Thieves' Market the next week to sell the refurbished merchandise at a mark-up. (Every now and then a well-dressed man in an expensive car will drive up and get out and buy large quantitites of available items. I am told these are second-hand store owners.)[84]

On the Bowery the "stock" tends to be less diverse and expensive than in Pacific City. Secondhand shoes, old magazines, sandwiches, and old clothing are representative of the merchandise offered:

A man stands holding a presentable looking pair of leather sandals. "Five cents," he asks. "I need a nickel more to make a phone call." Another man sells a half-used, small bar of Ivory soap for a dime. New, it would cost only eight cents. An old man buys six dirty fedoras from a young Puerto Rican for ten cents apiece. "They'll come in handy in the winter," he tells me. Most of the men stand individually and hold the wares they hope to sell. Occasionally, a man walks through muttering, "nice razor, ten cents." Items that sold well . . . were clothing, eyeglasses, combs, paperback books, and sandwiches and oranges from the Men's Shelter.[85]

Bendiner's description of the homeless man's interaction with the secondhand dealer catches the spirit of the Thieves' Market and at the same time demonstrates the continual exploitation of the homeless.

The principle of the "thieves' market" is to get rid of all that encumbers the present moment. If the weather is warm, sell your coat. If your beard isn't too bad, sell your razor.

This sort of trade provides an obvious opening for enterprising businessmen who can buy what the Bowery Men shed on warm days and sell it back to them—at a profit—on cold days. And here they are—the dealers in the leftovers of men's lives. They stand on the crowd's fringes. There is a seediness about them but they are nonetheless easily distinguished from the Bowery Men.

As if it were a badge, each dealer carries a rolled newspaper under his arm. Years ago one used to see these men wandering through the back courts of New York apartment houses, slapping their thighs with their papers and calling: "I cash clothes!"

Now they stand about on a Sunday afternoon, seeing only the objects for sale, not the sellers. Occasionally a dealer will reach out and pinch the sleeve of a jacket to see if his fingers feel each other through the threads.

The seller smiles wanly, obsequiously holding the jacket, daring to hope only this much—that by nightfall he will have the price of a drink or a flop.

If the dealer turns away without a word, the ragged man moves on. Sometimes he turns his head so that the dealer cannot see and his lips frame the word "Bastard," but he murmurs it without passion as if he were saying "Good day."

There isn't much money on the Bowery but what there is is readily available. A man receives his pension check, and once it is cashed he does not dream of saving anything. A farm hand has his summer earnings to blow in; the itinerant, occasional dishwasher has his pay. And now and then the Bowery turns up a treasure. Gold watches—leftovers from a forgotten past—have been snatched up by the watchful dealer for five dollars apiece.

Bowery Men are easy people to deal with. They rarely bargain.[86]

Our treatment of the social organization of skid row—the formal and informal structure there—has been a combination of summary of research findings and personal reports by participants or trained observers. We described the physical layouts of the lodging houses, the services they offer, and the criteria by which their quality is ranked by skid row men. Life in the lodging house was illustrated in depictions of three Bowery hotels based on the field notes of interviewers stationed there. Also considered were the distinctive programs of skid row gospel missions and the essentially negative attitudes of most skid row men toward them. The role of bars as the "heart" and "life" of skid row was highlighted, and interaction there was described. Two types of institutions typically given short shrift in descriptions of skid row—the blood banks and the junk dealers—were singled out for special attention. Finally, there was some material on public shelters to supplement the descriptions of shelters found in other chapters.

The discussion of informal relationships began with an extensive analysis of the most famous informal grouping on skid row, the bottle gang. We moved from a statement about its practical and emotional functions for its members to a description of its mechanisms of social control and its processes of birth, activity, and dissolution. The greater frequency of solitary and bar drinking as opposed to bottle-gang drinking was emphasized. Next, we noted the absence of cohesion among skid row men, the tenuousness of their friendship ties, the pervasive sense of distrust for their fellows, and the isolation of most of the men from close friendships of any kind. As in the previous section, these generalizations were supported by field researchers' reports and the statements of skid row men. We also drew upon one of the few studies of racial discrimination on skid row to point up the informal racial discrimination in the streets and parks and the bars. Finally, there was a brief depiction of another unique skid row institution, the thieves' market.

Up to this point we have considered the nature and history of homelessness and skid row, the characteristics of skid row men, the diversity of people's perceptions of skid row and its men, and the social organization of skid row. In the next two chapters we turn to the more specialized topics of homeless women and social control and rehabilitation programs.

6 | Homeless women[*]

Homeless men have been widely studied, but there is no comparable body of literature on homeless women. Occasional studies on the female drunkenness offender[1] point to the fact that some women alcoholics are homeless, but few follow-up investigations focusing on the life histories of these women have yet been undertaken. Explicit discussions of homeless women alcoholics almost always are singular accounts of their unsavory character and bizarre way of life. For example, there is the incredible case of Marie, a chronic alcoholic who lived in New York's public library by day and in the subways by night.[2] Another published account is the case of Miriam, who had roamed the streets of Manhattan since her early adulthood. At age fifty-four, she was a "bottom level" alcoholic, physically disabled, destitute, and without family or friends.[3] Accounts of this type constitute tangible evidence that homeless women exist,

* Gerald R. Garrett is the co-author of this chapter. The description of the Women's Shelter includes portions of Gerald R. Garrett and Dinah Hirschfeld Volk, "Homeless Women in New York City: Observations at the Emergency Assistance Unit and Women's Shelter," New York: Bureau of Applied Social Research, Columbia University, 1970 (mimeographed). For a more extended discussion of homeless women see Gerald R. Garrett, "Drinking Behavior of Homeless Women," Washington State University, 1971, unpublished doctoral dissertation.

but, provocative as they are, such case histories have failed to stimulate much social research.

The scarcity of studies of homelessness among females may be attributed to a number of factors. In the first place, skid row women are rare. The survey of Minneapolis's skid row found only one female for every twenty-three males.[4] A similar study in Philadelphia identified a total of twenty-eight presumably homeless women,[5] and only 3 per cent of Bogue's Chicago respondents were female.[6] Among drunkenness offenders in jail men outnumber women by approximately twelve to one.[7] Since women are rarely present in the places where social scientists have studied homeless people, it is understandable that they have been overlooked. Furthermore, because homeless women are not ecologically concentrated in areas such as skid row, they have not been perceived as threatening the social order or as neighborhood problems. Politicians and neighborhood organizations have not been concerned with "cleaning up" areas where "unattached" women live, and as a result there has been little interest or financial support for the study of these women.

Finally, the definitions of homelessness used by sociologists have usually been operationalized in such a way that women are, for all intents and purposes, excluded.[8] For example, if homeless people are defined as those who participate in facilities and institutions of skid row, the probability of encountering a woman is exceedingly low.

Nevertheless, there are compelling reasons why careful attention should be given to this population. For one thing, unlike the "conventional" female alcoholic, the homeless woman may find it difficult to remain a "hidden alcoholic." Moreover, investigations of the drinking behavior and misbehavior of homeless women may greatly increase the value of present findings about the homeless men. Although some comparative data on male and female alcoholics and problem drinkers are currently available, we have not been able to locate any studies in which the homeless man has been compared to a population of females in a comparable life-situation. Since the course and patterning of alcoholism is influenced by social position, a straightforward comparison of these two populations could provide important information regarding sex differences in the etiology of alcoholism. Equally important, such a comparison could reveal important sex differences with respect to the role of excessive drinking in the etiology of homelessness.

In the initial part of this chapter, we review literature about female alcoholism, only part of which is directly relevant to homeless or skid row women. Following the consideration of research about alcoholic or skid row women, we describe a shelter program for homeless women. Finally, some illustrative case histories are presented.

Antecedents of alcohol abuse among women

One of the most important studies of female alcoholics is Lisansky's detailed analysis of the social histories of problem drinkers at an outpatient clinic and at a state reformatory.[9] Her contribution is especially noteworthy for two reason. First, she illuminated important differences in the life histories of outpatient and state reformatory women which implied a difference in the dynamics and etiology of alcoholism. Her work firmly established the importance of investigating drinking histories and pathologies of women in varied settings—clinics, AA, skid row, and hospitals. Second, Lisansky's study also provided a detailed comparison of the characteristics of female and male alcoholics, and supported the position that certain etiological factors were unique to female alcoholism. Thus, Lisansky's work set forth important guidelines for subsequent research. Studies by Rosenbaum; Cramer; Fort and Porterfield; Cramer and Blacker; Johnson, DeVries, and Houghton; and Kinsey, each investigating female alcoholics in varied institutional settings, have extended and amplified Lisansky's pathfinding work.[10]

Comparative research on male and female alcoholics has been largely directed at specifying the ways in which these two populations differ on various sociological, psychological, and physiological variables. Investigators have assumed that there are significant differences between male and female alcoholism, and that these dif-

ferences can be discovered through careful study of early-life experiences, life histories, and adult drinking patterns.[11] Research on
sex differentials may be especially significant because the findings
carry implications for differential treatment strategies and prevention programs.

Early life and family experiences. A number of studies have attempted to isolate childhood experiences related to the development
of problem drinking and alcoholism. Most of these investigations
have begun with the assumption that early-life and family experiences are important determinants of personality and, therefore, are
relevant to understanding adult drinking pathologies. Events or
situations which appear frequently in the life histories of alcoholics
generally have been interpreted as important etiological factors.
Thus, the experiences of a broken home, sibling rivalry, uhappy
peer-group encounters, inadequate parent-child relations, and parental alcoholism have been cited as elements predisposing an individual toward alcoholism or problem drinking. However, it should
be emphasized that no single factor or set of childhood experiences
is viewed as a necessary condition for the development of alcoholism. Rather, unwholesome early-life experiences have been interpreted as exerting stressful influences on the personality structure
and thus increasing the vulnerability to alcoholism.

Parent-child relationships. Research conducted in a variety of settings has shown that alcoholic women have had unhappy child-
hoods. Nearly one-third of Lisansky's sample of female alcoholics
at an outpatient clinic described their mothers as strict and controlling; roughly 10 per cent characterized their fathers in similar
terms.[12] Hospitalized women alcoholics tend to preceive their fathers as gentle and lovable and their mothers as aggressive and
severe.[13] A sample of sixty-nine women alcoholics undergoing clinical treatment described their mothers as being the dominant authority figure in the family household; 17 per cent mentioned the
father as dominant.[14] These findings have been corroborated by

many other researchers; a strict, unloving mother is seen as a source of childhood emotional deprivation among female alcoholics.[15]

Cramer and Blacker investigated factors associated with time of onset of problem drinking among inmates at a women's reformatory.[16] The women's histories revealed a constellation of problematic family relations including lack of affection from at least one parent, sibling rivalry, severe treatment from at least one parent, at least one alcoholic parent, and inconsistent parental control. The researchers concluded that problematic parent-child relations increased the risk of alcoholism in female offspring, and that the more problematic the family relations, the greater their facilitating effect upon early problem drinking.

Kinsey's examination of the life histories of forty-six female alcoholics revealed that almost all respondents reported unhappy relationships with their parents during early family life. A subsequent in-depth analysis further suggested that the general character of parent-child relations reported by these women was unfavorable to the development of a positive self-image.[17] Kinsey's results supported the hypothesis that female alcoholics do not form strong attachments to either parent. Ambiguity of status in the family was also found: 63 per cent of the subjects felt that parents or guardians had favored other siblings.

Contrary to some earlier research,[18] a pattern of parental domination or overprotection was not revealed in the family histories of the alcoholics studied by Kinsey. In the five cases where domineering parents were located, the subjects were usually single (or had married late), and their drinking problem appeared to be linked to the death of their parents. Kinsey's findings strongly confirmed the hypothesis that female alcoholics were reared in families with maladjusted fathers. Finally, it appeared that control of the family was primarily the mother's responsibility, and she was a strict disciplinarian. The father, on the other hand, was usually described as being indulgent or ambivalent in his use of authority.[19]

Alcoholic parents. There is evidence that if one or both parents are alcoholics the risk of problem drinking in their female offspring is increased.[20] In fact, when siblings and other close relatives are considered, the relationship between alcoholic family background and female alcoholism is quite striking. Johnson *et al.* found that two-thirds of all subjects from an Alcoholics Anonymous sample and from a physician's treatment group reported at least one relative who had a history of alcoholism or problem drinking.[21] Similar results are reported by numerous others who have examined the social and family background of samples of female alcoholics, problem drinkers, and drunkenness offenders.[22]

Broken homes. Although the quality of parent-child interaction is usually considered more significant in the etiology of alcoholism than the physical presence or absence of a parent, the broken home has been seen as a general indicator of social and emotional deprivation during childhood. The absence of a father is usually interpreted as depriving the child of a significant interpersonal relationship with an adult male as well as complicating family interaction through financial hardship.

No less important are the events leading to the removal of a parent from the family. Divorce, separation, or desertion may be preceded by a sequence of family tensions such as parental conflict and child neglect. Death of parent poses the risk of psychological trauma which may have detrimental effects on personality growth. Thus, a causal relationship between the broken home and chronic disruptive and stressful influences during socialization is postulated.

Almost all studies of the life histories of female alcoholics have revealed that a substantial proportion were reared in families where one or both parents were absent. Six of every ten female alcoholics in Linsansky's reformatory sample had experienced a broken home, as compared to roughly 40 per cent of the outpatient respondents. Mayer and Green's research on female alcoholics at a state reformatory and Rosenbaum's investigation of married women alcoholics undergoing hospital treatment produced rates comparable to Lisansky's: 60 per cent in the prison sample and 40 per cent among the hospital alcoholics had experienced a broken home.[23] In another study, Kinsey found that 50 per cent of a sample of female alcoholics at a state hospital had been raised in a one-parent family. In most cases, the father was the absent parent. When he was present in the home, there was a high probability that he was either a chronic inebriate or psychotic.[24]

While there is some question about what constitutes a "high" rate of marital disruption, and of the role of the broken home as an antecedent of alcoholism among males,[25] there is little doubt that among female alcoholics the broken home is a more common experience than among other women of corresponding social-class background.

In addition to the literally "broken" homes common in the histories of female alcoholics, there are many marriages which are "psychologically" broken or extremely unhappy. In a sample of clinic and hospital alcoholics, for example, Wood and Duffy observed that all respondents considered their parents' marriage to be an unhappy relationship and lacking in mutual affection. In almost all cases the mother assumed the dominant role in the family.[26] Lisansky, Rosenbaum, and Lolli have described the relationship between parents of female alcoholics as characterized by conflict, tension, instability, and an absence of strong affectional bonds.[27] In summary, the family background of almost all female alcoholics can be seen in terms of a disorganization syndrome, which may include inadequate parental rearing practices, conflict in the home, maternal domination coupled with submission and instability of the father, and parental alcoholism.[28]

Marriage. A few researchers have focused on the marital relationships of female alcoholics.[29] Kinsey requested his respondents to evaluate their marital relationships along several dimensions, and his findings suggest that for most female alcoholics marriage was a painful and disillusioning experience. Out of a total of sixty-three marriages, forty-nine were described as characterized by cruelty, physical abuse, chronic infidelity, and extreme jealousy on the part of the husband. Only seven of the marriages were rated as satisfactory, and in four of these respondents were widowed at a early age. Among subjects who had been married more than once, subsequent marriages typically were evaluated as being even less harmonious than the first ones. In a separate analysis of widows and divorced subjects Kinsey found that most respondents began to withdraw from social participation and to experience prolonged states of loneliness and despair immediately following the breakup of their marriage. Although Kinsey does not provide evidence directly linking periods of loneliness with an increase in alcohol consumption, an inference to this effect seems justified since most of these women reported that they began frequent visits to bars and cocktail lounges soon after their marriages collapsed.

Other studies have produced similar findings. Married subjects in Rosenbaum's survey of hospitalized women alcoholics disclosed that marriage had been unhappy due to unwanted children, "untimely" pregnancies, and frequent quarrels with the husband. In almost all cases, respondents identified intrafamilial tensions as the precipitating cause of their drinking episodes. In addition acute feelings of loneliness, depression, worry, and general boredom, all due to marital unhappiness, were cited as secondary or contributing causes of their drinking sprees.[30]

Although there are several studies of the wives of alcoholic men, there are no systematic studies of husbands of alcoholic women. A few findings about husbands of alcoholic wives have appeared in works devoted to other topics. Lisansky observed that alcoholic women in her reformatory sample said that irregular employment, heavy drinking, and abusive treatment of the wife were common among these men. Such characteristics did not appear among the husbands of a comparison sample of outpatient female alcoholics.[31] (Since over half of the outpatient sample had husbands who were employed in business and professional occupations and overt abuse of wives is generally less characteristic of upper- and middle-class males than of lower-class males, this finding is not very surprising.) Kinsey found that an unexpectedly high number of alcoholic women were married to alcoholic men. Moreover, the tendency to marry chronic inebriates was even more pronounced for second and third marriages.[32] Rosenbaum noted that a majority of her respondents had been married to men who were at least heavy drinkers, and essentially the same results are reported by several others.[33] Whether heavy drinking was characteristic of the husbands before marriage or whether it developed during marriage, however, has not been firmly established.

Drinking and symptoms of alcoholism: history and patterns

Since Jellinek's well-known study on the phases of alcohol addiction, a major approach to the study of alcoholism has been to outline the natural history and course of alcoholic symptoms.[34] This approach assumes that typically each disorder has a sequence of symptoms which progresses from the prodromal to the terminal phases of the illness. In 1952 Jellinek applied the natural-history approach in a questionnaire study of male alcoholics. His findings indicated that the course and patterning of alcoholic symptoms fall into four sequential stages: prealcoholic symptomatic, prodromal, crucial, and chronic. A configuration of behavioral, psychological, and medical symptoms comprises each of these phases.

Using the natural-history approach, a number of researchers have attempted to discern differences in the drinking history and patterning of symptoms among various alcoholic populations. Since differences in symptom patterns in particular have been seen as indicating differences in etiology, the issue of symptom differentials assumes major importance.

First drinking experience. Many students of alcohol have assigned special significance to a person's first drinking experience. Critical foci in past research have been the age of introduction to drinking, whether drinking is periodic or regular thereafter, who sanctions the activity and how it is sanctioned, and the purposes and motivation for drinking. It is assumed that a person's initial experiences with alcohol reveal important information about the cultural setting in which this activity occurs and about the values associated with it, both of which influence his drinking behavior as an adult.

There is considerable evidence that the first drinking experiences of females differ from those of males. On the basis of a series of comparative studies of college students, Ullman concluded: 1. Women are more likely to remember the circumstances in which they took their first drink; 2. men are considerably more likely than women to experience intoxicating effects; 3. women are much more likely to take their first drink in their own home; 4. women are more likely than men to take their first drink in the company of their parents; 5. men are more likely than women to have a second drinking experience within a few days or weeks after their first. However, Ullman did not find a significant difference in age of males and females at first drink.[35]

Using Ullman's results for "normal drinkers" as guidelines, Kinsey gathered comparable data for women alcoholics at a state hospital and found that: 1. Most respondents (77 per cent) took their first drink before age twenty-one; 2. nearly 60 per cent took their first drink outside the home (taverns, bars, etc.); 3. approximately six out of every ten women indicate that their parents would not approve of their drinking; 4. group pressures were given by most of the respondents as the major reason for imbibing; 5. half of the women reported that they experienced feelings of guilt and anxiety concerning the drinking episode; and 6. a majority of the women began drinking on a regular basis almost immediately following their initial encounter with alcohol. Essentially the same findings were reported by Cramer,[36] in a study of problem drinkers at a state reformatory for women.

Although Ullman did not observe differences in the age that male and female "normal" drinkers experienced their first drink, there is evidence that a sex differential in age at first drink exists for alcoholics. Lisansky, for example, found a significant difference between the mean age of first drink for outpatient men (17.0) as compared to outpatient women (20.8).[37] Hughes' investigation of male and female alcoholics admitted to a midwestern psychiatric hospital produced similar results: In most cases women reported a first-drink experience at a significantly later age than men.[38]

Onset of heavy and excessive drinking. It has been widely held that alcoholics exhibit the premonitory signs of pathological drinking relatively soon after their first imbibing experience. For example, in comparing a sample of alcoholics to a group of "normal" drinkers, Ullman observed that many of the alcoholics, unlike "normal" drinkers, began drinking heavily almost from the very first drinking experience.[39]

The progression from controlled drinking to the onset of alcoholism appears to be more rapid in women than in men. Several investigations have shown that women alcoholics begin drinking at a later age than men, but they appear in clinics or hospitals after fewer years of problem drinking. Kinsey and Lisansky observed that women who began drinking comparatively late in life (usually in the late twenties) experienced more rapid development of alcoholic symptoms within two years after their first drink. Moreover, the average span of development was significantly shorter for late drinkers than for early drinkers.[40]

Socioeconomic status also appears to influence the rate of progression of alcoholic symptoms. Findings from Cramer and Blacker's analysis of female drunkenness offenders suggest that problem drinking develops much more rapidly among high-status than low-status women,[41] and Fort's study of members of Alcoholics Anonymous provides indirect support for this point of view. In the majority of cases the span of development was shorter for those respondents who experienced severe repercussions (e.g., loss of family, job, or husbands) as a consequence of their heavy drinking. Since upper-income women almost always reported more severe repercussions than the lower-income group, Fort's findings imply a positive relationship between economic status and the rapidity of the development of alcoholism. Fort also observed that neurotic patterns of behavior seem to influence the onset and progression of alcoholic symptoms. An early onset of alcoholism was more likely among neurotic women than among non-neurotics.[42]

Precipitating circumstances of heavy drinking. In recent years a growing number of sociologists, psychologists, and clinicians have posited that excessive drinking is more closely associated with a specific crisis situation among women than among men. In his classic study on female alcoholics, Wall concluded that "excessive drinking [among women] is more intimately associated with some concrete situation than is true among men."[43] Similarly, Lisansky found women to be twice as likely as men to cite a specific past experience, such as a divorce, separation, an unhappy romance, a parent's death, and postpartum depression, as a precipitating factor of their uncontrolled drinking. Kinsey also found that female alcoholism was closely related to serious disruption of social ties and to family and marital difficulties. Examining the drinking histories of male and female alcoholics, Lolli found that "women abstained or . . . drank alcoholic beverages only moderately until some late and overwhelming difficulty precipitated excessive and uncontrolled drinking whose progression exhibited a malignancy far greater than that observed in alcoholic men."[44] Rosenbaum specifically addressed the problem of precipitating factors by asking sixty-seven married female alcoholics to designate primary and secondary causes of their drinking episodes. In the vast majority of cases the configuration of primary factors revealed a theme of immediate stress of situational crises such as marital conflict, problems with children, death of a relative and physical ailment.[45] Finally, results from a survey of 161 physicians indicate widespread consensus among physicians that women drink for different reasons than men, and that female alcoholics are more apt to report that their drinking problems developed in response to a crisis than are male alcoholics.[46]

Personality disorganization. A number of researchers contend that alcoholism reflects a more serious state of personality disorganization in females than in males, and that the alcoholic symptoms of females appear more bizarre and pathological. On the basis of a series of clinical studies, Karpman concluded that

alcoholic women are much more abnormal than alcoholic men. The reason for the difference probably lies in the fact that even in this sophisticated age women are still subject to more repression than men, and in attempting to solve their conflict, they must seek outlets that are still within the limits of conventional social acceptance of their sex.[47]

In addition there is evidence that women are more difficult to treat in a therapeutic setting.[48]

While differences in symptoms exhibited by male and female alcoholics are clearly observable, the general validity of the "greater pathology" viewpoint has been severely attacked. Lisansky inquired, "Does 'much more abnormal' refer to deviation from a single norm of behavior for both men and women or does it mean that women alcoholics deviate more than the norm of feminine behavior than do men alcoholics deviate from the norm of masculine behavior?"[49] The fact that no standardized criteria for evaluating the extent of personality disorganization have been established undermines the over-all validity of the "greater pathology" hypothesis. In addition, it has been suggested that much of the data alleged to demonstrate "greater pathology" (e.g., focus on female deviations from role performance, such as sexual promiscuity) is more a reflection of the traditional double standard in America than of personality aberration.[50]

Patterns of drinking. Inasmuch as clinical records almost always contain information on past and current drinking practices, empirical reports of drinking patterns and habits of outpatient and hospitalized alcoholics are abundant. The analyses of Horn and Wanberg, Kinsey, Wanberg and Knapp, and Lisansky are particularly illuminating.[51] Among their findings: 1. Women are more apt to drink alone than men. Frequently reported patterns are "bedding down at night with a bottle" and sipping at frequent intervals during the day. In contrast, male alcoholics are more inclined to imbibe in public drinking places, particularly bars and taverns. 2. Even in public places, women are more likely than men to drink alone. 3. Women are more likely than men to drink wine and spirits.

In addition to differences in drinking patterns of men and women, a few investigators have isolated social-class differentials associated with drinking styles of female alcoholics. Cramer and Blacker's study of female drunkenness offenders analyzed drinking patterns by social-class background. Solitary drinking at home, for example, was much more prevalent among the high-status women, whereas lower-status women reported that they frequently drank alone in bars and taverns. Additional comparisons revealed that higher-status alcoholics reported more "respectable" drinking habits than the lower-status group (fewer benders, less drinking in unconventional places, and more periodic drinking). In general, upper-status women alcoholics were less likely than lower-status women alcoholics to be arrested for public drunkenness.[52]

Lisansky's analysis of social class and drinking among women alcoholics at an outpatient clinic and at a state reformatory identified two types of female alcoholics: 1. the "respectable" alcoholic whose drinking was relatively concealed from public view and who, because of high status and a relatively high degree of integration in the community, typically sought treatment in an outpatient clinic or similar private facility; and 2. the female alcoholic whose drinking behavior was visible because of her frequent encounters with the law. These two types differed markedly in the type of drinking pattern and in the ways in which alcoholism fit into their pattern of life. Among the clinic group, addictive and solitary drinking were usually prominent features of their drinking. Nevertheless, these women had retained a relatively high degree of integration in the community, at least until they reached the more advanced stages of alcoholism. In contrast, women in the institutional sample were more often habitual-symptomatic drinkers, usually drank in public places and in the company of others, and had lengthy histories of "problem" behavior (public drunkenness arrests, vagrancy, sexual promiscuity) which accompanied their heavy drinking.[53]

Sexual Maladjustment. Many studies of female alcoholism have discussed the apparent relationship between female sexual maladjustment and alcoholism. Sexual promiscuity, for example, is commonly cited as a concomitant of excessive drinking in women. Wall's classic study of hospitalized alcoholics in New York City indicated that the heterosexual adjustment of these women was "far from normal" and that loose heterosexual activities were characteristic of both married and unmarried female alcoholics.[54] Although sexual promiscuity has not been clearly defined, the majority of studies suggest that sexual promiscuity and sexual maladjustment in general are primarily a matter of psychosexual disturbances and not a direct consequence of chronic inebriety, except insofar as drinking itself may increase a woman's vulnerability to sexual exploitation. For example, Lisansky concluded that sexual promiscuity was more characteristic of the public drunkenness offender than of other types of female alcoholics. Often such offenders also showed signs of serious pathological disturbance.[55]

Wood and Duffy found no evidence of promiscuity in the sixty-nine women who were subjects in their study. Levine reported that the basic sexual problem of female alcoholics is frigidity, sexual inhibition, and lack of interest in sexual activity. Essentially the same conclusions were reached by Curran and Massot. Finally, Kinsey reported that the women alcoholics in his sample had never achieved adequate psychosexual adjustments even prior to the onset of alcoholism, and their maladjustment was reflected in high rates of frigidity and homosexuality.[56]

Some clinicians have hypothesized that the alcoholism rate among prostitutes is disproportionately high, but it has not been established empirically that alcoholism and prostitution are related. Some researchers have observed a high correlation between homosexuality and alcoholism,[57] but much of the evidence rests on inferences drawn from clinical studies of psychiatric patients. Since hospital samples are not representative of either the universe of alcoholics or homosexuals, the generality of the relationship remains in doubt.

Social isolation and alcoholism. Using Jellinek's phases of alcohol addiction as a model, many researchers have proposed that the progression from controlled to uncontrolled drinking represents a series of withdrawal stages in which the drinker becomes increasingly isolated from social relationships. As the drinker's behavior becomes more alcohol-centered, he begins to avoid interpersonal relationships, particularly those that intrude upon his drinking. According to Jellinek, the tendency to withdraw from social relationships (e.g., loss of family, friends, job) is especially pronounced in the "crucial" phase.

There are no in-depth studies specifically focusing on isolation as a factor in female alcoholism, but a few studies have provided findings that bear indirectly on the problem. For example, it is commonly believed that extent of solitary drinking represents a gross measure of an alcoholic's interpersonal involvement. If solitary drinking is the predominant pattern of drinking, it is presumed that the alcoholic is relatively isolated from social relationships.

There is some evidence that female alcoholics are more likely to be solitary drinkers than male alcoholics. Lisansky found that solitary drinking was the predominant drinking pattern in 55 per cent of the outpatient female alcoholics as compared to 21 per cent of the male outpatients. Several other researchers have reported that solitary drinking was characteristic of approximately half of their respective samples of female alcoholics. More recently Wanberg and his associates have compared the symptom patterns of male and female alcoholics and found that women were more likely to drink alone and generally less gregarious in their drinking pattern than men. Even at the more advanced stages of alcoholism men were much more inclined to drink in the company of others than were women.[58]

Although knowledge about extent of solitary drinking may indirectly shed light on the social isolation of a drinker, a much more reliable picture may be obtained by constructing a profile of social affiliations. For example, the frequency of contact with members of the immediate family, parents, relatives, friends and the frequency of participation in social clubs, political organizations, and other associations presumably reflect the extent of one's interpersonal involvement. On the basis of Jellinek's model, the number of these social relationships will decrease as the drinker's behavior becomes increasingly alcohol-centered.

A few investigators have examined interpersonal relationships at various time periods in the drinker's life. Kinsey's research suggests that female alcoholics are likely to be isolates even during adolescence. In the majority of cases his respondents reported that their participation in social activities in school, dating, and peer-group associations was very limited.[59]

Findings about the marital histories of alcoholics from previously cited studies are in essential agreement that female alcoholics and problem drinkers generally have unsatisfactory relationships with their husbands and families. Most studies have shown that approximately half of the women who enter "official alcoholic statistics" (AA, hospital, jail, and clinic) are either unmarried or no longer living with a husband. Cramer and Blacker have provided a more extensive picture of the family contacts of alcoholic women. Respondents were asked to rate the extent of contact with their husband and children (if any) for a given period of time. Only 15 per cent of the sample reported that they had had at least an "occasional" contact with their husbands in recent months. Interaction with their children, however, was more frequent. Two prominent trends were apparent: 1. There was an inverse relationship between a respondent's age and the frequency of her interaction with husband and children; and 2. high-status respondents generally had fewer family contacts than low-status respondents. The latter difference suggests that alcoholism in upper-status females produces a more complete dissolution of family ties than in lower-class women.[60]

There is evidence that even while the family is intact, the frequency of interaction with the husband and children decreases as a woman's drinking increases. Analysis of interview data from two samples of women alcoholics (AA members and a private therapy group) indicated that respondents progressively avoided their husband and family as their drinking became heavier. Surreptitious drinking was an especially prominent drinking pattern. Typically these women often contrived an excuse to leave the house in order to drink in private.[61]

There is also empirical evidence indicating that extrafamilial relationships of female alcoholics become progressively more limited in the later stages of alcohol addiction. Johnson, DeVries, and Houghton observed that most women in their sample, all of whom were in the relatively advanced stages of alcoholism, had few "active" friendships. In addition a majority of respondents reported that there was no one (family or friends) to whom they could turn for help and guidance regarding their drinking problem.[62] Similarly, Cramer and Blacker found that the majority (63 per cent) of their sample of problem drinkers had no friends whatsoever, and of those who reported active friendships, the frequency of association was only an "occasional basis." It is also noteworthy that approximately half of Cramer and Blacker's sample reported that they lived alone, and this pattern was most pronounced among older respondents in the higher-status group. Thus, female alcoholics who are older women of high social-class background were extremely likely to be isolated from social and family contacts.[63]

Perceptions of loneliness have also been widely used as general indicators of social isolation. Although it is conceivable that one might experience chronic feelings of loneliness and, at the same time, maintain a vast network of social contacts, such cases are seemingly rare, especially for female alcoholics. Cramer and Blacker show that while a majority (67 per cent) of all alcoholic women in their sample experience chronic feelings of loneliness, the most isolated respondents, who lived alone and had no friends, were most likely to describe themselves as being lonely. Several studies have also reported that loneliness was an especially prominent psychological characteristic of female alcoholics.[64]

The concept of anomie is also believed to be a general indicator of social isolation and withdrawal. Although the concept has been variously defined (and frequently misused) by theorists and researchers, its most popular usage has been in reference to the psychological conditions resulting from certain strains in the social system which are created by discrepancies between socially defined goals and institutionalized means. Referring to the psychological dimension, MacIver conceives of anomie as "The state of mind . . . in which man becomes spiritually sterile, responsible only to himself, responsible to no one."[65] Using essentially the same definition of anomie (anomy, anomia) several investigators have shown that alcoholic men and women tend to be highly anomic.[66] Kinsey and Phillips' research suggests that the relationship between anomie and alcoholism is contingent upon the developmental state of alcohol addiction. Thus, incipient alcoholics are less anomic than middle-phase alcoholics, who, in turn, are less anomic than their counterparts in the last stage.

On the basis of the findings from the studies above, it appears that isolation is related to excessive drinking in two ways. First, there is evidence that female drinkers are comparatively isolated *before* they begin drinking heavily. Second, as the drinker progresses from controlled to uncontrolled drinking, social involvement (as reflected in the frequency of social interaction with friends and family) decreases. Thus, social isolation appears to be both an antecedent and concomitant factor in a vicious circle: Deviant drinking occurs as a response to social isolation; excessive drinking increases social isolation, which in turn leads to heavier drinking.

The preceding review of the literature on the antecedents of excessive drinking among women is relevant for two reasons. First, alcoholism is one of the most serious problems of skid row women, and it is their dominant trait according to the popular stereotype. Second, most of the research on female subjects even roughly comparable to homeless women has been research on drinking behavior.

The women's shelter

The description of the Women's Emergency Shelter which follows is based on fieldwork conducted under the direction of Theodore Caplow and Howard Bahr during 1968 and 1969. It is not intended as a portrayal of current conditions—the location, bureaucratic arrangements, and operating procedures of the Shelter have changed since that time. Rather, the account and the case histories which follow are intended to illustrate the treatment and characteristics of homeless women in New York City at that time.

The emergency assistance unit

The Emergency Assistance Unit (EAU) in lower Manhattan operated on a twenty-four-hour basis to provide temporary assistance for emergency cases. The EAU fell under the administrative jurisdiction of the Department of Social Services, the coordinating body for New York City's vast system of welfare organizations. Emergency cases handled by the EAU ranged from clients who requested carfare to destitute and homeless persons. The latter, provided they met certain eligibility requirements, were referred to the Men's or Women's Emergency Shelter, both of which were located in Manhattan's Bowery district.

All cases were supposed to be handled in accordance with official procedures.

The client reports to the intake desk which is manned with a receptionist and one or two policemen. Following a brief questioning period, the client is sent to an appropriate casework division depending upon the needs presented. If she is a homeless woman, she is sent to booth one or two, where she will talk to one of two caseworkers who deal only with homeless women. Often, particularly during peak hours, the line at the intake desk is long and the client is usually required to wait before seeing the caseworker. Rows of chairs are provided in the center of the lobby, which is lined with casework interview booths. We observed women in the office for as long as five and six hours. The caseworker conducts an interview, fills out an intake interview form . . . an Application for Public Assistance or Request for Care, . . . a Resource Summary, and has the client sign a Consent and Release Form. After each interview, the caseworker records a summary of the interview together with comments and opinions on the History Sheet.

Perhaps because of the huge volume of questionnaires and interview schedules caseworkers were required to complete in authorizing and dispensing services, they made irregular use of the official forms. In some instances, questionnaires were half-completed, thereby omitting vital information about the client; in other files the standard documents were missing altogether. The extent to which EAU staff members attend to official details of handling clients is reflected in comments made by caseworkers and secretarial employees:

Most of these forms are obsolete to begin with. I know the case files are disorganized. Now, this is because whether or not a worker fills out the forms is left up to him. Nobody really checks the files. . . .

There's really no need to fiddle with most of that stuff. We don't use it anyway. Besides, the way things are around here, I, for one, don't have time to complete them anyway.

While a somewhat casual regard for processing clients in a routine way seems to promote organizational problems, the "quick pace" of operations itself, especially during the working day, makes the work situation even more difficult. These working conditions are aptly summarized in the comments of fieldworkers:

. . . At peak periods of the day, especially during the afternoon hours, the masses of clients and workers circulating through the main intake-reception room make it almost easier for a caseworker to telephone across the hall for a file rather than make the trip in person. . . .

Today I attempted to speak with two caseworkers in their intake booths. The noise muffled most of our words. In the course of 15 minutes, the interview was interrupted eight times: five telephone calls and three interruptions by clerks.

. . . The EAU is characterized by disorganization, a lack of coordination, and a shortage of staff and facilities. This is amply illustrated by the state of the files as well as the general operational level of the agency. The outer room where clients wait is crowded so that as many as 30 must either stand or sit on the concrete floor. This is particularly so in the afternoon hours; at 9:00 in the morning when the Center opens, the line at the intake desk extends out the front door. We have observed many clients waiting for an entire morning or afternoon because there are not enough caseworkers.

Permission to interview clients at the Women's Emergency Shelter and to examine case records at the EAU had been obtained from the Commissioner of New York City's Department of Social Services. Despite this high-level approval, the idea of publicity for the Women's Shelter in particular was seen as a controversial matter by some caseworkers. On one occasion a staff member expressed the opinion that "it is not good for the women to see someone talking about them," and another worker objected to "publicizing the misery and despair of these women." Some caseworkers, however, argued that it was important that Shelter clients have exposure to publicity and visitors.

The women's emergency shelter

At the time of the pilot study in 1968, the Women's Emergency Shelter had just recently been placed under the jurisdiction of the EAU, and it shared the same secretarial staff, files, and facilities. By 1969, a gradual shift of management to the Shelter itself had taken place; case files for almost all Shelter clients who had been admitted within the past two years were kept in the Shelter's intake office.

THE NEIGHBORHOOD

The Women's Shelter was housed in the Pioneer Hotel, a commercial hotel establishment located in the heart of the Bowery district. Nearby were the traditional institutions of skid row: bars, "flophouses," cheap restaurants, barber colleges, secondhand shops, missions, and liquor stores.

Perhaps the most distinguishing feature of the Bowery is the presence of many drunken men propped in doorways, lying in the street and on the sidewalk, and occasionally under parked automobiles. It was this feature of the Bowery, more than anything else, that seemed to irk the Shelter women (although, ironically, most of the women themselves had been intoxicated in public at one time or another). Often, comments such as the following would be made during an interview.

Bums on the street—layin' around. They're all sick—sick in the head.

They're drunken bums. Always sleepin' in the streets. That's the problem with the Bowery. It's no place for a lady.

They're poor people. They're homeless drunks. Let's rehabilitate these God-awful winos.

All you find is alcoholics down here; your derelicts. Lost men and women.

Although many women had misgivings about associating with Bowery men, only a few were afraid to roam the Bowery area. In fact, a few of the more adventuresome clients appeared to find a certain exciting quality about the neighborhood. As one woman put it, "I sit in the park sometimes, watch all the interesting people go by. And, then, there's all sorts of interesting shops—jewelry shops, the lamp stores, things like that. Lot's of good bars, too [respondent laughs]."

The Bowery had other attractions. Several of the Shelter women indicated that the neighborhood was especially good for panhandling. One explained, "You've got to know where to go, though. Myself, I make a good living down on Canal Street; sometimes on Lafayette and around Mott [Chinatown]. Even better, I like the banks on Friday afternoon!" Still other women commented that the Bowery was a suitable place for them because it was "easy to bum a pint off of the Bowery bums."

FACILITIES

The City of New York had a lease contract with the Pioneer Hotel for occupancy of most of the rooms located on the main floor. The remainder of the hotel space was handled on a commercial basis. Fieldworkers provided a description of the facilities at the Pioneer:

Men and women use the same entrance to the hotel. To the left of the lobby is a hall which leads to the hotel rooms, bathroom facilities, and offices (converted hotel rooms) for the caseworkers. On the right of the lobby, there are two sitting rooms with television sets. One of these is for the women. Most of the women remain in the television room throughout their waking hours. The matron's office adjoins the women's sitting room. There are three rooms used by the caseworkers. In addition the Shelter has eight sleeping rooms with forty-six beds and several bathrooms. The remainder of the hotel is used by male guests, though the Shelter can rent these if there is not sufficient room for their population.

There were no dining facilities at the Pioneer Hotel. Meals were taken at a restaurant a few blocks away. Menus were planned by a dietician in the Welfare Department. In the words of a Shelter matron:

The girls do get very good meals. For breakfast they have juice, dry cereal, a cup of milk, a scrambled egg, roll and butter and a beverage—coffee, tea, or milk. A lot of us don't get that. They get it 365 days a year. For lunch they have soup, a sandwich, a cupcake and something to drink. For supper they have something like meatballs and spaghetti and bread and butter or they have baked ham sometimes and vegetables . . . dessert and coffee.

Complaints about the food were like those encountered in most institutions. Women complained that portions were too small, meat was too fatty or tough, or that they were unpalatable altogether. Matrons almost invariably discounted the complaints about food: "Well, they just have to have something to gripe about."

ADMISSION AND REFERRAL TO THE SHELTER

Women may be directed to the Shelter in a number of ways. Though the majority of cases are authorized through the central welfare office (during the day) and the EAU (after 5:00 P.M.), a small number of clients come to the Shelter as self-referrals or are referred by policemen, community charity organizations, psychiatric institutions, state or city hospitals, and particular city agencies such as the Women's House of Detention. Not all referrals, particularly those dispatched from non-welfare organizations, are accepted as clients at the Shelter. Policy regarding accepting clients was explained by the casework supervisor:

We get lots of people, especially "after hours" who are just plain looking for a hand-out. They want something for nothing. A lot of times somebody will bring a gal here for us to take in when we can't do anything for her. I usually tell them that they should go to the Welfare center.

Even within the welfare system the problem of inappropriate referral is evidently common:

We get four or five inappropriate referrals every two or three days, and I just won't accept them. We got rules here which we have to abide by. We got a referral from Gramercy just this morning; they should have sent her to Church Street. They should know better. So, I called up the Welfare Center and let them know about it . . . And, then, the client needed carfare to get back to her caseworker . . . If they would just follow the rules things would be a lot better.

Regarding the Shelter's admission procedure, a number of women with whom interviewers spoke complained that they were the victims of a disorganized and uncoordinated welfare system. One client summarized the difficulties she encountered in receiving authorization to enter the Shelter:

. . . I had lost my apartment, like I said before. I didn't have nowhere to go. . . . So I went to see my caseworker at the ———— Welfare Center on —th Street. . . . Miss S. told me to report to Pioneer Hotel on Broome at Bowery; she said I could stay there. . . . Well, I only had a quarter, and I was saving that for a coffee and donut, so I asked for carfare. Well I took the subway downtown, but you see, I didn't know exactly how to get there . . . I got off on Houston, I think, and walked and walked and walked. You know, we'd just had that big snow the day before, and it was real hard to get around, especially with my ankle swollen like it was. I fell two or three times, I did. . . . Well, I asked an officer and he explained how I should get there. . . . By the time I arrived at the hotel it was half past noon. The caseworker made me wait for half an hour, then had the nerve to tell me I had to go to

Church Street to get authorization; said my caseworker, Miss S., shouldn't have sent me here. . . . I walked to the Church Street Center—sat there for an hour—and then some woman told me I had to get authorization or something from my caseworker since I was under her care. I'm telling you the truth: I walked all the way from Church Street up to 63rd Street. When I got there, Miss S. had already gone home and they said I'd have to wait until Monday to see her. I told the lady my problem and she called the office on Bowery, and he told her I had to go to Church Street . . . it was close to midnight time I got there, and then the matron says she can't take me in after 10.

While official criteria define eligibility for referral to the Shelter, it became increasingly clear throughout the study that caseworkers recognize client needs other than the objective circumstances of poverty and temporary homelessness. As one caseworker put it, "There is a 'shelter type,' I think." Comments from caseworkers and supervisors elaborate on the "informal policy" that governs referral and admission to the Shelter:

I think the department defines the clients as you [the researchers] do. We have something known as a "shelter type." I think the Department defines them as disaffiliated, without fixed family ties and residence as opposed to people who can't manage funds. That's the way a lot of people there define it.

Most of them just aren't hospital cases. Sometimes I feel like we function like a nut hospital for those few . . . that need the security. They live alone in some furnished room somewhere. . . . Part of it's due to the fact that they're drinkers . . . it leads to emotional problems. If you're . . . how could you say it? . . . straight . . . you could do that . . . you could live alone all right. . . . So the women are really afraid to get on public assistance.

The Shelter is designed for women who can't function in the community, who need a protective environment and supervision. Alcoholics, the mentally disturbed—these are people who can't manage their own affairs. . . . These women need the protective facilities of an institution. Left on their own they could get into trouble.

Most of the people are on the borderline between being in the community and not being in the community. Some become accustomed to shelter living. Like a club membership. They don't have to make beds, they get clean linen, there's a TV to watch, they're locked in at night, a matron turns the lights out. It's a return to a real childish state.

They are sick if they're alcoholics . . . chronically ill. They can't cope with society and they become immature. They can't seem to function on their own and they're better off in an institution with friends. . . . If they had to live in a room alone they would starve. We don't know why it is but it's a true fact. You wouldn't believe it but it's true.

You see, on public assistance they get $15 a week for room. Where can you get a room for that? Some place on the West Side. There are addicts, prostitutes around. The women are protected in the Shelter. They're not molested, except from the outside. Not often because the police are there. They could get mugged in an apartment. At the Shelter there's security. They have an appointment once a week with a caseworker . . . some of these women . . . if you offered them the White House they wouldn't go. They're dependent. They come to get a ticket for the Shelter where they're secure. That's a lot of them. Some just vegetate there. We don't want them to get dependent but some just sit there the whole day and don't do anything.

Welfare puts them in a room somewhere . . . it's terrible. I think it's worse than being here. They drink themselves to death then. That really happens in some cases. I remember one woman who just drank herself to death. It's worse than it is here, I think, because they're all alone.

Since its inception, the Women's Shelter has exchanged clients with Bellevue Hospital and with nursing homes in metropolitan New York. From time to time the Shelter admits clients who are recently discharged patients from Bellevue, and Shelter clients who show signs of severe psychiatric disorders are sent to Bellevue. Commitment for psychiatric treatment, however, seems not to rest solely on medical grounds. When the Shelter psychiatrist, who spends one morning each week at the Pioneer Hotel, was asked if he often recommends hospitalization, he replied:

No. There is a reluctance . . . not that there isn't a need. Hospitals are more and more reluctant these days to admit people. . . . There's no good place to go. . . . We usually commit them only when they're a danger to themselves and others.

DAILY ROUTINE

The Operations at the Shelter were routine during the regular work week. Almost without exception, a "typical" day followed this schedule:

The client is awakened at six (sharp) in the morning; breakfast is at 7:30 to 8 in a local restaurant located two blocks from the Hotel. Meals are provided by the restaurant under a special contract with the City Welfare Department. Lunch is served at 1:00 P.M. on weekdays; 12, on Sundays. Dinner is served at 5:30. Twice daily refreshments are served to the women by the matrons: coffee and cookies at 10 in the morning; juice and cookies in the evening.

The sleeping rooms are locked during the day; at 7:30 in the evening they are opened. Lights are put out at 10 and each woman must be in her bed then. Violation of this policy brings about cancellation of her meal and lodging privileges.

When a woman arrives at the Shelter, having first negotiated check-in procedures with the casework staff, she is required to take a bath; soap and delousing shampoo are provided. Each bath is recorded in the matron's "bath-book." Nightgowns and bathrobes are issued by the matron. A woman is never permitted to sleep in street attire; neither is she allowed to sleep nude. If an intoxicated client returns to the Shelter, her clothes are withheld until she has achieved sobriety. Sundry items and toiletries are provided by the Welfare Center; special items are obtained through a request-for-cash. The management of the Pioneer Hotel provided linens and towels as well as a housekeeper.

Aside from television, reading materials, and a few games and art supplies (which were seldom used by the women), there were few diversions in the monotonous routine. More than half the clients with whom interviewers spoke said that they remained in the television room all day. Responses to the question "what do you do most of the day" reflect the dismal surroundings and uninterrupted monotony:

What do I do? I sit. Period. I sit all morning before lunch; I sit all afternoon before dinner; and I sit all evening until bedtime at 10. That's all. Besides going to the cafe, 'bout the 'farthest' I go is to the toilet in the other room!

What the hell *is* there to do around here! That's a better question! We don't do nothing. The same goddamn thing every day. Except, maybe the food gets worse over to the cafe each day. Why, we even get the same awful cookies every day. . . . I take walks.

Well I usually sit in the dayroom, you know. I like to look out the window, out on the street. I watch them tear that building down. . . . Oh, and I have some friends, I talk to them; but mostly just sit and look out the window.

Nothing. That's what I do. Nothing. You can't watch TV; them girls— especially the colored devils—are yelling and screaming all day and night, too.

Sit. I sit in the TV room; I sit in the recreation room; I sit outside on Broome Street; I sit in the park on Grand Street; I just sit. Oh, on Thursdays, I go to the King's County Hospital—to the alcoholic ward. Otherwise I just sit . . . unless, of course, I'm drinking. Then it's another matter.

Walk around, usually. Yesterday I walked all the way to 42nd Street and back . . . there isn't much else for me to do.

I don't go nowhere. I sit in the dayroom. Talk to a few of the ladies, watch TV. That's about it.

SOURCES OF DISRUPTION

Although the operations at the Shelter followed a routine time schedule, the "normal" day also included occasional disputes, fights among the women, and other problems. Policemen and matrons at the Shelter said that the women, especially those with a drinking problem, frequently became abusive, threatening, and occasionally violent:

There's a lot of fights . . . a lot of fights. . . . It gets nasty. Especially when the (welfare) checks come in on the Bowery. When there's money around the men buy the women drinks. They come back here and get nasty. . . . They fight like cats among themselves.

Theft was evidently the major cause of fighting among the women. In addressing the problem of stealing personal belongings, one caseworker said:

There's a lot of stealing around here. There's always some stealing but you can't do much about it. . . . The personal belongings of these women are important to them, probably the only thing they have. That's why they carry all their belongings, what little they've got, with them, even when they go to the restaurant. Of course we always lock the sleeping rooms every day, but that don't seem to stop the thievery.

The matrons reported that homosexuality was an occasional problem in handling Shelter women. When complaints of homosexual activity occurred, the usual practice was to reassign the suspect client to separate quarters. As for drug use, caseworkers explained that addiction rarely was a problem among Shelter women. Known addicts were immediately referred to other agencies, and drug users seldom behaved in abusive or violent ways. Regarding prostitution, informants indicated that only a small minority of the women were practicing prostitutes.

SHELTER STAFF AND SERVICES

Professional staff. The Shelter had a staff of five professionals: the director, a case supervisor, two senior caseworkers, and a junior caseworker. All had previously worked in other divisions of the Department of Social Services.

While the staff seemed to "know" the behavior and habits of their clients in the professional sense, each staff member suggested that the Shelter personnel were not particularly suited or qualified to handle this type of case. As one senior member of the staff remarked at the time of the exploratory investigation:

To be frank most of us don't have the background. I've been here two years but I have a major in economics. Caseworkers are just assigned to the Shelter—it's ridiculous. These cases should be handled by an MSW with special training in alcoholic women. . . . Someone with training in medical social work.

At the same time, some staff reported that their ineffectiveness in working with Shelter clients was a consequence of personality conflicts. Explaining his situation, one caseworker commented:

I'm getting out (of the Women's Shelter) . . . (I'm) going to something else in a year or two. At first it was very interesting but it gets boring after awhile. . . . I can't get along with these women. You know, some people can't get along with them at all.

Caseworkers are assigned to the Women's Shelter by the EAU. According to one source, members of the EAU night staff who work especially well with the women or who do not like night work are the most likely to receive Shelter duty. In questioning staff and administrators about job-assignment, it became clear that professional qualifications per se played a relatively minor role in determining assignment to the Shelter. In speaking of the issue of recruiting qualified personnel for the Shelter, the director remarked: "We have a pretty high turnover rate here. I don't know that the department really killed itself trying to recruit."

Recruiting qualified personnel for the Shelter was further complicated by the fact that, from a professional standpoint, the Shelter was not a particularly desirable assignment. Caseworkers remarked that the Shelter woman was one of the most difficult types of client to handle. One worker remarked: "You just can't develop a meaningful relationship with them. It's hard to handle women like that . . . I don't know whether it's due to their alcoholism or not. I suspect so."

The matrons. The Women's Emergency Shelter employed twelve matrons, at least two of whom were on duty during the day. Shifts were allocated on the conventional eight-hour basis. One matron explained her duties:

We do no social work here. We maintain the place and the people. We make sure order is kept. We cooperate with the caseworkers. We don't overstep our part. . . . We do the best we can.

The role of the matron included duties of a peacemaker, housekeeper, and maid. If a dispute erupted among the women, she acted as arbiter; when the women lodged complaints about their treatment at the Shelter, she lent a sympathetic ear; if there were medical problems, she summoned a doctor; if a client's personal problem became acute, she called a social worker; and if the facilities were in a state of disorder, she acted as the official cleaning lady.

The matrons did not serve the clients in a professional capacity, but it was evident that the women perceived the matron as a powerful figure in the organizational structure. Indeed, some women indicated that the matron wielded more power than a member of the casework staff. This observation is not altogether surprising, however, in view of the fact that it was the matron who distributed most of the goods and services provided in the Shelter. Commodities such as cigarettes, ice cream, and candy were particularly precious, and it seemed to make little difference whose command or generosity made these items available; it was the matron who dispensed them and she inevitably received the credit.

Well, she's just as nice as can be. Why, she brings us some cookies and juice every night. Every now and then she gives me a cigarette, too.

Oh, she's just a wonderful thing. She brought me dinner when I was sick.

While the matron enjoyed a certain halo effect in her role as quartermaster, at the same time she took the blame for the variety of decisions that limited clients' freedom. The following excerpts from field notes illuminate the flow of "negative halo effects":

There just ain't no good reason why we have to have the light off by ten. None. She's just plain mean, that's why.

On Wednesday, the caseworker evidently told the matron, Mrs. B, that Mrs. N. should not be assigned to the lower sleeping quarters. . . . Later, Mrs. N. remarked: "Oh, she's a goddamn devil, she is. Pardon me, I don't swear you know, and I don't like to say anything bad about anybody. . . . I wanted to share a room with Lillian. She and I are good friends, you know. And that bitch, pardon me, said that the caseworker had given her orders that I couldn't room with Lillian. Well, she's a damn liar, excuse me; I hate to say it, but she *is*. . . . She doesn't like me; it's a darn shame; she doesn't like me . . .

Special service policemen. At least one policeman is on duty at the Shelter at all times. According to their handbook, their function is "preventative protection," and they have the authority to place a client under arrest if "circumstances, in the opinion of the officer, warrant it." Generally speaking, the officer on duty assumes the role of watchdog over the Shelter: inspecting the rooms periodically for various types of contraband (especially alcohol), monitoring the flow of visitors to and from the Shelter, and occasionally subduing an aggressive client. During the period of the study, interviewers witnessed one violent scene.

As I entered the TV room, Mrs. G. was hurling insults, though she seemed not to be addressing them to any particular woman. A few moments later, Mrs. S., who had been drinking most of the day, entered the room. Almost immediately, Mrs. G. began directing her insults at Mrs. S. A short time later, Mrs. G., unprovoked, leaped from the couch and assaulted Mrs. S. in a stranglehold. At that moment, the policeman on duty raced to the rescue. He grabbed Mrs. G. by the throat and threw her across the room. (Notably Mrs. S. took this opportunity to strike a blow with her purse on Mrs. G.'s forehead.) Again, the policeman grabbed Mrs. G. and this time tossed her into the hallway. At last, he pushed her down a short flight of stairs, yelling, "Goddamnit. You get the hell out of here and don't you come back." That ended the incident and the policeman returned to reading the evening newspaper.

Among the women, opinions about the policemen seemed to be determined by whether or not they have experienced some run-in with an officer. Observers reported that one officer was seen by the women in a particularly unwholesome light:

He's always saying mean things about the women.

He'd hit me if he dared. . . . He hit two women who were walking down the stairs. . . . One of them was in the hospital for three weeks. . . . There's no need for a stick in here.

In contrast, one caseworker reported to observers that:

Many of them (Shelter women) have quite a relationship going with the police. They think of them as public servants and will usually call them if they need help. The men (Bowery men) certainly don't see them as helpers. When some of the women go out, they'll stick close to the side of the street where the police call boxes are.

MEDICAL SERVICES

A physician was on duty at the Shelter each morning during the regular working week. Although medical facilities were limited to a small examination room, the medical services given to the women were perhaps the most successful part of the total program at the Shelter. A substantial number of newly admitted clients entered the Shelter with a variety of ailments, the most common being malnutrition, skin disorders resulting from poor personal hygiene, respiratory ailments, and venereal disease. For this reason, it was standard practice to require all new admissions to undergo medical examinations.

Women with acute medical problems arising from prolonged drinking often were referred to the Alcoholic Clinic at King's County Hospital in Brooklyn. At the time of the pilot study, several women were undergoing therapy; consequently, a woman's attendance at the Clinic was usually sporadic.

PSYCHIATRIC SERVICES

A psychiatrist visited the Shelter on a weekly basis, but he acted as a consultant only and provided no psychiatric treatment per se. If a client showed signs of a severe psychiatric disorder, institutional treatment was recommended. A recommendation by the psychiatrist, however, seldom resulted in actual hospitalization: "Hospitals are sometimes reluctant to accept Welfare clients, and, of course, most institutions are seriously overcrowded, which limits acceptance to those with the severe disturbances."

According to a Shelter psychiatrist, the prognosis for treatment of these women was poor. He characterized them in the following way:

I could speculate about it. . . . I would guess that they are particularly more self-defeating than other people. They have a greater feeling of failure. You know, it takes a lot of effort to wind up on the
Bowery . . . at the Shelter . . . it really takes work . . . you have
to want to go there . . . you have to work at it.

These people are at the lowest level of existence. . . . And for long-
term chronic schizophrenics . . . who can't function on their own
. . . even with a tremendous effort made at a day hospital with a good
rehabilitation program. . . . You can have this kind of program without hoping for even a good percentage of good results. The people at
the Shelter are not temporary cases with temporary problems. . . .
They're long-term problems with chronic difficulties in managing in the
community.

Most of the people here are on the borderline between being in the
community and being out of the community. This is the last place to
go before being sent to a hospital or elsewhere. . . . Rehabilitation
is a tremendous effort and useless. . . . They aren't terribly motivated.

ALCOHOLICS ANONYMOUS

Each Sunday and Tuesday members of Alcoholics Anonymous
held meetings at the Shelter which were conducted in the traditional manner. Women with drinking problems were encouraged to
attend AA meetings even though it was recognized that they were
unlikely to develop any long-range commitments to the program.
The underlying assumption was that discussion of one's drinking
problem at any level constituted an initial step toward permanent
sobriety.

Observers at the Shelter reported that most women seemed to
view their involvement in AA in a serious light, and a few women
identified AA as their only organizational affiliation. But while the
women manifested a serious attitude toward AA, reports indicated
that the spirit of fellowship, perhaps the hallmark of AA organizations, was absent among the Shelter group. Rather, the women
seemed to view their fellow members as a disinterested audience.
Although no statistics on post-Shelter drinking are available, it is

notable that the bulk of clients who regularly return to the Shelter are those with long-standing drinking problems.

Most caseworkers estimated at least half of the Shelter clients were chronic alcoholics, and the substantial majority had experienced some type of acute drinking problem earlier in their lives. In fact, caseworkers assigned special significance to excessive drinking as a cause of the predicament of Shelter women.

Yes, I think their problems are caused by alcoholism.

She brought it all on herself through her drinking . . .

I think the kind of person you find around the Bowery—men and women—are mostly alcoholics. If you could take away their drinking, they would never have had the problems they have.

Regarding a twenty-five year old client, one worker remarked, "Sure, she's a chronic alcoholic. She told me that she gets drunk once, sometimes twice, a week."

Not unexpectedly, caseworkers took a rather dim view of the chances of recovery for these women:

I'm afraid they're pretty much hopeless cases.

When you have an addict, you get him away from dope and he goes through a withdrawal period. How can you get an alcoholic in an environment like this (The Bowery) to withdraw from alcohol? . . . You can't.

Case histories

The foregoing discussion has illuminated certain aspects of the life histories of homeless women, but a review of research findings alone provides limited insight into the meaning these women attach to significant events in their past. It is one thing to point to the characteristics of family deprivation, broken parental marriage, marital instability, and social isolation, and quite another to show how these women interpret their early-life and family experiences, their marriages, and their present-life situations. The remainder of this chapter consists of four case histories that illustrate some of the family experiences and personal lives of Shelter women. These histories draw upon several sources, including interview schedules, fieldwork observations, and clients' case history folders at the Women's Shelter. Of course, these four cases cannot be considered as "typical" of all homeless women, but they nevertheless mirror several characteristics that were reported by almost all of the women interviewed in our 1969 survey of Shelter women. First, the most outstanding feature of these life histories is an unhappy childhood. Most respondents reported long years of unhappiness and misfortune during childhood or adolescence. The four cases considered here are particularly interesting in this respect because each represents a distinctive family situation, ranging from child neglect and financial hardship to circumstances posed by parents who were very strict disciplinarians. Second, these accounts (particularly the first three) also capture the "isolation dimension" in the life histories of Shelter women. They illustrate not only the circumstances leading to the severance of marital and family ties but also suggest that the subjects' present-day isolation is at least partly self-imposed. This situation is placed in bold relief in the cases of Gladys and Carrie,[67] both of whom boldly assert, "I want to be left alone." These cases may reflect examples of independence and isolation more extreme than usual among Shelter women, but the fieldworkers did report a stated preference to avoid close interpersonal relationships among a striking proportion of the women. Finally, the following case histories are useful in highlighting the lifestyles of homeless women—how they live, how they support themselves, and how they make their way as "women alone."

THE CASE OF GLADYS

"Gladys" was white, fifty-five years old, and lived at the Women's Shelter off and on for three years. She said she had no permanent home other than the Shelter. At the time of interview the Shelter was serving as a convalescent home while she recovered from a recent injury. She described the place of the Shelter in her life:

When I'm beat and "had-it" I come to the Pioneer for a rest. Lots of
the girls here are that way. . . . You know how I came here this time,
you know why? I been livin' in the streets and the subways for the
past month. I got hold of some cash last Monday. Tied one on, I did.
. . . I was so drunk I never knew what hit me. . . . I was crossing
Houston up here. A truck, he hit—plow! The doc says I'll be ok after a
few weeks rest here. . . .

Gladys was born in Lancaster County, Pennsylvania. She was
raised in a large family (eleven brothers and one sister) of Mennonite faith. "We lived the way all good Mennonite families live.
We farmed, we prayed, and we went to church every Sunday—
never fail."

Her early-childhood and adolescent years were unhappy but relatively uneventful. At the age of twelve (in keeping with the Mennonite practice), she quit school to help out on the family farm.
She recalled:

The most unhappy years of my life were when I was growing up. I
hated the religion; I hated the bonnets, the black dresses down to your
ankles. I always wanted to be like other girls. I was actually glad when
I quit school cause it was embarrassing to have my friends see me in
that "get-up." . . . Life was miserable. I stayed home. Worked, that's
all I ever did. The Mennonite folk think it's good for the soul, you
know, to work. Well, my soul musta been pretty healthy, I'd say. . . .
The only ambition I ever had was to get away from there.

The day following her eighteenth birthday Gladys moved to a
nearby Pennsylvania town where she was hired as a seamstress in
a garment factory. Soon after she began work, she rented an apartment with an older woman who was also working at the factory.
"We had a great time. I was doing things I'd never done before.
Going to parties, meetin' men, and just doing what I wanted."

At age twenty Gladys began dating a man she had met at a tavern. They were married a year later and moved to another city in
Pennsylvania. Her husband worked as a truck driver for the first
few months of their marriage, but later he was fired for drunken
driving. Gladys described him:

That sonofabitch never did an honest day's work. We lived together for ten years and I supported him the whole time. . . . He was a hypochondriac. His mother told him he was sickly and he believed it. He was always complainin' about somethin' or another. . . . Yes, we both drank a lot then. We was young; didn't know no better. We was both drunk two or three times a week. It was embarrassin'. The difference was, though, I'd pull myself together. He never did. . . .

After ten years of marriage, she finally left her husband on grounds that he failed to support her: "I just packed my bags and left. Never did get a divorce. Figured why should I sink more money into that good-for-nothing." A short time thereafter, she moved to New York City. "I didn't have no reason to go 'cept that I'd always wanted to go to a big city. One day a driver down to the ammunition factory offered me a ride, so I took it." For the next two years, she worked in garment factories, but she lost many jobs because of her heavy drinking.

Oh, I got work OK. Had no trouble at all. I'd work for a couple of months, even got one raise after another. Trouble is I'd get to drinking. I'd take up with some man, stay with him a few nights, we'd do some drinking, and before I knew it I'd be so under-the-rug I couldn't go to work. I was ashamed, too. I'd never go back to pick up my last paycheck. I just couldn't face 'em. . . .

She spent more than ten years like this, going from one job to another. On three separate occasions, she lived with a man for as long as six months, but she describes these relationships as transient affairs.

. . . It was nothin'. They were no-goods. Two were alcoholics—bad as me—and the other was a junkie. We'd get in a fight over somethin'. That was that. . . . No, the men I've met—if this is what men are like —I want no part of them.

Since age forty-five, Gladys had lived alone in New York either in a hotel or rooming house. In recent years drinking had prevented her from holding a job for longer than a month. "I spent most of the time in the hospital—sick or hurt—or drunk on the Bowery." She summarized her present life:

As for me I got nothin'. I'm probably nothin' more than a hopeless alcoholic—no better than the winos around here. . . . But I don't want no part of men or marriage, and I don't want to see my family. . . . I want to be independent. I don't want nobody; I don't need nobody.

THE CASE OF CARRIE

Carrie was born in Brooklyn in 1914. Her parents had immigrated from Russia. She remembered them as "poor people who were hard workers." Carrie was the second of two daughters. Her sister was "sociable, extroverted, and not at all like me. . . ." When Carrie was four years old, her family moved to Manhattan's Lower East Side where her father opened a small shoe store. Carrie and her sister used to tend shop while her father peddled shoes from a cart in the streets of Manhattan. "He worked hard, maybe sixteen, seventeen hours a day. Used to come home exhausted. . . . He never had much time for family life; too busy working all the time."

Carrie's early years were uneventful. However, she reported that the "Jewish way of life" created an unhappy childhood for her:

I went to Synagogue once or twice, and that's because I *had* to go. But I didn't care for it. That ritual. It's phony. I finally told them I won't go anymore; I don't want any part of that life. . . . My parents said they understood, although I always felt like an outcast from that point on. . . .

Carrie left school during her first year in high school, and went to work in her father's shop. She explained:

I was a good student, top of my class. . . . But school was too confining. It was boring for me. Never got along with the other students, either. So I quit. . . . What I lost in schooling I gained in freedom. . . . I did all sorts of things, but *always* (her emphasis) alone. Used to take long walks on the Bowery—I grew up here, you know, right here, two blocks from Broome and Bowery. I know this neighborhood better than anybody else. . . . I used to spend hours on end walking, sitting in the Park by myself, watching people do things. But, I'd always keep to myself . . . didn't *ever* (her emphasis) talk to people.

A year after she left school, Carrie went to work in a garment factory, but she continued to live with her family. Later she began dating a German immigrant whom she subsequently married. In commenting upon this period in her life, she recalls:

He was my first date. Imagine that. My first date. I was nineteen and he was thirty-nine. . . . He had just come over from Germany; been here a month. He made good, tho'. Made *good* money as a boiler-maker. . . . Those were the happiest years of my life. I had everything. Life was secure.

Neither she nor her husband wanted children. When she became pregnant they agreed that she would have an abortion. A few years later she became pregnant again, but lost the child as a result of a self-induced abortion in the eighth month of pregnancy.

After ten years of marriage her husband died of cancer. The tragedy of his death completely rearranged Carrie's life: "My whole life ended. That was the beginning of the most unhappy time in my life. . . . Now I got nothin'. . . . When he died, I stopped being with people; I stayed to myself; I was lonely. Nothing was worthwhile without him. It was terrible."

When her husband died Carrie returned to her parents' home. Soon afterward they both died within a span of six months. She was quite unprepared for the sudden bereavement: "I had no one except my sister, but she was married. I had no place to go. I just wandered around the neighborhood for the next few months."

Carrie was twenty-nine years old. After that she never had a permanent home. Nor did she work or receive public assistance monies, or financial assistance from friends or relatives. She described the past twenty-five years of her life as reflecting self-imposed isolation:

Since my husband died twenty-five years ago I've kept to myself. I don't talk to people. I want to be left alone; I enjoy being alone; I'm individualistic. I just don't like people. . . . They make demands on you, so I stay away from them. . . . The only person I ever . . . (saw was) . . . my sister. I lost her last June. She was the only person I knew, the only one who understood me, who cared about me . . . I don't have any friends; I don't want any friends.

. . . I don't like to work. Last job I held was when I was eighteen. I get by; I have for 25 years and not on welfare, either. People give me money. I'll be walking around on Canal Street or on Times Square and people just give me money. I don't know why. . . . Sometimes I find money. Oh, occasionally, when my luck is down, I'll ask somebody on the street for a dime or something. I get by.

For most of the past twenty-five years, she had lived in New York's subways, in public parks and rest rooms, and in condemned office buildings and warehouses near the Bowery. She lived eight months in the ladies lounge on the second floor of one of the city's largest office buildings. Another time she lived for nearly a year on the rooftop of an office building located near the Battery. She said:

You've got to have ingenuity. You've got to know New York, its people, how to get around. I sleep in the subways nowadays. It works out fine. . . . You can't sleep there when an officer's on duty. That's from 8 (P.M.) to 4 (A.M.). So, I go there about 10 (minutes) till 4; sleep to noon, usually. . . . I like the Eighth Avenue line. Less stops. I sleep on one of the front or back cars; never the middle. Too many disturbances. Works out just fine, just fine. I get a good night's rest.

Although Carrie avoided close interpersonal relations with others, she said that she sought only limited isolation: "I like to be around people, to watch people, to see them; I just don't like to talk to them, to be friends. . . . People are interesting if you don't have to talk to them."

At the time of the interview, Carrie had just returned from Newark where she had been living alone in a shanty house she had made from railroad ties and pieces of cardboard. She commented, "You might say that I was on vacation. It was my first time away from the City since I was born."

THE CASE OF SAUNDRA

Saundra first came to the Women's Shelter in June 1969. She said she had been living in the streets and sleeping on park benches or in condemned warehouses a few blocks off of Canal Street since the previous February.

Saundra was born in 1945 in Lawrence, Kansas. She was an illegitimate child. Six months after her birth, she was made a ward of the state on grounds of parental neglect. Child custody was given to her grandparents (in Lawrence) who raised her until she was five years old. Then she was sent to New York City to live with her mother, who had been married and divorced since Saundra's birth. "I was only five, but I remember it well. My grandmother and father put me on a train in Kansas City. I went the whole way alone."

Her mother, who now had another child, worked as a waitress in a midtown bar for a short time, but was later fired for reasons unknown to the respondent. Excerpts from the interview with Saundra reveal a very unhappy childhood:

I lived in New York until I was eight or nine. My mother was never home. I used to live on peanut-butter sandwiches. I fed them to my stepbrother when he was only three. . . . I remember that my mother used to come home with all sorts of strange men. There were always men at home. I always used to ask her if one of these men were my father. . . . My mother drank a lot. One day I came home from school and she had fallen down the stairs with a bottle in her hand. She was cut badly. . . . One day she said that Johnny (stepbrother) was going away; she packed all of his things in a large shopping bag. She gave him away. I've never seen him since. . . .

When Saundra was eight years old, her mother remarried. A short time afterward, they moved to a Los Angeles suburb where her stepfather worked in a factory. In Saundra's view the addition of the stepfather to the family was not an improvement:

He ordered us around a lot. He was mean. If I'd be late for dinner I'd be whipped. When my mother was late in getting home they'd have terrible arguments and he'd hit her. I hated him. I hated him even worse than my mother.

At age fourteen, Saundra's stepfather ordered her out of the household for reasons that she did not fully understand. She said, "I don't really know why he wanted me away. I think he thought that I was coming between him and my mother."

Her mother sent her to Tucson, Arizona, to live with some close friends of the family, and she remained there until she finished high school. Then she hitchhiked to New York City. "I wanted to find a good job and be independent. I never wanted to see my mother or stepfather again. . . . I tried to get a job as a dancer, then an actress. It was useless." Eventually she was employed as a governess for a family in a New York suburb but she was fired after nine months on grounds that she was an unwholesome influence on the children.

So Saundra returned to New York City. She was twenty-one years old. She said that she drifted around New York's East Village area for nearly three months. "I slept in doorways most of that summer, bumming what I could off people." I then met a man who "promised to make me a famous artist." She moved into his apartment in West Village, but they were never married. Her relationship with this man was in many ways a turning point in her life:

I must have been blind. The first two months were beautiful. Neither of us worked, but we got by somehow. . . . Then we started to have arguments, arguments over everything. . . . He wanted sex every day and I didn't. He got to be like an animal; he hurt me. Then he started to bring other women home—even when I was there. . . . I'll say this, though. He showed me some beautiful, beautiful experiences; I discovered myself. He used to bring home barbituates and STP. . . . Whenever I was lonely or sad or depressed I'd feel better by taking a pill. It was simple.

Although Saundra's relationship with her common-law husband became increasingly unsatisfactory to her, she stayed with him because he supplied her with drugs. Their relationship ended when he was convicted on charges of burglary. After that time Saundra drifted about Manhattan until she came to the Shelter. In the months preceding the interview she was raped three times, robbed ("right on Eighth Avenue, right in Times Square"), and badly beaten by two teenagers. Despite her misfortunes, however, she was optimistic: "Life will be better for me. I know now what I want. I want to be alone, to be independent. Maybe have my own farm so I can be away from people and work with my hands. I'll make it."

THE CASE OF MARGARET

Margaret came to the Women's Shelter for the first time during midsummer of 1969. Apart from being homeless and without means of support, a major reason for her seeking welfare assistance at this time was that she had been informed that the Department of Social Services would provide medical and dental services which she badly needed.

Margaret was white, forty-five years of age, the eldest of three children. She grew up in a small coal mining town in western Pennsylvania. Her father was a coal miner, and her mother worked as a clerk in a department store. She said that she had a very unhappy childhood up to about age five. "My old man was a no-good drunkard and gambler. When he finally deserted us I was glad. . . . Even when I was little I'd try to get away from home as much as I could. I liked to be with other children; I was happy then." After her father left, Margaret's mother began drinking heavily, and the neighbors complained that she was an unfit mother. Margaret and her two sisters were sent to a Catholic foster home in Philadelphia; a year later she was placed in a foster home (a married couple without children of their own). After six months she was returned to the orphanage in Philadelphia because her foster parents complained that she was an unruly child. At age eight she was again placed in custody of foster parents but was returned to the orphanage almost immediately. She was then transferred to another Catholic orphanage in suburban Philadelphia. She said life in the orphanage was among the happiest years of her life: "I was always happy with the children. I loved being with them and I was never, never lonely. In the foster homes I was always lonely. I was mistreated. I hated it."

When she was fifteen, Margaret was sent to live with her mother, who was living in Akron, Ohio. She remained with her mother until she was sixteen. Apparently her mother was a domineering woman who "made life miserable for me." She escaped the tensions at home as soon as she could. "I just had to leave. She just nagged all the time, all the time. I could never do anything right. . . . To make matters worse she was three-quarters drunk all the time."

Margaret lived with a man for four years and then married him. They lived together for sixteen years, and had ten children.

The only thing that made me happy was my ten children. I was always happy when I had my children. . . . But my husband, he wasn't alive. He never did anything. I couldn't work; I couldn't do anything.

At the end of the fifth year of marriage, Margaret was experiencing prolonged states of depression. "It was more than just loneliness. It was a kind of sadness that wouldn't go away." During these depressions she began drinking heavily. Following one of her drinking episodes, she attempted suicide by cutting her wrists with a razor blade. She was then confined in a sanitorium for a year. After her release, "my life seemed to be rearranged. Everything was different. For the next ten years . . . I just sort of existed. I have no 'memories'—nothing stands out. I only know I was bored." And her marriage got worse.

We argued about everything. Money was a problem with ten kids. He was drinking too much and so was I. . . . When I found out he was supporting another woman I started steppin' out on him and then he complained that I was away too much. . . . We disagreed on how to raise the children. He wanted to take them traveling, wanted them to be refined by going to a private school. I disagreed.

At the end of the twelfth year of their marriage, Margaret left her husband and moved in with her sister in Akron. She worked as a waitress, then as a clerical worker at a rubber manufacturing plant. A year later she became involved with a man whom she met in a tavern in Cleveland. They lived together for almost a year and then were married. Her second marriage was less successful than the first:

It's funny in a way. When we were just living together everything was fine. As soon as we were married, all legal-like, it wouldn't work out.

. . . He was worse than my first husband. He even drank more. Every week he'd beat me up till I was black and blue. . . . What was worse, his drinking caused bed problems, you know. Men are like savages.

Two months after the marriage, Margaret left her husband. She later learned that he had never divorced his first wife.

After that she said she "lived a loose life." "I took up with any Tom, Dick, or Harry that came by." Two months before she was interviewed at the Shelter, she met a truck driver in a restaurant where she was working. He was on his way to New York City, and invited her to "come along for the ride." She came.

7 | Control and rehabilitation

Chapter 7 contains a review of historical and contemporary treatment programs for homelessness and alcoholism, including several illustrative cases. It begins with treatment for vagrancy, which at the turn of the century was seen as the primary disorder of homeless men. Later vagrancy was superseded by alcoholism, and social control programs changed their focus from neutralizing wanderlust to maintaining sobriety. The negative experience poor people have had with representatives of the law is summarized, and the aspects of that experience most familiar to homeless men—police behavior on skid row and the "revolving door" of arrest, jail, court appearance, jail, and then the street again—are discussed. Having considered the operation of the law, we will turn to specific kinds of therapy and treatment, including "rehabilitation on the streets" (community organization or street project work), Salvation Army Men's Social Service Centers, hospital programs for alcoholics, treatment programs in prisons and jails, long-term residential centers, detoxification centers, halfway houses, and Alcoholics Anonymous. One of the critical problems in treatment of chronic inebriety and other aspects of homelessness has been the virtual absence of scientific evaluation programs; Pittman identified the lack of critical evaluation as the greatest weakness of alcoholism treatment in

America and Europe. Our review of types of therapy and their efficacy contains sections on insight therapy, aversion therapy, the lack of established criteria for successful treatment, and the problem of individualizing treatment to meet a man's special needs.

Treatment of vagrancy

Vagrancy used to be an important social problem in this country, and a great deal of professional attention was devoted to methods for treating or controlling the vagrant. One type of vagrant was the alcoholic, and treating his alcoholism was part of the larger problem of treating vagrancy and homelessness. Nowadays, alcoholism has superseded vagrancy as the more general disorder, and the only homeless men who receive much attention are the chronic alcoholics. It follows that the dominant feature of treatment programs for skid row men is treatment for alcoholism.

In the late 1800's and early 1900's treatment programs were structured about the moral inferiority of the homeless and the need to protect good citizens from contact with such undesirables. Unemployment and wandering were vices (frequently attractive ones) and it was society's responsibility to make indulgence in them costly enough that miscreants would reform and end their social parasitism.

Agents of social control in England and the United States were urged to follow the lead of several European countries which had adopted severe, sometimes repressive measures against vagrants, including the establishment of detention camps and labor colonies.[1] The idea of establishing labor colonies was attractive because it not only put the vagrants to work but also kept them from associating with the non-homeless. In 1895, John McCook, an authority on homelessness in Massachusetts, proposed to the National Conference of Charities and Correction that "the Tramp Problem" be solved by giving tramps prison sentences of indeterminate length. Presumably the open-ended sentence would give prison authorities as much time as necessary to complete the rehabilitation process.

He also called for unsympathetic repression of hobo camps to prevent these attractive nuisances from winning children to a life of
vagabondage.[2] Germany's remedial program for the eradication of
begging, including antibegging societies, national shelters, labor
colonies, and the imprisonment of beggars, was described in glow-
ing terms in the *Annals of the American Academy of Political and
Social Science*, and the feasibility of applying such measures to
homeless people in New York City was assessed.[3] A speaker at the
1903 National Conference of Charities and Correction suggested
that the constraints on the homeless in urban areas should be extended to rural tramps. Feeding tramps and sending them away
merely encouraged their vagabondage, he said. Instead, they should
be given a choice between labor and imprisonment.[4]

Compulsory labor was a popular solution. Its proponents pointed
out that it served to separate the truly poor from those whose indigence was a direct result of their laziness.[5] By 1881, Detroit had
adopted a "tough" approach to homelessness which included forced
labor. A British advocate of the "labor test" proposed that unemployed beggars be assigned to areas which had a labor shortage.
Relief programs would furnish work, not food or money.[6]

Many students of the problems of homelessness recognized the
need for rehabilitation as well as punishment. Edmond Kelly, author of *The Elimination of the Tramp* and *The Unemployables* and
one of the advocates of labor colonies in the United States, recognized the difficult problem of finding a balance between rehabilitative and custodial aims in programs for the homeless.[7] One innova-
tive proposal was that municipal lodging houses serve a screening
function for the vagrant population, identifying the honest unemployed men, the unfortunate impoverished, and the "social parasites." Within the municipal lodging houses, facilities would be segregated and each type would receive appropriate rehabilitative
care.[8]

In the 1920's and 1930's proposals for more centralized, concentrated care of the homeless began to be made. With the Great
Depression the federal government had moved into the "treatment

of vagrancy" business on a large scale, and interagency overlap and public and private duplication of programs and services increased. The problems of chronic inebriates and many non-alcoholic vagrants were serious and diverse, and frequently many different agencies shared responsibility for them, but at the same time no single agency was equipped to treat them. The need for reorganization and centralization of welfare agencies was not new. It had been recognized as a serious problem in Paris in 1893.[9] But in the United States, it did not become a dominant theme until after the Depression.

A 1937 evaluation of Chicago's care for homeless men concluded that homelessness should be seen as part of the larger problem of poverty and advocated a more coordinated, integrated approach by the disciplines and agencies concerned.[10] After World War II "comprehensive plans," "interdisciplinary programs" became popular phrases. In 1961 a rehabilitation expert argued that skid row could be eliminated if comprehensive community plans for rehabilitation were instituted, including inputs from the fields of internal medicine, psychiatry, psychology, sociology, and religion.[11] Treatment programs established in the late 1950's and 1960's often reflected the view that alcoholism and homelessness were complex problems requiring "comprehensive" approaches. Many were largely referral programs, operating on the assumption that the skid row man did not know about, or for some other reason could not take advantage of the helping programs already available in the wider community.

A 1928 paper on "psychopathic vagrancy" argued that bread lines encouraged vagrancy, and that vocational assistance was ineffective in keeping derelicts off the streets. A more appropriate solution was segregating them from society. The responsibility for the confinement and treatment of the homeless, it was proposed, should fall upon the police and the psychiatrists.[12] The psychiatrists did not rise to the challenge. There were not enough of them to handle the middle- and upper-class people with problems let alone the homeless wanderer. Law enforcement and rehabilitation were left to the police, the courts, and the jails. In the past forty years there have been some imaginative model programs, and some recent legal reforms augur well for the homeless man in the 1980's. But the primary agent of social control on skid row continues to be the policemen, and the most common rehabilitation program the sequence of arrest and confinement.

Homeless men and the law

"The poor have almost always had uniquely bitter experiences with the legal process," writes Jonathan Weiss. He goes on to note that the poor tend to be dependent, and to react passively to everyday situations.[13] They face the institution of the law as they face other institutions in society, with an anticipation of negative outcomes. Not only is their access to legal forums constricted as compared with other citizens', but their "durability" or staying power is weak. They lack resources to continue legal fights, particularly when the matters at issue are essentials of their own continued existence, e.g., an indigent mother must live on something while she tries to demonstrate her right to welfare payments to the court. In addition to their limited access and durability in legal process, often the poor are a specially treated group for whom special laws may apply or laws may be differentially enforced.[14]

The legal difficulties of the poor are most starkly illustrated in the experience of homeless men and the law. If the poor have peculiar legal problems,[15] the peculiarities are most apparent among the most indigent—the homeless. Homeless men are more passive, more dependent, have less access to legal forums and fewer resources for enduring extended legal processes than any other segment of the population. Perhaps the skid row man's most frequent encounter with the law is his arrest and jailing for chronic inebriety. The revolving door trap for indigent alcoholics is aptly summarized in the following statement:

The "revolving-door" cycle, one extremely unfortunate sociological outgrowth of alcoholism, affects the homeless alcoholic in particular.

Such a person is inextricably caught in the cycle of intoxication, arrest for being publicly in that condition, conviction, confinement, release, and return to the street where, because of his complete lack of control over his drinking, the cycle begins again. This cycle has become so common that the number of arrests for public intoxication is higher than that for any other offense. The courts and jails are overburdened, the cycle continues, and the essential problem—the sickness and anti-social behavior of the indigent alcoholic—remains unabated except for periodic "dry" spells in jail.[16]

Recent landmark court decisions involving chronic drunkenness offenders include *Driver* v. *Hinnant* and *Easter* v. *District of Columbia,* in which Circuit Courts of Appeal ruled that chronic drunkenness offenders could not be criminally convicted of public intoxication. However, in *Powell* v. *Texas*, the Supreme Court addressed the significance of the "disease concept of alcoholism" for the criminal law but refused to reverse the conviction for public intoxication of Leroy Powell, largely on the basis that testimony for the defendant was "utterly inadequate." Four of the five justices who affirmed Powell's conviction joined in the opinion that since no effective treatment of alcoholism is known and treatment facilities were lacking, a short jail term was preferable to an indefinite therapeutic civil commitment.[17] Excellent discussions of the background, nature, and implications of these decisions are readily available.[18]

Hollister has suggested that despite the *Powell* decision, states could create a common-law defense to charges of public intoxication by invoking the mens rea standard of criminal responsibility.[19] At present, however, with a few notable exceptions, the revolving door continues to operate in American cities.

In 1969 approximately one of every four arrests was for public drunkenness. When arrests for disorderly conduct and vagrancy are combined with drunkenness, 38 per cent of all arrests are accounted for. High as that figure is, there is some comfort in the fact that it represents a substantial decline in the number and proportion of arrests for drunkenness and related offenses. In 1960 more than half of all arrests were for one of these three offenses, and arrests for public drunkenness alone represented 38 per cent of all arrests.[20]

It is estimated that only about 3 per cent of a given city's alcoholics live on skid row, but men from the row may make up as much as 45 per cent of all arrests for public drunkenness.[21] Moreover, a fraction of the skid row population bear the brunt of the differential arrest rates; some of the heavy drinkers on skid row are arrested over and over again. For example, in Los Angeles, one-fifth of the total number of persons arrested for drunkenness accounted for two-thirds of all arrests for that offense. In Pacific City three-fourths of the annual arrests for public drunkenness were repeat arrests, arrests of men who had already been arrested for that offense at least once that year.[22]

Individually, "repeaters" who are caught in the revolving door of arrest, incarceration, release, and re-arrest may spend large portions of their lives in jails, in a sort of life sentence on the installment plan. For example, six chronic offenders in the District of Columbia had been arrested 1,409 times and had served a total of 125 years in jails and prisons. A 1965 newspaper account told of a man appearing in police court for the 277th time on public intoxication. In all he had served 16 years in the penitentiary, and on this 277th time he was sentenced to an additional six months.[23] A Seattle man, first arrested for public drunkenness in 1947, was convicted over 100 times between that time and 1968 for the same crime. He was sentenced to jail 74 times, receiving in all more than 14 years of sentences.[24]

Figures on public drunkenness arrests alone may seriously underestimate the extent of the problem. In Washington, D.C., and Atlanta, Georgia, drunkenness arrests accounted for more than 50 per cent of all arrests in 1965. However, when arrests for disorderly conduct and vagrancy were included, more than *three-fourths* of all arrests during the year were accounted for. Also, there is substantial variation from place to place in the enforcement of public drunkenness and related statutes. During the same year that Washington, D.C., and Atlanta achieved the percentages noted above, only about 6 per cent of the arrests in St. Louis were for public drunkenness; when disorderly conduct and vagrancy arrests were included, the total was a comparatively low 19 per cent.[25]

The police on skid row

One of the most provocative analyses of the work of policemen on skid row is Egon Bittner's study of "peace keeping."[26]* He identifies two distinct and relatively independent kinds of police roles: one as "law officers," in which their behavior is oriented to the prospect of a case in the courts, and the other as "peace officers," in which they operate with reference to constraints other than law enforcement. Their peace keeping activities include many routines not directly related to making arrests.

Among the situations which do not demand the invocation of the law, and where the policeman is free to decide what to do and how to do it, are the following five circumstances:

1. The supervision of some licensed services and regulation of traffic.

2. The decision not to arrest persons who have committed minor offenses.

3. The invocation of police authority in situations which frequently contain no criminal or legal aspects.

4. The monitoring of mass phenomena, e.g., crowd control.

5. Duties with respect to persons not fully accountable for their behavior or judged "abnormal" in some way, e.g., the mentally ill, the underage, vagabonds, ex-convicts.

In his response to all of these "demand conditions" the police officer may make arrests and invoke the criminal process, but much of his behavior in these situations does not involve arrests. Such be-

* Excerpts from Egon Bittner, "The Police on Skid Row" are reprinted by permission of The American Sociological Association.

"Don't look at me!"

havior tends to be outside the pale of direct administrative control
—"policemen act in the role of 'peace officers' pretty much without
external control or constraint."[27]

The job of the skid row police officer is to "contain" skid row.
The methods of containment are not officially defined. The usual
practice is to make assignment to skid row fairly permanent, and,
within broad limits, to allow the patrolmen to run things their own
way. Part of the socialization into the role of the skid row peace
keeper is the acquisition of a definition of skid row and its men.
The stereotype of skid row held by the policemen who work there
is that it is a place for people who are incapable of leading "normal" lives.

In general, and especially in casual encounters, the presumption of in-
competence and of the disinclination to be "normal" is the leading
theme for the interpretation of all actions and relations.[28]

A dominant element of the policeman's stereotype is the notion
that on skid row "all enterprise and association is directed to the
occasion of the moment." In other words, the prevailing spirit is
one of fortuitousness. The past and the future have only limited
relevance. To a large extent, the future is unpredictable: "It is a
matter of adventitious circumstance whether or not matters go as
anticipated. That which is not within the grasp of momentary control is outside of practical social reality." "Irresponsibility takes an
objectified form on skid-row," and the social relations and activities
of skid row residents are not meaningfully connected over time.
Consequently, ". . . life on skid-row lacks a socially structured
background of accountability . . . in the life of a skid-row in-
habitant every moment is an accident."[29] This drastically reduces
the policemen's power to find people when they want them; the
skid row man has reduced visibility for the police because the web
of predictabilities that make up the life space of the "normal" person does not exist on skid row. Also, because the skid row residents
are perceived as being outside the "controlling influences of the
pursuit of sustained interests," they are viewed with apprehension

by members of the larger society: "As they have nothing to for-sake, nothing is thought safe from them."[30]

Despite the presence on skid row of criminals who have com-mitted crimes outside of that area, and despite the public concern about containment, the skid row patrolman's basic job is keeping the peace and enforcing the laws within the skid row area. In effect, this means protecting potential exploiters from each other. To aid him in maintaining control, the patrolman uses an approach that includes three elements: 1. He acquires "a richly particularized knowledge of people and places in the area." 2. Strict culpability before the law is not the most important determinant of a sanction (after all, everyone on the row is "guilty"). 3. The use of coercion is determined by the nature of the particular situation at hand with little regard for long-range effects on individual skid row men.[31]

The patrolman's particularized knowledge of people and places on skid row means that he knows the "regulars," both residents and persons who are employed on skid row. He has a detailed knowl-edge of public and private places, and has an historical perspective based on numerous past events about which he can cite names, dates, and places with precision.

The skid row policeman perceives himself as having a right to know about everything that happens in his area. In interaction with skid row men and representatives of the institutions which serve them he allows a bantering informality, provided the object of his attention does not question his right to know whatever he wishes to know. The officers recognize that their direct approach and the ex-pectations that accompany it encroach upon the civil liberties of skid row men, but they justify it as "in accord with the general free-dom of access that persons living on skid row normally grant one another."

. . . people are not so much denied the right to privacy as they are seen as not having any privacy. Thus, officers seek to install themselves in the center of people's lives and let the consciousness of their pres-ence play the part of conscience.[32]

The officers also see their "aggressively personal approach" as an aid to the residents of skid row. Only if they know what is going on can they provide necessary services. The patrolman knows that persons in dire need are a potential source of trouble, and besides it is part of the role expectation that the officer can do something about the sick, the hungry, and the victimized.

The domain of the patrolman's service activity is virtually limitless, and it is no exaggeration to say that the solution of every conceivable problem has at one time or another been attempted by a police officer. In one observed instance, a patrolman unceremoniously entered the room of a man he had never seen before. The man, who gave no indication that he regarded the officer's entry and questions as anything but part of life as usual, related a story about having had his dentures stolen by his wife. In the course of the subsequent rounds, the patrolman sought to locate the woman and the dentures. This did not become the evening's project but was attended to while doing other things.[33]

The "restricted relevance of culpability" in skid row peace keeping means, in practice, that while persons arrested are presumably technically liable to arrest, the law is invoked not because of the manifest violation but for other considerations. "Thus, it could be said that patrolmen do not really enforce the law, even when they do invoke it, but merely use it as a resource to solve certain pressing practical problems in keeping the peace."[34] Bittner maintains that the reduced relevance of culpability is not readily apparent because most arrested persons were found in the act alleged in the arrest record. It is most apparent when the legal grounds for arrest could be questioned, as in the case of "preventive arrests." Again, the point is that in a situation where everyone is presumed guilty— and that is the way the patrolman views skid row—it is not feasible to arrest everyone, and it is more practical to use the coercive sanction of arrest only when other ends than law enforcement are served thereby. The attitude of police officers in this matter is illustrated in these two statements:

. . . patrolmen adopt the view that the law is not merely imperfect and difficult to implement, but that on skid-row, at least, the association between delict and sanction is distinctly occasional. Thus, to implement the law naively, i.e., to arrest someone *merely* because he committed some minor offense, is perceived as containing elements of injustice.

The patrolman maintained that . . . "these people take things from each other so often that no one could tell what 'belongs' to whom." In fact, he suggested, the terms owning, stealing, and swindling, in their strict sense, do not really belong on skid-row, and all efforts to distribute guilt and innocence according to some rational formula of justice are doomed to failure.[35]

The patrolman's ad hoc decision-making in minor offense arrests usually is justified in terms of "protecting" the arrested person, or, more infrequently, on the grounds that the arrest protects other skid row residents. When he uses force, it is dictated by an "intuitive" grasp of the situation, and is incidental to the major task: "An ideal of 'economy of intervention' dictates . . . that the person whose presence is most likely to perpetuate the troublesome development be removed." That removal frequently occurs at the same time that equally "guilty" practices in the situation are not subject to arrest. The tactic of arresting one or two men as "examples" is used even in cases where trouble is not likely to develop:

Thus, when a patrolman ran into a group of four men sharing a bottle of wine in an alley, he emptied the remaining contents of the bottle into the gutter, arrested one man—who was no more and no less drunk than the others—and let the others disperse in various directions.[36]

Other exigential factors which increase the probability of arrests rather than other sanctions are whether the skid row man is in a conspicuous place, how far he is from his home, and whether the police van is nearby.

Precisely because patrolmen see legal reasons for coercive action much more widely distributed on skid-row than could ever be matched by interventions, they intervene not in the interest of law enforcement but in the interest of producing relative tranquility and order on the street.[37]

As for rationalizing the effects of their "making an example" of particular men, or arresting certain men who are no more guilty than others, the patrolman does not seem to think that his arrest works any particular hardship on the arrestee.

It is difficult to overestimate the skid-row patrolman's feeling of certainty that his coercive and disciplinary actions toward the inhabitants have but the most passing significance in their lives. . . . Indeed, it happens quite frequently that officers encounter men who welcome being arrested and even actively ask for it. Finally, officers point out that sending someone to jail from skid-row does not upset his relatives or his family life, does not cause him to miss work or lose a job, does not lead to his being reproached by friends and associates, does not lead to failure to meet commitments or protect investments, and does not conflict with any but the most passing intentions of the arrested person.[38]

Thus, the same factors which make the skid row man relatively immune to any but physically coercive sanctions also serve to justify the application of those sanctions.

Police in Ontario are reported to exercise similar "discretion" in their choice of arrestees. To be arrested, a drunk has to be creating a disturbance, likely to do so, or in danger of coming to harm.[39]

Part of the reason for the class-linked discrimination in enforcement of public intoxication statutes is the relative powerlessness of the homeless person. Giffen has noted that the "over-zealous and indiscriminate" use of arrests for public intoxication among the middle-class employed would create public opposition to interruption of role performance for "a trivial offense of no political significance." Especially the necessary court appearances during working hours would not be tolerated. The system is "obviously attuned to a clientele that is predominantly jobless and without duties to families or other organizations."[40]

The revolving door

The policeman's decisions are reinforced in the judicial screening process. In principle, judges are expected to decide each case on its merits. Yet the drunk court operates on an assembly line basis. Sometimes "platoons" of men are sentenced at once, and the time per decision may average as little as 30 seconds per man. A court observer in Pacific City noted that "on the average, cases take between 45 seconds and one minute to dispose of."[41]

In drunk court the judge's decision is usually the type of sentence, since most men who appear before him plead guilty. Hence, his role is one of classifying the defendant, and the available categories include "overindulgent social drinker," "chronic drunken bum," and "sick alcoholic." The primary criteria for assigning men to a type appear to be general physical appearance, past performance, and social position. Derelicts who look rough or men with previous arrest records are most likely to serve time and get long sentences. To help the judges in their instantaneous appraisal of the men who pass before them, assistants familiar with skid row and its residents may be employed as "court liaison officers" who make informal suggestions about the kind of judicial treatment likely to benefit a man. The court atmosphere tends to be informal, or even jocular. Judges justify the extra-legal nature of the proceedings by defining the men as patients and the arrest and incarceration process as at least potentially helpful.[42]

The skid row man is outraged by the group-sentencing procedures and the seemingly extraneous factors that determine a sentence.

It's law on the assembly line. That's how it really is. No judge would admit it though. He's got a nice, soft, plush $15,000 or $18,000 job which hinges on this.

The situation here [in jail] could stand a lot of improvement, but the court situation is much worse. When you go down there to court each individual in the courts of the United States is entitled to individual and separate trial. You go down there and they run you into these courts, 30 or 40 at a time, and they sentence you accordingly. The front row first.[43]

Apart from the obvious costs such as time lost and exposure to socializing influences that favor the skid row way of life, other consequences may stem from arrest and imprisonment.

. . . an isolated arrest without incarceration may have little influence on the personality. . . . But the psychological impact of a continual process of arrest and incarceration on the individual and on his self-conception are of a different order. Imprisonment, which occurs in American society in a framework of repression, authoritarianism and rigidity, is not conducive to the development of initiative and maturity in the individual . . . society's accepted manner of dealing with the public drunkard is to place him in a county or city jail or penitentiary, along with other misdemeanants, where the framework is one of repression instead of treatment. In the process, the resources of the individual suffer further deterioration and the development of the institutionalized offender occurs—one whose pattern of life becomes a constant movement from incarceration to release and reincarceration, with increasing dependency on the institution.[44]

The optimistic hope voiced by some judges that involvement in the revolving door may do the chronic inebriate some good must be weighed against the hygienic and psychological consequences of his stay in the "drunk tank." The "tank" is a barren cell where the drunk sobers up before seeing the judge. It may be so overcrowded that there is no room to lie down, or even to sit. Frequently, sanitary facilities and ventilation are very inadequate. The chronic alcoholic may be suffering from a variety of ills other than his drunkenness, but medical aid is not available.

After a night in the drunk tank, the offender appears in court. He may be released, sent to jail, or sent to some other rehabilitation center. If he is released, he finds himself without money, job, or specific aims, and is likely to return to skid row. There he may be re-arrested almost immediately. The defense counsel for one homeless alcoholic reviewed the number of arrests his client had experienced during a period of approximately four months and concluded that the man had been arrested "once out of every two days that he appeared on the public streets of the District of Columbia."[45]

A graphic account of the operation and consequences of the "revolving door" is found in James Spradley's *You Owe Yourself a Drunk: An Ethnography of Urban Nomads.*[46] Spradley insists that the skid row men are caught in the revolving door not primarily because of what they do, but because of *who they are.* "These men do their life sentences on the installment plan because they have been *discredited and stigmatized* by other Americans."[47] For the chronic inebriates, Spradley argues, the revolving door is an initiation ceremony, a *rite de passage,* which strips away old elements of one's identity and creates a new self-image.[48] Stages in the ceremony are street, call box, paddy wagon or police car, elevator, booking, padded drunk tank, mug and print room, cement drunk tank, court docket, courtroom, holding tank, delousing tank, time tank, trusty tank, and the street again.[49] As a man cycles through these stages, he is continually treated as defective or even non-human, and to the extent that his previous self-concept is shaken he is vulnerable to the labels "sent" by the social control agents who direct the action at the various stages. Spradley's description of the vulnerability of the person of the arrested urban nomad is revealing:

Although being clubbed or smashed against a wall symbolically reminds a man that his body, the most intimate dimension of his self-concept, is vulnerable, it also has another important meaning. Like a rehearsal before a dramatic performance, it forcefully instructs the tramp to play the part of a dependent and passive actor within the bucket. The longer a man has been in the world of tramps, the more he learns to respond as if he were an animal whose master had broken his will.[50]

Thus the personal ("as if he were an animal") and moral defectiveness of the homeless men are emphasized to him. As he "revolves," he faces his "marginal human" status again and again:

In all these experiences—the public humiliation, the waiting, facing the judge without any means of defense, the physical discomfort involved—tramps feel that underlying the whole process they are looked upon by the officials of the society as objects to be manipulated, as something less than human. The worst thing about court is being "herded around like a bunch of cattle—dumb animals."[51]

At last, stigmatized, his new identity affirmed and his old ties attenuated, the chronic inebriate knows who he is and who "his kind" are. Among the defectives—the cripples, ex-cons, drunkards, and derelicts of skid row—he can find temporary peace and at least the appearance of comaradarie. Here the incongruity between his image of himself and society's image of him can be minimized.

Society, which has swept them out of sight and in the process cut them off from their former selves, now views them as bums or common drunkards. But in jail there has developed in these men an identity vacuum, along with powerful motivations to fill it, not only because of their material losses, but because inactivity, restraint and oversensitivity to the staff create pressures to act, to become and to gain a new sense of personal identity and a new set of values to replace what has been lost.

The novice who repeats this experience several times may first seek to escape it by travel to a new town, but once there he usually goes to Skid Road for ready acceptance. Sooner or later, for many men, the world and culture of the tramp become a viable alternative to replace what has been lost in the ritual of making the bucket. In that culture he may still be alienated from the rest of society—but *not from himself* or others like him.[52]

If the revolving door has such negative consequences, why does the process continue? The "overriding consequence" of the cycle is the perpetuation of the very behavior the process is supposed to curtail.

One function is that arrests for public drunkenness may reduce the number of rootless men in circulation, thus protecting the general public from some proportion of the "idle rogues and vagabonds." Police in Ontario were strongly in favor of retaining the public intoxication statutes because of the role of the revolving door process in preventing crime.[53] However, the evidence shows that chronic alcoholics rarely commit offenses against the person, although they frequently are victims of such offenses.

Another possible function for the arrested men is a benefit from "drying out." Giffen has suggested that "In terms of their physical welfare and perhaps survival the net result of having their drinking bouts terminated by arrest is beneficial."[54]

A third possible function is the "sorting out" of alcoholics for treatment suited to their individual needs. Of course, given the typical rapidity of trials involving drunkenness offenders and the inadequacies of the facilities available for "rehabilitation" either in the community, the hospital, or the prison, the "sorting out" function does not operate to the arrestee's benefit. He is not evaluated so that an informed decision about his future can be made, but even if the evaluation were done properly, there are no facilities for carrying out the requisite treatment. Frequently the judges recognize the incongruities of their position with respect to the drunkenness offender.[55]

Perhaps the most generous evaluation of the positive functions of the revolving door is the statement about "effect on the offender" by the President's Commission on Law Enforcement and Administration of Justice:

The criminal justice system appears ineffective to deter drunkenness or to meet the problems of the chronic alcoholic offender. What the system usually does accomplish is to remove the drunk from public view, detoxify him, and provide him with food, shelter, emergency medical service, and a brief period of forced sobriety. As presently constituted, the system is not in a position to meet his underlying medical and social problems.[56]

Therapies and treatment facilities

A comprehensive review of modern psychological approaches to the treatment of alcoholism is beyond the scope of this book. Blum and Blum's exhaustive work devoted to that purpose considers treatment, stages and hurdles in the treatment process, and treatment evaluation, and devotes a separate chapter to each of ten distinct forms of treatment for alcoholism (psychoanalytic treatment, conditioning and learning, group therapies, educational group therapies, live-in facilities, outpatient group treatment for resocialization, activity groups and psychodrama, psychodynamic group therapies, drug therapy, and total push programs).[57]

Following their exhaustive review Blum and Blum comment on defects in treatment efforts for alcoholism. Among the problems singled out are two that are especially detrimental to homeless alcoholics, namely, the shortage of treatment personnel and "the striking apathy and almost willful disinterest that has been seen among citizens, professionals, and public authorities when it comes to the support of *treatment* for alcohol-related problems."[58]

Part of the difficulty in helping the homeless has been that their rehabilitation has never had a very high priority. Their position as expendables and the justification for the chronic shortage of resources which has plagued skid row treatment programs are clearly set down in the report, "What to Do About the Men on Skid Row." The authors of that document assert that homeless men are multiproblem men, and list among their deficiencies unhealthy attitudes, lack of employment skills, problem drinking, old age, and illness. Incredibly, the same sentence containing that profile of negative characteristics goes on to say:

. . . we do not recommend extensive or elaborate attempts at rehabilitation for the men nor do we favor a permanent municipal shelter or "halfway" house for all the men that has been proposed from time to time. Such major private and public social service funds that are available to the Philadelphia community should be expended on families with children or persons with greater promise.[59]

The next sentence states that it is "for the interest of the community to assume some responsibility for the men of skid row." Major funds, public and private, are for *worthwhile* projects. It is in the community's interest to do something for the skid row man, but not very much. He has negative attitudes, is unskilled, drinks too much, is old and sick. He is so needy that he is not worthy of major expenditures. He has too little "promise."

The question of what to do about the men of skid row is answered separately for each type of skid row resident. The answers include making publicly supported facilities for the aged available to the homeless, getting more federal and public old age assistance, making public housing available for the physically disabled, employing marginal workers in the state department of forests and waters, providing vocational rehabilitation for some, and referring the mentally ill to state institutions. It is also suggested that skid row men should be referred to outpatient facilities in hospitals, that university experiments in the rehabilitation of problem drinkers be encouraged, and that better records be kept of men brought before the magistrate court. Finally, the wage earners on skid row, the "better-class" residents there, were said to fill an economic need, and it was recommended that arrangements be made for private establishments to provide lodging facilities for them.

Following the recommendation that the city set up records of public inebriates which would be available to guide judges and other interested parties, there appears the following statement shifting the responsibility for protecting the civil rights of skid row men to "groups interested in civil rights."

The question of the civil rights of vagrants is raised from time to time. It must be remembered that civil rights do not include a right to be a public nuisance or a charge on the municipality. Groups interested in civil rights should come forward with specific proposals for protecting the interest of the community as well as the civil rights of the men. Drafts of improved legislation might be prepared by a local school of law.

Within existing circumstances the skid row "revolving door" from street to lock-up to Magistrate to House of Correction to street is just about inevitable.[60]

In a chapter devoted to special treatment problems, Blum and Blum discussed programs for homeless alcoholics. Their inventory of treatment modes included rehabilitation on the streets, Salvation Army Men's Social Service Centers, other religious and charitable centers, Synanon, community hospitals, foster home placement, halfway houses, rehabilitation centers, facilities for permanent supervision, halfway houses for jailed offenders, and programs that structure correctional facilities as treatment centers.[61] We shall consider several of these in detail. Others are treated extensively in recent books about skid row, and others are alternatives that have not been used by many homeless men.

First, a brief note is needed about some of the programs we will not treat at length. The numerous private organizations which offer aid to the homeless tend to be poorly integrated with other community facilities, often are undersupported, and sometimes stress religious exhortation without providing opportunities for temporal rehabilitation.[62] As for Synanon, although it is described as an alternative for homeless alcoholics unable to accept the religious emphasis of AA or the Salvation Army, few chronic alcoholics have defined it that way. In the first decade of its existence fewer than 1,000 people were treated at Synanon, and most of these were addicted to drugs other than alcohol. Similarly, foster home placement has had more currency as a suggestion than as practice. Given public abhorrence of the skid row man, its practicality on any large scale is questionable.

Rehabilitation "on the streets." This kind of treatment is fairly new to skid row. Blum and Blum refer to it as "community organization" or "street project" work in which the change agent works and lives among members of a deviant or disadvantaged minority subculture, helping the members of that subculture to organize and help themselves. In their words,

It is our recommendation that major efforts be made to reach urban homeless alcoholics by having street workers live in the sub-culture. Their job would be to establish confidence, to offer guidance that would channel the homeless to appropriate community agencies, and to accentuate the interpersonal resources of the naturally occurring groups somewhat in the way that activity-group therapists now work.[63]

The notion of organizing the skid row community is not new. Early in this century skid row was a fertile seedbed of protest, and radical labor and political organizations worked among the homeless with some success. However, by 1940 the labor and fraternal organizations on skid row had disappeared, and whatever community orientation to collective goals they had fostered died. The decline of skid row and its gradual evolution into an open asylum have been described in detail by Rooney.[64] The political organizers abandoned skid row, perhaps because its "naturally occurring groups" had too little longevity to support organized action on any scale.

The present residents of skid row seem too disaffiliated to respond to even the most skillful organizer. However, two very recent developments, one a proposal and the other a report of community organization among homeless people only slightly more affiliated than the skid row residents, suggest that rehabilitation on the streets may prove to be a viable approach, at least as part of experimental programs.

Joan Shapiro has conducted a series of projects designed to organize tenants of single-room-occupancy buildings (SRO's) in New York City. Reacting to a demonstration project, which had revealed "a shocking picture of chronic physical and mental illness, loneliness, and deprivation" among SRO residents,[65] Shapiro and her associates planned caseworker intervention in the SRO milieu. Each of the SRO projects had a female social worker who, following the model of the "detached" group worker assigned to a street gang, attempted to use "only herself"—her personality, skills, creativity, and integrity—to influence the behavior of an existing group in its home territory. In the first attempt, the social worker served as a catalyst in a building where 71 per cent of the tenants were on welfare, 62 per cent had major chronic medical disabilities, and 90 per cent evidenced major psychosocial maladaptation patterns. She was available to mediate crises and to participate in group activities, and she was "explicitly maternal in behavior, touching, feeding, and establishing contact with individuals." As a consequence of her intervention, tenant meetings were held; a recreation program was begun; biweekly group dinners were organized, prepared, and served by the tenants; and a rehabilitation program was set up.[66]

In subsequent projects social workers identified charismatic leaders in many SRO's.[67] All were women, and the organization of the buildings was quasimatriarchal. A major challenge was the establishment of working relations with these "natural" leaders. The role of the social workers was finally defined as to increase the referral skill and range of contacts of the charismatic leaders, thus enabling them to provide better care for their "families."

The work of Shapiro and her associates is pioneering and exciting, and promises improved problem solving and community spirit among disaffiliates who live in SRO's. Whether it will work among skid row men is another question. One characteristic of skid row that might decrease the impact of such work there is the salient role played by female SRO residents who served as dominant maternal figures in their buildings. Such "mothering" is unlikely to be found on skid row, where the absence of women is one of the primary characteristics. Still, the idea of binding the skid row men into pseudofamilies by sending in full-time, maternal caseworkers to work among them is provocative.

One of the more imaginative proposals for the control of alcoholism on skid row is Rubington's suggestion that alcoholics can rehabilitate themselves if they are paid to keep the peace on skid row. He would establish an alcoholic control unit, located in a hotel on skid row and employing skid row men. Employees will be assigned to foot patrols and auto patrols, divide up the skid row area, and police it. They will make no arrests, but will help other homeless men who need help and will move men sleeping in the streets to the unit building, where they can sleep off their drunk in safety. The men on foot patrol will carry movie cameras and photograph fights, robberies, and other incidents. They will also intervene in altercations where possible and practical. Wearing special uniforms, they should deter crime and establish some visible moral order in the community. Also, the visible demonstration that alcoholics can treat each other with greater respect may lead the general public to accord greater respect to skid row men. Finally, the activities of the proposed unit will help members of the skid row community to recognize that minimal rules of public conduct should apply even on skid row.[68]

Salvation Army men's social service centers. The work of the Salvation Army among skid row men is well known. In 1961 there were 124 centers, providing over 8,000 beds to homeless men and alcoholics.[69] An insightful account of the process of "spiritual salvation" sponsored by organizations like the Salvation Army is found in Wiseman's *Stations of the Lost*.[70] Her discussion of "Spiritual Salvation: The Last Resort" examines the "Christian Missionary's" program as seen by the Christian Missionaries themselves and as perceived by the skid row men it serves.

The basic assumptions of the "Christian Missionary" approach is to err is human, recidivism is the rule, the worker must be willing to continually labor despite the backsliding of his charges. A long-range rehabilitation program involves living "under the protection and tutelage of one of God's helpers and messengers" and working in the Missionary's salvage operation. In contrast, many skid row men see the Christian Missionary's program as exploitative, hypocritical, and stagnating.

The therapy program includes spiritual and religious therapy (twice-weekly religious services, daily meditation periods, voluntary Bible study groups, and semivoluntary "self-denial" campaigns), work therapy (a five-and-a-half day work week in Missionary salvage enterprise), companionship therapy (enforced group living), group therapy (psychoanalytically oriented therapy groups which men may be invited to join), vocational counseling therapy, and structured milieu therapy (clearly stated rules about property, dress, room maintenance, and so on, with punishments for violations).[71]

As a consequence of their selective intake procedures, Salvation Army clients are better educated and have held better jobs than other skid row men. According to Katz, rates of abstinence increase by two-thirds among program participants and employment increases by 40 per cent. Extent of improvement seems to depend upon the duration of a client's participation in the program.[72] For further details the reader is referred to Wiseman's *Stations of the Lost*.

Hospital programs. Most hospitals will not treat alcoholism unless it is accompanied by other obvious medical disorders. However, there is a trend toward an increasing involvement of physicians in the treatment of alcoholism and a recognition by them that treatment of the alcoholic is as clearly within their responsibilities as treatment of the diabetic. As with his other patients, he will feel responsible for the alcoholic twenty-four hours a day. Physicians have been cautioned to time their treatment of alcoholics in terms of years rather than weeks; otherwise they and their patients are likely to become discouraged. Moreover, according to some physicians, the doctor's responsibility is not limited to treatment; he also has a role to play in diagnosis, prevention, and in influencing the mores of the community which affect the consumption of alcohol.[73]

One of the more successful alcoholism treatment programs in general hospitals is that at Sparrow Hospital in Lansing, Michigan.[74] Alcoholism is the third most common diagnosis at Sparrow Hospital, and there is a separate nineteen-bed ward set aside for the treatment of alcoholism. One of the unusual features of the Sparrow Hospital program is immediate admission. Alcoholics make their way directly to the alcoholism ward, where nurses make decisions about admission and assign unattached patients to doctors. There is always a vacancy in the alcoholism ward. The intoxicated alcoholic who has decided he needs help gets first priority, even if that means shortening the stay of someone already there. Nurses have a standard set of guidelines for treating inebriates admitted to the ward, and only unusual cases require special attention from a physician. Another innovation is that there is unlimited food for the patients. A well-stocked refrigerator is available twenty-four hours a day.

There is no anonymity in alcoholism treatment at Sparrow Hospital. Visitors are welcomed on the floor, the diagnosis of alcoholism is honestly recorded on appropriate insurance and hospital records, and patients are encouraged to discuss their disease with employers, ministers, and others. There is also an intensive educational program, occupying three hours of every day and taught by a variety of volunteers. Content is haphazard, the aim being not so much what is taught as the demonstration that people in the community are interested in alcoholics and that alcoholics are worthwhile people.

Treatment for alcoholism at Sparrow Hospital is open to almost everyone. Only after a man has been through five or six times might he be excluded. The staff do all they can to involve spouses in therapy, and Alcoholics Anonymous meetings are held every night. The hospital staff takes the responsibility for "sorting out" people whose problems are more serious than alcoholism; psychotics and psychopaths who might upset the milieu of the alcoholism ward are transferred or discharged. Finally, the patients are involved in caring for each other: "This enables one alcoholic to see how repulsive he may appear to his wife when drunk. Involving as many as possible when there are rum fits or delirium tremens on the unit can change a group of resentful or apathetic patients in short order."[75]

Richard Bates, director of Sparrow Hospital's alcoholism program, views involvement of the alcoholic in the treatment of others as "a primary goal in the therapy of any compulsion or addiction." Stages in physicians' treatment of alcoholism include convincing a man he is an alcoholic ("even a man with appendicitis won't submit to therapy until he is personally convinced of the diagnosis") and then involving him in medical treatment, either as an outpatient via Alcoholics Anonymous or as a patient in a hospital alcoholism unit. In the latter situation, initial therapy may involve detoxification. Then the medical staff is responsible for "intermediate therapy," educating the patient that he is a typical alcoholic who can never drink again, that he can achieve sobriety if he works at it, and that he will need continuing therapy to deal with the personality deviations he has previously treated with alcohol. Long-term therapy is defined as beyond physicians' responsibility, although they assist in continued medication. These four steps, recruitment into therapy, detoxification, education, and referral for long-term treatment, comprise medical treatment of alcoholism according to Bates.[76]

Another distinctive hospital program at the Northhampton (Massachusetts) Veterans Hospital begins with the proposition that harmful drinking is a kind of activity instead of a disease. In this perspective, harmful drinking is defined as a "special or *defective* way of acting" (emphasis added), and the ramifications of this de-

fective acting for the ongoing functioning of the individual are assessed. Working from this "drinking as activity" model, treatment
aims at creating or re-establishing effective activity under the assumption that one's self-image is related to what one does: the
more accurate one is in problem solving, the better is one's self-
image.[77]

Patients are scheduled to stay for ten to twelve weeks. Among
the less common techniques incorporated in the program are audio-
video feedback, self-other description, and relaxation training. Recordings are made of the patient when he enters the hospital, when
he is inebriated, and at other times throughout his treatment. The
patient reviews the recordings as he reassesses his personal history
and self-image. In self-other description the patient describes himself on paper, and then his descriptions are the basis for discussion
at large group meetings. Relaxation training is a process in which
the patient makes the connection between his states of stress and
the circumstances which produce them. Gradually he learns to disassociate the tension responses from those circumstances, and to
substitute other responses.

The program also stresses physical fitness; there are formal calis-
thenics and a variety of athletic pursuits, both individual and team.
Sensitivity and encounter sessions encourage direct, uncensored reactions to the deviant situation. Tape recordings are made of interviews and evaluation sessions and given to the patient. At his own
leisure he may listen to himself express opinions and feelings. Also,
there is peer group confrontation. If the patient drinks while in
treatment, he must discuss the episode with a committee from the
Patient Government. Finally, more traditional techniques are available at the V.A. hospital. There is group therapy, Alcoholics Anonymous, disulfiram therapy, educational therapy, and aversion conditioning.[78] A preliminary evaluation of the effectiveness of this
program showed that among patients whose average time since release was over eleven months, 31 per cent said they had been abstinent since discharge and approximately 60 per cent were not
drinking at the time of the follow-up. The evaluation was flawed by

the lack of a control group. However, there was a comparison group of men who did not complete the program. On most variables this latter group was very similar to the group of alcoholic subjects who completed their stay in the hospital. However, two substantial differences did appear. A higher proportion of men who completed their program had maintained complete sobriety since release—the differential was 11 per cent—and they were almost twice as apt to be attending Alcoholics Anonymous at the time of the follow-up.[79]

Treatment programs in prisons and jails. Homeless alcoholics frequently are jailed, and the jail would seem a logical place for extensive treatment programs aimed at rehabilitating them and preventing their being jailed again. However, most jails do not offer treatment for alcoholism. The California correctional system has attempted widespread use of group counseling for alcoholic inmates of prisons and jails, but the program has been notably ineffectual. In one evaluation less than one-third of the staffs of state correctional institutions felt that the program was being carried out as well as could be expected, and "it was noted that the officers in charge tend to exhibit little overt enthusiasm for the results obtained by group therapy."[80]

Some of the difficulties associated with institutional programs for alcoholics are illustrated in Wiseman's description of the "Jail Branch Clinic" in Pacific City.[81] Originally, the clinic was established as a demonstration project aimed at reforming incarcerated chronic drunkenness offenders, but it achieved little success with the original target population. Staff members blamed the chronic alcoholics' unfitness for group therapy and the prison context. The alcoholics' apathy, insincerity, and disinterest, combined with a sentencing system which produced too many potential patients and then released them before the group therapy had had time to produce results, led the staff to change the focus of the group therapy program so that patients who could "benefit" were allowed into the program and others were screened out. In practice this meant that most of the chronic drunks were screened out, and "more satisfying

patients," such as drug users, sexual deviants, gamblers, and potential suicides, replaced the alcoholic as the target population.

The incarcerated alcoholics are embittered because one of the
manifest justifications for their imprisonment is that there is treatment available in the jail. In fact, there rarely is any treatment, and
when there is, the therapist is perceived as inept or heartless and
his therapy useless. The dishonesty of being promised "therapy"
when none is available is especially frustrating: "Judges know there
isn't any therapy here—but they know it sounds better if they say
they are sending us to get some."[82]

A short-term treatment program for inmates with drinking problems at the Cleveland House of Correction has been evaluated by
McCaghy, Skipper, and Bruce.[83] The treatment facility was Trusty
Hall, a special unit to which motivated chronic inebriates suitable
for minimum custody were transferred for short-term treatment.
The program was "an attempt to separate inmates with drinking
problems from other offenders, to provide them with an awareness
of consequences of drinking, to acquaint them with means by which
these consequences may be avoided, and to provide them with some
assistance upon release, if necessary."[84] At the time the evaluation
was conducted, treatment included AA meetings three evenings a
week, a weekly "alcohol and health" class designed to teach inmates
about the physiological and psychological aspects of alcoholism,
weekly group religious meetings "geared to create an awareness of
the moral issues involved in behavior prompted by uncontrolled
drinking" and to give inmates a chance to talk to a clergyman, and
a "pre-release plan" under which arrangements were made for
newly released inmates to obtain food, shelter, or other aid from
alcoholic rehabilitation programs, private and public agencies, employment offices, and poverty programs.

The researchers were beset with unanticipated problems during
their evaluation. A change in court practices made it impossible to
acquire a sample as large as intended; the director of Trusty Hall
became ill and died and only portions of the program were carried
on after his absence; alcoholism night clinics whose records were to

provide information about inmates after release proved to have had incomplete attendance records and even, in one case, a "questionable existence." The validity of reports on participation in AA meetings became so questionable that the variable "AA contact" was eliminated; and another phase of the follow-up—personal contact with the subjects, their employers, and families—proved to be so expensive and time consuming that it was abandoned. In the end, the evaluation of the treatment program hinged on a single variable, arrest and commitment for alcohol-related offenses.

During the evaluation, inmates eligible for admittance to Trusty Hall were assigned to experimental or control groups randomly. The control respondents served out their time in "ordinary confinement," and men in the experimental group were transferred to Trusty Hall. Comparisons of the number of post-release alcohol-related offenses, number of commitments for such offenses, and number of months between release and first commitment revealed very slight differences between the experimental and control groups. The evaluators' summary of the program effectiveness read:

It appears safe to assume that the Trusty Hall program . . . was at least minimally successful in influencing men to avoid further contact with the law. But the over-all success of the program appears to be very modest. It would be presumptuous to conclude from our measures that the program had a positive influence on all, or even a majority, of the men.[85]

The evaluators concluded, as have many other students of alcoholism treatment programs, that the men who tended to avoid further arrests and commitments for drinking-related offenses had the same characteristics whether or not they participated in the Trusty Hall program. Success-linked characteristics included low residential mobility, living with spouse, receiving calls or visits from relatives and friends during incarceration, few previous alcohol-related arrests, and positive motivation to control drinking as indicated by planning for release and use of disulfiram. Positive effects of the Trusty Hall program seemed limited to improving the probabilities of success for men who already had a high probability of success. For those who had an unfavorable prognosis, there was no evidence that the program had any significant positive effect.

The researchers' recommendations about Trusty Hall are striking examples of the tendency in alcoholism treatment to continue programs of dubious value, apparently because of inertia and the feeling that one should be doing something. In the absence of sure knowledge about what would be right to do, continuing a program of questionable value entails few short-term risks. The evaluators recommended:

Despite our conclusions concerning the program's minimal if not negligible success among the "poor risks," we recommend the continuation of the program for *all* types of individuals whose encounters with the law stem from drinking difficulties.[86]

Part of the justification for this recommendation is the argument that the "traditional confinement-and-punishment orientation" is known to be ineffectual and to deprive inmates of degrees of space and freedom which they are not denied in Trusty Hall. However, I find the argument unconvincing; it does not justify a change from one ineffectual program to another. There are other options, and the efforts and resources poured into both ineffectual programs should be diverted into more productive approaches. The evaluators also repeat a theme familiar in the alcoholism treatment literature, namely "the real need is to gear the program to identify individuals' particular vulnerability to failure and to concentrate treatment efforts accordingly."[87]

Long-term residential centers. Except for prisons and mental hospitals, there are few long-term residential centers for homeless men. These facilities are expensive, and the skid row man's low priority as a public problem does not justify the expense of maintaining large numbers of the homeless in such facilities. We shall describe two long-term residential centers, one a large-scale camp capable of handling over 1,000 inmates, and the other a small "milieu-therapy" project in which social control agents and carefully selected homeless men live together in a rural farmhouse.

Camp LaGuardia is an institution for homeless men operated by the Department of Social Services of the City of New York.[88] It is a voluntary institution; inmates are free to leave when they wish. Admittance is granted through the Shelter Care Center for Men (Municipal Men's Shelter) and, once in the camp, men may stay as long as they wish. The usual stay is not longer than a few months, but some have lived there for a quarter of a century.

The camp is located about sixty miles from Manhattan, near the town of Chester, New York. In 1968 the grounds consisted of 268 acres, much of it leased to local farmers. A three-story main building had administrative offices, a dining hall, recreation room, chapel, laundry, tap room, infirmary, and other service facilities, as well as sleeping quarters. Three other buildings nearby have beds for about 700 men. Counting the dormitory space in the main building, the camp can sleep as many as 1,050 men.

Camp LaGuardia began in 1934, when a vacated women's farm colony was given to the Department of Public Welfare for a work camp for homeless men. Welfare officials had the idea that many homeless men could be rehabilitated if there were employment for them, and if they could be moved away from the negative environment of the urban shelters. The camp was to be "self-supporting"; in practice this meant that during the early years it operated on federal Works Progess Administration funds. There was little emphasis on rehabilitation. Its major function was providing employment, and there was no attempt to evaluate its effectiveness in preparing residents for employment outside the camp.

After World War II the camp became a facility for aged Bowery men rather than a place for the unemployed. Residents interviewed in a 1966 survey identified the camp as a place where one could retire, recover health after heavy drinking, get "cleaned up" and acquire new clothing, and avoid the stresses of life on skid row. In fact, the contrast between life on skid row and life at the camp operates to keep men at the camp longer than they originally intended. It also serves as a way-station for skid row men on their way to work in resort hotels in upstate New York. For some men, the camp seemed to be a place to rest up and gather energy for an attempted escape from skid row life.

Officials of the Department of Social Services view the camp as "good for the men," especially as a therapeutic environment for recovery of health. Getting a man off the Bowery, even if only temporarily, is seen as something of a moral victory. Also, officials argue that it is cheaper to support a man at the camp than on the Bowery, especially when costs to the City hospitals and jails are taken into account. Finally, a significant proportion of the Bowery population—perhaps as much as one-sixth to one-eighth of the total at any one time—are housed off Bowery, thereby reducing the visibility of homeless men and easing the political pressure from citizens and businessmen for Bowery clean-up programs. These alleged benefits all rest on the assumption that camp men would be on the Bowery if they were not at the camp, and that they would not be contributing to their own support.

An official view of the benefits of Camp LaGuardia is summarized in one of the annual reports of the Bureau of Shelter Services for Adults:

First, it provides long-term protective care and services for elderly and permanently debilitated skid row men. Secondly, it provides medical, psychiatric, vocational and related restorative services for other categories of homeless men.

The former program—really the equivalent of a home for the aged—provides a necessary and important service to men who for reasons of age or infirmity can no longer manage even on the low level of adequacy of Bowery living. The Camp offers a highly satisfactory answer to their needs and is also a benefit to the general East Side community by reducing the homeless population of the Bowery.

The latter program provides a variety of services ranging from drying-out, to physical, medical, psychological and vocational rehabilitation opportunities. These are pitched to the level of the capacity, potentiality and motivation of the individual. Many of the men cannot relate to the demands of full substantive rehabilitative measures but can benefit to a limited or temporary degree.[89]

Most of the work at the camp is done by the residents. The resident–staff ratio is extremely low. Every resident capable of working
is given a work assignment. Usually the assigned duties are light,
shared by several other men, and easily completed by noon. More
responsible "payroll jobs" are also held by some residents. Apart
from these assignments, the only compulsory scheduled activity is
a weekly shower. Recreation rooms open early in the day, and television sets are turned on late in the morning. The most frequent
forms of recreation are walking, reading, and watching television.
Some men play cards or pool. The tap room is open every evening
and beer may be purchased. (In 1967 it cost seven cents a glass.)
Movies, AA meetings, bingo, and other organized entertainment
are held at night. The general "spirit" of the camp is evident in a
researcher's comment about activity there:

The pace of life is very slow. One rarely sees a resident walking rapidly
and purposefully, and it is conspicuous when one does. The aim of
most men is to stretch out their activities to consume as much time as
possible. There is no need to conserve time.[90]

Each man receives a weekly allowance of one dollar from the
Department of Social Services. In addition, men with payroll jobs
receive up to twenty dollars a month extra. Each day a few men are
given passes to go into the nearby town. Usually such trips are for
buying and drinking wine. No one objects to this unless a resident
tries to smuggle wine back into the camp or returns drunk and
creates a disturbance.

Henshaw assessed the effects of life at Camp LaGuardia by comparing a sample of current camp residents with a random sample of
Bowery men. Some of the men interviewed on the Bowery were ex-
residents of the camp. His findings showed that despite the interdependence, population density, and relatively secure social context
at the camp, its residents were only slightly more apt to interact
with each other than were Bowery men:

. . . campers do not take full advantage of their opportunities for social interaction. For example, the residents scatter the lawn chairs in-

dividually around the grounds rather than arranging them in groups so that they can sit and talk. Residents usually eat their meals very quickly without talking to the other men sitting at the same table. One never sees an extra chair pulled up to a diningroom table to allow a man to join his friends. The factors determining the rate of interaction of the men are psychological—the men's defenses—rather than structural—the opportunities provided by the social structure of the camp.[91]

Comparison of attitude scale scores for residents, ex-residents, and other Bowery men revealed that the camp residents were less misanthropic, alienated, and anomic than were ex-residents or Bowery men. However, there was no relationship between length of stay at the camp and positiveness of attitudes. It was suggested that the more favorable attitudes of camp residents reflected changes that occurred soon after a man arrived at the camp. The positive effects on camp residents were especially noticeable for younger men and heavy drinkers. Henshaw concluded that "The resident society embodies more positive attitudes than the Bowery society and tends to influence the attitudes of the men who become integrated into it."[92] In any case, the attitude changes were temporary; ex-campers on the Bowery had very high scores for anomia, alienation, and misanthropy.

For younger men, a prolonged stay at the camp was associated with low self-esteem, but this was not so for older residents. Apparently, deprivation of occupational status was costly in self-esteem to younger camp residents, but not to older ones. A man of working age might justify a temporary stay at the camp as "resting up" for future work, but after a few months this justification no longer works and his self-esteem is likely to sag. But an older man or a disabled man might legitimately withdraw from the labor force, and for these kinds of men there was no link between low self-esteem and duration of stay at the camp.

The only substantial sanction used to control behavior is expulsion from the camp. It serves to remove the most disruptive and seems to restrain the rest effectively. The expulsion sanction is accepted by the men and creates little resentment, probably much less than would a graduated scheme of punishments for little things. The voluntariness of the institution further legitimates the order at the camp; men who do not like it or are unwilling to abide by the rules are free to leave.

The camp's goals are modest; there is little expectation that "rehabilitation" in any long-term sense will occur, and little need to justify its existence by seeking out "success" stories. In a very real sense the camp has adjusted to its inmates, rather than the reverse. Men can buy beer cheaply, there are few compulsory activities, scheduling is loose, work is light, there are recreational facilities and the food is excellent. Men may leave to drink and later be readmitted with no questions asked. Compared to the drunk tank or prison, it seems an ideal institution.

Another distinctive long-term treatment program is an experimental rural residential treatment center, "Bon Accord Farm," in Ontario, Canada, sponsored by the Alcoholism and Drug Addiction Research Foundation. Its general objective is to learn the extent to which the behavior of members of the skid row alcoholic subculture can be changed in a "controlled but democratic" setting organized according to the principles of learning theory.[93]

In 1966 directors of the newly established rehabilitation program toured a number of American and Canadian facilities for the rehabilitation of public inebriates. Various rehabilitation agencies, missions, hospitals, clinics, halfway houses, and alcoholism agencies were inspected. The directors concluded from their tour that there were few programs for public inebriates that had treatment goals; instead, the major goal of most programs seemed to be containment of a deviant group. Staff members at most treatment centers were pessimistic. Their programs had ill-defined objectives: keeping men away from drink and finding them employment. Moreover, the centers were organized in such a way that a frequent outcome of treatment was a client more dependent on institutions than before.

Having concluded that short-term custodial treatment had little efficacy, the researchers decided to adopt a long-term residential "habilitation" program, aimed at increasing patients' receptiveness to rehabilitation. The aim of the program was to structure an inebriate's environment so that alternatives other than retreat to drug dependency or withdrawal from social relationships would be realistic responses to stressful situations. The creation of rewarding experiences which reinforced the alternate responses was considered more important than a goal of abstinence.

Characteristics of the habilitation community designed to provide a setting for exposure to and reinforcement of alternate responses were physical distance from skid row, suitable control techniques, a variety of possible social, recreational, and vocational experiences, reinforcement schedules, and staff members to serve as role models. It was important that the setting be a democratic one, that the clients experience some feeling of control over their environment, and that interpersonal relationships be maximized.[94]

In many respects, the habilitation community was like a family. Dependence upon it was encouraged as an important step toward healthy adult role behavior. The intent of the program is aptly summarized in the sentence: "In the habilitation community, we break off a segment of the Skid Row alcoholic society, mix it with 'squares' from the normal society, and endeavour to reshape its values and goals." In other words, the program is "an involvement of staff and residents at a warm, human, social level, a mixing of squares and deviants, of socially involved people and disaffiliates, with the aims of rediscovering the meaning of human community and risking commitments to its values."[95]

In achieving these aims, a 193-acre farm was purchased. The farmhouse was renovated, but its "family setting and layout" was maintained. One small room in the house served as an office for the staff, and its size forced the seven staff members to interact with the clients. In the somewhat cramped quarters of the farmhouse—there was little room for indoor recreation, sometimes three men per bedroom, overnight accommodations for staff "just sufficient for sleeping"—staff involvement with residents at all times of the day and evening was enforced, interchange of roles and a "rather fluid hierarchy" among the staff was fostered. During the first two years of the program, staff morale remained high enough that only one staff member left the project.

The program at Bon Accord was an attempt at "community building" among men who have lost their sense of community and been socialized into a subculture which lacked community goals. Previous attempts to rehabilitate them had usually been "insight therapies" which emphasized the "cause" of their problems, or the nature of their "disease." At Bon Accord the object was to emphasize health, increase accomplishments, pay attention to the present situation, and avoid allowing residents to play the "alcoholic game" or get "psychiatric kicks." Realistic standards of behavior were a part of the program; neither staff members nor residents were allowed excuses which shifted responsibility for their actions.[96]

During the first two years of the Bon Accord program, a total of fifty-five residents was served. Criteria for selection included being identified as a chronic drunkenness offender (at least three arrests for drunkenness in the past year), being "integrated members of Skid Row society," and being able to do physical work. In the second year of the program, men with less favorable prognoses were also admitted. Details of the program changed somewhat over the two-year period, but the general emphasis continued to be having the men take as much responsibility as possible and to teach them to select alternative positive behaviors rather than drinking:

We endeavour to bring a man to a point where he will choose not to overdrink because of his responsibility for the resulting negative effect on the community. . . . Staff conferences with men in conjunction with group sanction avoids reinforcement of the maladaptive behavior. Severe intoxication is interpreted to the man as destructive of relationships rather than solely a destroyer of the man's sobriety.[97]

Detoxification centers. One of the encouraging developments of the past decade is the establishment of "detoxification centers" where public inebriates receive short-term medical attention and referral services. Despite widespread public acceptance of the disease concept of alcoholism, more alcoholics are being treated by being put in jail than in all health facilities combined. The personal costs of a drunk tank experience and the kind of abuses which attend this system are starkly portrayed in *You Owe Yourself a Drunk*.[98] The detoxification center is an attempt to "short circuit" the revolving door, or, at worst, to substitute a more humane kind of revolving door. Such centers have proved successful in a number of countries including South Africa, Czechoslovakia, and Poland.

A detoxification center is a facility where people who are drunk in public can receive medical attention. As a substitute for treatment by arrest, incarceration, and judgment, the use of detoxification facilities by the police, civilian squads, or even walk-in patients makes treatment for public drunkenness a problem of civil rather than criminal process. There are five advantages to this change: 1. the stigmatizing effects of involvement with the criminal law are avoided; 2. the medically oriented detoxification center is more sanitary and humane than the drunk tank; 3. expert medical help is available with a minimum of red tape; 4. law enforcement agencies are freed to devote their resources to more serious crime; 5. there is a chance for referral and the potentiality of rehabilitative therapy.[99]

The oldest and best-known American detoxification program is the St. Louis Detoxification and Diagnostic Center for Intoxicated Men, which began operation in November 1966. Initially, the center was housed in St. Mary's Infirmary, a centrally located facility near the areas where most arrests for drunkenness were made. Administratively linked to the police department, the program is aimed at men who otherwise would be processed through the criminal system. Only men brought in by the police are admitted to the detoxification center. The usual stay at the center is seven days. In addition to being a sobering-up station, the St. Louis center attempted to meet rehabilitative objectives by providing therapy during a patient's stay and by making appropriate referrals.

Even before the establishment of the detoxification center, the St. Louis arrest rate for public drunkenness was comparatively low, in part because of official departmental policy that made the arrest of drunks low priority police activity, and in part because of an atypical independence of police from pressures in the community to "do something" about drunks in the streets. The drunk arrest was viewed as "an unnecessary diversion, to be used only where other means could not be employed to dispose of the man and the circumstances indicate that he could not be ignored."[100]

At first the location of the detoxification center made it easy for patrolmen to use it, even if they were skeptical about the efficacy of treatment for skid row men. A newspaper report contrasted the three and one-half hours needed for arrest, booking, and court appearance under the traditional system with the twenty minutes it required to take a drunk to the detoxification center.[101] The patrolmen used the facility because it was convenient for them, not necessarily because of any desire to help homeless men.

After a year, the detoxification center was moved to the outskirts of the city, and its use by patrolmen dropped off. It no longer was convenient for them to drop drunks at a centrally located center; instead, they had to drive the inebriates to the outskirts of the city, a thirty-minute trip each way. Sometimes when they made the trip, it proved futile because there were no beds available at the detoxification center. Also, they were frustrated by the new program because they saw men they had taken for detoxification reappearing on the streets, drunk again. Finally, the police department continued to consider time spent processing drunks as "low quality" time. The admissions rate at the detoxification center declined, and by 1969 it was necessary for the center's director to make personal requests that police districts bring a quota of men to the center each evening.[102]

The achievements of the St. Louis program have been assessed by Raymond Nimmer, a research attorney for the American Bar Foundation, who has studied several detoxification centers.[103] First, it must be recognized that the program is limited to those who would otherwise be arrested for public drunkenness, and in St. Louis this represents only a small fraction of the homeless population. Unquestionably, the detoxification process is more humane than jailing the drunks. Also, holding a man for a week at the center and giving him good medical treatment and good food benefits his health. But there is no reliable evidence that rehabilitation occurs. Nimmer reports that only 12 per cent of the patients accepted aid in improving their housing.[104]

Nor is it clear that the St. Louis center represents a reduction in public costs. Few drunks were processed by the St. Louis criminal system even before the detoxification system. Since the center's move to its present location, taking a drunk to the center consumes only one-third less time than that required for arrest, booking, and court appearance. Finally, the center may not represent a public benefit because the cost advantage to law enforcement agencies is compensated by increased expenditures in public medical facilities.

Thus, while the St. Louis detoxification program is not a complete failure, it certainly is not an overwhelming success. Nimmer warns that the growing tendency to view the detoxification concept as a panacea for the ills of the criminal system in processing the public intoxicant is not warranted in light of the St. Louis experience.[105] The program suffers from its ties to the police department; "the extent to which the police fail to bring in destitute intoxicants in need of these services limits the success of the new program." Because police are in charge of intake, many of the men who need the facility most never have a chance for admittance. The St. Louis program is described as "a one-half program," because it cannot deal with either the skid row derelict population or the entire destitute public intoxicant population. Even if they wanted to, the police could not serve a much wider clientele because of the limited available bed space. On the other hand, if there were more beds available, they would not be filled under present police policies because of internal departmental pressures and traditional priorities.

Nimmer argues that the present program's emphasis on both rehabilitation and detoxification raises public and police expectations and greatly increases the cost of the program, reportedly averaging forty-two dollars per man-day at the center. He proposes that the length of stay in the center be reduced to two days. Patients who wanted additional treatment might then transfer to another facility.[106] In any case, the St. Louis experience has highlighted some of the difficult structural problems and policy issues encountered in attempting to upgrade procedures for handling the public inebriate.

Another detoxification center opened its doors in November 1967 in Washington, D.C. It was designed to deal with "simple intoxication" only: to function as an improvement over the police drunk tank, but not as a substitute for the hospital. Unlike the St. Louis center, it aimed to serve both voluntary patients and inebriates escorted in by the police. These limited objectives are appropriate for the center's role as one component of a comprehensive alcohol treatment system. It had to be located in an area easily accessible to potential patients and police, to be designed so that patients could be managed efficiently and cheaply, and to be structured so that it did not look or "feel" like a jail.[107]

In the first years of the program, only about one-fifth of the patients were brought to the center by the police. Almost half voluntarily applied without formal referral, and 29 per cent were referred by other health facilities and community agencies. After implementation of the District of Columbia Alcoholic Rehabilitation Act in 1968, the number of police escorts increased to about one-half of all admissions.[108] The police were more conscientious about arresting inebriates than they have been about bringing them to the detoxification center. In fiscal 1969 only 3,610 persons were brought to the center by police, but prior to the Alcoholic Rehabilitation Act, there were over 43,000 drunkenness arrests annually.[109]

The detoxification center is not set up to handle unmanageable patients, but despite dire warnings in this regard, as it turns out few unmanageable patients have applied to the facility. Admission is quick and efficient, rarely lasting over twelve minutes. Medication is by standing order. Following admission, patients are cleaned up and lodged in the acute care area. Later they can be moved to the self-care section. Patients receive vitamin and mineral supplements, and a high protein diet. Sunday church service and AA meetings are available.

The stay at the detoxification center may last up to five days; the average stay is almost four days. Where possible, a patient's immediate needs for clothing, lodging, food, and employment are arranged for before release, and he is encouraged to enter a psychiatrically oriented alcoholism aftercare program. When a patient leaves, he is clean, his clothing is tidy, and he is proud of the way he looks. Among the demonstrated advantages of the Washington, D.C., detoxification center over a drunk tank are better medical care, a more positive environment, better nutrition, and more encouragement for patients to use appropriate community health and welfare resources after their discharge.[110]

In New York City, a combined effort of city agencies and private groups developed the Manhattan Bowery Project. The Vera Institute served as coordinator of the plan, and support was obtained from the Ford Foundation and city, state, and federal agencies. The Manhattan Bowery Project opened its detoxification center in November 1967. In contrast to the St. Louis and Washington, D.C., centers to which inebriates must apply or be escorted, the Manhattan Bowery Project operates an outreach program. A plainclothes police officer and a rescue aid patrol the Bowery twelve hours a day in an unmarked police car. This rescue team approaches derelicts who seem to need assistance and offers to take them to the detoxification center. And although there is no coercion either at the time of initial contact or at any other stage of the program, two out of every three men approached agree to come with the rescue team.

At the detoxification center, patients are screened by a physician, signed in by a correction officer, cleaned up and put to bed by medical aides, given a complete physical examination and medication by a physician, and then are under constant medical supervision for three days. After that time the patient moves into a recuperative ward where he may use television and recreational facilities. He also sees a caseworker and makes tentative plans for aftercare. Usually a patient leaves the project on the fifth day.

As a result of the first year's experience, two new treatment facilities were established, one which provides outpatient care for

project patients and the other an emergency care clinic capable of
providing aid to more than 200 men a week. The latter facility was
necessary because the detoxification center could only handle ten
admissions a day. As a consequence many homeless alcoholics remained on the streets and police department roundups continued.

By October 1969 the detoxification unit had admitted over
5,000 patients, the average stay was 5.5 days and the average cost
was $38 a day. Three-fourths of the patients were brought in by
the street patrols. The project's annual report stated that even if
few men were substantially improved as a consequence of five days
of detoxification, the substitution of the medical facility for the police court–prison system was certainly a more humane kind of revolving door.[111]

Since the Manhattan Bowery Project did not expect dramatic
results in terms of rehabilitation, there probably were fewer expectations of "success" among its professional workers than among
the staff of many rehabilitation agencies. Nevertheless, the report
of the first year's activity noted the strains to project staff resulting
from the skid row man's low stress tolerance, dependence and inability to make decisions, rejection of after care, and other personality problems. Despite the low expectations of success, those
staff members who were most "cure directed" found the recidivism
of their patients most frustrating: "Strenuous medical care, careful referral, all seem to come to naught when so many men resume
drinking."[112] Sixty-two per cent of the admissions during the year
were first admissions, the others were repeaters. One of every ten
had been to the center at least three times before. As for "success,"
a preliminary study of 100 men three months after their discharge
revealed that one out of six were still sober and either employed or
in an organized rehabilitation program.[113]

Confronted with fairly high recidivism rates and a program designed for short-term care, the staff of the Manhattan Bowery Project scaled down their definitions of rehabilitation and their ideas
about how it could be achieved. The more limited rehabilitation
goals were "standardized" against skid row practices rather than

the ideals of the broader society. Goals such as permanent sobriety, stable employment, and acquisition of other social ties are seen as unattainable for many skid row alcoholics because of the men's age, mental and physical disabilities, and the costs of treatment. The rehabilitation goals substituted—substantial steps relative to Bowery life—are to increase the period of time between benders, to help the men hold better paying jobs for longer periods, to teach them to use the city's health resources more efficiently, and to give them the alternative of combating stress via prescribed drugs rather than alcohol.[114]

Halfway houses. Halfway houses are recommended aids for reintegrating marginal people, and are frequently helpful to people who have been living in total institutions such as mental hospitals or jails. Their structure varies, but generally some supervision and treatment continues while the resident tries to establish social networks in the wider society that will make it possible for him to leave the halfway house. Halfway houses have been widely recommended for treatment of chronic alcoholics,[115] but relatively few of them have been available to skid row men. There is also some evidence that halfway house programs are more effective for middle-class than for lower-class men.

They have been widely used for middle-class alcoholics. In California alone there were some fifty independently owned and operated "recovery houses" in 1964 where residents stayed an average of three months while continuing treatment and at the same time obtaining outside employment and making other steps toward full rehabilitation.[116]

One of the first halfway house programs for skid row alcoholics began in 1950, when one ward of a 300-bed dormitory for indigent alcoholics at Boston Long Island Hospital was set aside for a special treatment program. Patients who volunteered took part in a four-phase regimen which included: 1. daytime employment in the city; 2. return to the hospital nights and weekends; 3. taking disulfiram each day; 4. attempting to re-establish family relationships, if possible. The effects of the program were evaluated in 1962 by comparing a "treatment group" of patients who had volunteered for the program in 1952 with a "comparison group" of skid row alcoholics admitted to the hospital that year who did not volunteer for the special program.[117]

Three possible effects of the program set down by the evaluators were "successful rehabilitation" (sobriety, employment, and restoration of family relations), "partial success" (sobriety and employment part of the time, typically while living in the hospital), and "failure" (no evidence of increased self-sufficiency; sobriety may or may not be maintained for long periods). After ten years, approximately one-fifth (22 per cent) of the men in the treatment group were classified as successfully rehabilitated. Another 24 per cent were classified as partially rehabilitated; they had manifested improvement only while living in the halfway house. The majority of those treated (54 per cent) were classified as failures.

The evaluators observed that patients who were successfully rehabilitated tended to be the least marginal, i.e., were younger, better educated, more occupationally skilled, were from families less dependent upon community agencies than the families of the "failures," and had been arrested and jailed less frequently than the other men. In other words, "the value of the treatment program was to offer men who, at one time, were able to care for themselves another chance to do so." Men who had never been self-sufficient were not rehabilitated by the program. It could not provide direction or skills to those who had always been aimless or helpless.

Certain critical points at which rehabilitation agents might intervene were noted, such as when a man is arrested for drinking three or more times within a given year, or when an alcoholic husband is arrested for non-support. The important point, however, is that there must be preventive and continuing coordination and follow-up by hospitals, alcoholism clinics, public welfare agencies, and other interested community groups:

> In its totality this problem is not solely a psychiatric or even a public health one, but one for the community at large. In general, these men

come from a group whose lives are so poorly organized in childhood that they ultimately end up totally unprepared for life as it exists in contemporary society.[118]

Alcoholics Anonymous. Alcoholics Anonymous is reputed to be one of the most effective programs for rehabilitating alcoholics, but its characteristics make it difficult to study. Its emphasis is on helping the sick alcoholic rather than making him a research subject. Membership is essentially subjective, and a tradition of anonymity impedes evaluation and follow-up efforts. Indications of the movement's growth are available in statistics on the number and location of local AA groups and the number of meetings the groups hold weekly, and these have been analyzed in a recent paper by Leach *et al.*[119] The first AA meeting was held in 1935; by 1965 there were 12,040 AA groups holding 15,991 meetings a week.

Alcoholics Anonymous functions to produce "a network of group controls for sobriety," by creating an intimate primary group which serves to inculcate a new subculture in its members. The major integrating force in the movement is a common system of norms:

. . . in addition to his local group, each A.A. member has a secondary group in the worldwide A.A. "fellowship," as it calls itself, sharing a common system of norms which is virtually the only unifying force in the movement, since it has no government equipped with enforcement powers and practically no formal, prescribed organizational structure.[120]

The essence of the AA rehabilitation program is contained in the statement that a new member becomes

. . . a part of a large group of former alcoholics who wish to help him. He is encouraged to tell his troubles and to ask for help at any time of the day or night that he feels the need. He is protected by anonymity and forgiven for backsliding. Eventually he is helped in his turn to become nurturant toward others like him.[121]

Details about the history and methods of AA are available elsewhere. Gellman's *The Sober Alcoholic*, Chafetz and Demone's *Alcoholism and Society*, and the AA's *Alcoholics Anonymous Comes of Age* are especially recommended.[122] Our brief discussion here will be limited to presenting some sociological views about why AA is effective.

Although the nature of Alcoholics Anonymous has operated to impede systematic evaluation of its effectiveness, its thoroughly positive reputation is at least secondary evidence of its frequent success. In fact, continued attendance at AA meetings following treatment is sometimes used as an indicator of successful therapy. Trice and Roman have suggested that the social processing of alcoholics by Alcoholics Anonymous results in positive behavioral changes because it is one of the few instances in which successful "delabeling" or destigmatization of deviants occurs.[123]

AA's success is in part because of their use of the "allergy" concept. The idea is that some people are physiologically allergic to alcohol and thereby predetermined to become alcoholic even before they begin to drink. The allergy concept allows the alcoholic to reduce the self-blame that accompanies the role of alcoholic. In addition, AA has made use of the "repentant" role, long a part of the American tradition, and the removal of the visible evidence of the alcoholic's stigmatization—i.e., his total abstinence from alcohol—is taken as evidence of more deep-seated changes. Moreover, the mythology that many skid row men are "skidders" who formerly were professionals serves to dramatize the upward mobility of skid row men who make good after "hitting bottom." Finally, AA's processing of stigmatized alcoholics is congruent with major American values.

Self-control, humanitarianism, emphases on practicality, and suspicion of established authority all are fundamental to its program and to the values of middle-class Americans. Yet these very types of treatment for alcoholism, it is not too successful with persons from the lower class. AA attracts a certain type of alcoholic values are also part of AA's weakness, because, like most other and is not effective at attracting or keeping other types in affiliation. A follow-up study of hospitalized alcoholics who had had extensive experience with AA during treatment revealed that those who continued their affiliation with AA after re-entry into the community had different personality features from those who did not affiliate.[124]

Rubington has identified several "barriers to abstinence" which contribute to the high relapse rates of chronic alcoholics and impede conventional treatment programs. The major barrier is the social expectation that people who try to stop using drugs will fail. Apparently what happens is at the same time the alcoholic decides to stop his drinking, his associates are preparing to accept him as a drinker, or even to require that he continue to drink.[125]

One explanation of treatment failure is that too often it involves unrealistic expectations for permanent abstinence. This means that relapses, when they occur, are further evidence of a patient's failure and provide additional support for the expectations for relapse which he and his peers have come to share. The patient comes to view his condition as irreversible. At the same time, continuing to participate in the alcohol subculture, he picks up ways of living which stigmatize him or in other ways cut him off even more fully from normal society. Finally, his companions in alcoholic dependency try to prevent him from leaving their group, or at least are ready to welcome him back after the anticipated relapse. All of these "social barriers to abstinence" decrease a treatment program's probabilities of success. As a consequence, the outcome of many treatment programs is not rehabilitation but rather stabilization in deviance. Rather than being surmounted, the social barriers to abstinence are sustained by the treatment.[126]

Rubington argues that AA and Synanon have been more effective than other treatment programs because they circumvent the abstinence barrier. They do this by "accepting drug dependence as a state of being, by offering a course of action based on that state, and by controlling."[127] Synanon and AA succeed because they offer instant acceptance, provide role models and status based on abstaining, and treat expertise in deviant skills as an advantage. Social action is controlled by insulating the patient from those who would want him to return to dependence on alcohol or drugs, and also by applying interpersonal pressures if there are indications he intends to leave the program.

Thus both self-help organizations make it possible for the drug-dependent to accept himself as he is at the moment. The member attains a set of ideas about himself which give him an identity, an increased degree of self-esteem, an acceptable explanation for his dependence, and a program for overcoming it in concert with a primary group of like-statused persons. The simple program is easy to follow, is observable, demands no vast repertory of social and technical skills, affords a role, and assigns status on the basis of observable results in cumulating days of abstinence. Finally the presence of a primary group gives protection against those who would belittle or would seek to engineer a relapse on grounds of group loyalties.[128]

Rubington also proposes that AA is best equipped to handle the solitary type of alcohol abuse, while Synanon is better prepared to treat dependence on drugs and on the deviant drug community. AA is also more involved in the outer community, in the sense that it is not insulated from that community. It functions as a kind of out-patient institution, whereas Synanon is a residential treatment center.

Program evaluation

In 1963 David Pittman identified the lack of critical evaluation as perhaps the greatest weakness of American and European alcoholism treatment programs.[129] The situation has improved in the years since that assessment was made, but program evaluation in the field of alcoholism treatment is still in its infancy. That Blum and Blum devote a chapter to "Evaluation Difficulties and Solutions" is itself a good omen, and in that chapter they summarize some important evaluation studies.[130]

They note that in addition to the formidable technical difficulties of evaluating alcoholism programs—including controls for matters such as why a patient came to a particular facility at the time and in the manner he did, the nature of his first contact with the facility, his expectations about treatment there and the cumulative cycling of his own and the therapist's expectations, his compatibility with those administering his therapy, the intensity and duration of treatment, extraneous factors operating during the treatment, the controlling for experience in previous treatment programs, following the patient after he leaves the program, estimating his success with reference to his own previous performance—there are additional sociopsychological obstacles to evaluative research. These include institutional resistance to any evaluation which assumes (and all evaluations should) that it is possible that an institutional treatment mode is ineffective, therapists' fears that evaluation will interfere with treatment, and the resistance of therapists to active involvement in the home environment of discharged patients. These latter factors are serious enough impediments that Blum and Blum recommend that some of the resources allocated for treatment research be devoted to analyses of therapists' resistance to treatment evaluation.[131]

One interesting pattern in the treatment of chronic alcoholism is that no one seems to learn from experience. When evaluation reveals that certain therapies do not work, a typical conclusion is that further studies are needed. Occasions when a form of treatment is abandoned because of evidence that it does no good are very rare. Where careful, systematic evaluation has been conducted, a typical finding, regardless of the form of therapy, is that the costly programs rehabilitate approximately the same proportion of patients as are rehabilitated by no treatment at all.

While there is little evidence that any of the methods of rehabilitating chronic inebriates are successful, there is evidence that some are more detrimental than others. For example, incarceration is the most common "treatment," and it is almost universally deemed a most ineffective aid to rehabilitation. In an overview of the variety and effectiveness of programs for rehabilitating the homeless Caplow concluded:

Hundreds of programs have been launched at one time or another—compulsory labor, compulsory abstinence, salvationism, job-training, psychotherapy, group therapy, halfway houses, guaranteed employ-

ment, hospitalization, dispersion, rehousing, communal gardens; even
hypnotism and group-singing. Every method shows a few successes
(mostly among men who have not been homeless for long or who have
experienced unusual downward mobility) and many failures. Since
every program provides a living for its practitioners, many programs
fit into the pattern of skid-row life and persist indefinitely. An antique
institution like a revival mission can often be found next door to something as modern as a group therapy center. Either type of program is
effective with a motivated client and a few such clients can almost always be found.[132]

Insight therapy. In part because careful scientific evaluation has
not been a characteristic of most alcoholism treatment programs,
there is little empirical evidence that certain programs are superior
to others, or to no treatment at all. The "recovery" rates of various
treatment programs are rarely greater than 35 per cent and usually
are much lower than that.[133] The forms of treatment preferred by
most clinicians and the general public—insight therapy with a psy-
chotherapeutic orientation—has not been demonstrated to be effective, and in fact the scientific evidence for its value in the treatment
of alcoholism is not much better today than it was thirty years
ago.[134] One critic laments: "Insight therapy of various sorts is still
the most widely used method of treating alcoholics; and still nobody has proved whether it works or not, or what makes the difference between therapy that works and therapy that does not."[135] In
fact, there is evidence that psychotherapy may be fairly ineffective
in treating many forms of mental illness. A review of controlled
studies of individual psychotherapies by Bergin reveals that people who had psychotherapy were no more likely to improve than
comparable people who did not.[136]

As many as 2 per cent per year of alcoholics may "mature" out
of their addiction with no outside help. In a ten-year follow-up,
this means that 20 per cent spontaneous recovery would be expected had there been no treatment at all. Thus it is a serious question as to whether insight therapy is better than no treatment for
chronic alcoholics.

Nevertheless, next to incarceration and physical labor, the most common treatment of chronic alcoholism has been some form of psychiatric or psychological treatment aimed at helping a patient acquire insight about the cause of his problems. It has been presumed that knowing about the psychological forces underlying the personality conditions of which alcoholism is symptomatic will enhance the chronic alcoholic's self-image and help prepare him for greater social responsibility. However, a growing body of research findings suggest that insight therapy is ineffective. An example is a study conducted under the auspices of the Alcoholism and Drug Research Foundation which systematically contrasted psychiatrically oriented insight therapy with recreational therapy The latter included opportunities for counseling if the patient desired. The criteria for success were whether there was a reduction of alcohol intake, an increase in responsibility for self and others, and an improvement in self-image. Using these criteria, 15 per cent of those exposed to traditional psychologically oriented therapy showed improvement. In the self-directed recreational therapy, two-thirds were unimproved and one-third improved.[137] The authors concluded that treatment programs emphasizing recreation were at least as effective as those aimed at producing psychological insights.

Probably no one would deny the long-term efficacy of establishing the "true" bases of things via self-analysis, but it may be that in terms of a limited objective such as treating alcoholism, a simple rest or diversion is more effective than a traumatic attempt to break down defenses and reveal the unsightly truth. If recreational therapy, which is simply a matter of making facilities and some resource persons available, is as effective as the protracted, costly searching for hidden causes which accompanies psychiatric treatment, there is no reason why we should opt for the more expensive treatment.

Aversion therapy. Aversion therapies are based on the assumption that if unpleasant effects are linked to alcohol during treatment, subsequent encounters with alcohol will evoke those same unpleasant responses and as a consequence patients will avoid alcohol use.

Aversion therapies in alcohol treatment typically have used emetic drugs (emetine and apomorphine), but electric shocks and scoline have also been used.

One review of literature on behavior therapy for alcoholism[138] concludes that while many applications of behavior therapy have included the precision of laboratory procedures, the field of alcoholism treatment is notable both for its gross errors in laboratory procedures and for the incomplete or incorrect reporting of research procedures. A frequent, critical omission in most behavior studies of alcoholism is the control and report of relations among stimulus events. It is almost as if there had been a decision that precise temporal relations were not important to behavior therapy in applied settings, but there is no evidence that this is so.

Another common error is the use of hospital readmission rates as indicators of the effects of conditioning procedures. In place of this gross, inappropriate variable, researchers should measure whether some conditioning takes place. The more immediate effects of behavior therapy should be assessed, rather than merely asking whether subjects have been rehospitalized within some follow-up period.[139]

The most impressive results from the use of emetic drugs is the work at Shadel Hospital in Washington State, where abstinence rates during the first few months after treatment have reached 85 percent. Researchers at Shadel hospital have reported that 60 per cent of those conditioned with emetine are abstinent for one year or longer, and 25 per cent for ten years or longer.[140] However, patients at Shadel are middle and upper income, highly selected, well motivated, and likely to have fairly stable personalities.

Another drug used in aversion therapy is succinylcholine (scoline). Scoline produces temporary paralysis of skeletal muscles and makes it difficult to breathe, but leaves the patient conscious. Results of the scoline conditioning are inconclusive and not very impressive. The most significant thing about it is the extent to which subjects describe the conditioning as a traumatic experience. Its use is attended by great fear and followed by a variety of behavior changes, many of which are not linked to abstinence from alcohol. Evaluations have revealed that treated patients are not more likely to improve than patients exposed to a control procedure. Abstinence rates are in the neighborhood of 20 per cent or lower after two months and apparently show little change from that level after twelve months.[141]

Some researchers claim that electrical shock is better than chemicals in aversion therapy because it is subject to better experimental control. Reported abstinence rate following electrical shock aversion therapy range from zero to about 50 per cent.

With the exception of the Shadel hospital studies, most of the evaluations of aversion therapy have used extremely small samples, or case reports. Studies of aversion therapy are continuing, and it is too soon to make a guess about the probable outcome of systematic comparisons of aversion therapy and other modes of rehabilitation. But the outcome is not very promising. To date, comparative studies of different treatment methods have not revealed aversive therapies to be the most successful. For example, Wallerstein's follow-up of patients treated by disulfiram, hypnosis, group therapy, and aversive conditioning with emetine, did not show aversive conditioning to be the most effective method. In fact, both disulfiram therapy and treatment by hypnosis produced higher rates of abstinence, the former producing 50 per cent abstinence after two years.[142] Finally, one of the most recent reviews of aversion therapy in alcoholism treatment concludes that "there is no good evidence that aversion procedures are particularly effective in the treatment of alcoholism."[143]

Criteria of "success." The evaluation of treatment programs for alcoholics has been further complicated by the lack of established criteria of successful treatment. Abstinence from alcohol has been a traditional criterion, but it may be an unrealistic or even inappropriate goal. At best it is a partial index of success; at worst, it may be positively misleading.[144] An evaluator of aversion therapies in alcoholism treatments has noted that abstinence should be viewed as a "rather unlikely steady state imposed upon the patient" and has concluded that while it may be desirable, "it is probably unrealistic to anticipate that alcoholics who have a particular difficulty in relation to drink should be able to perform better than normal subjects in this respect."[145] If after treatment patients report having less of a problem with alcohol, or even are able to resume social drinking, this also should be reflected in the measurement of progress or success.

Working from the assumption that outcome variability derives from both variable inputs and differentials in the treatment facilities, Pattison and his associates postulated a number of models of the relationship between variables linked to the successful treatment of alcoholism.[146] They evaluated treatment in three kinds of facilities: a private medical hospital specializing in alcoholism, a mental health clinic which emphasized treatment for alcoholics, and a halfway house. In the medical hospital the major emphasis was on the biochemical origins of alcoholism, the mental health outpatient clinic stressed the need for changing a prisoner's psychological and social functioning, and the halfway house facility aimed to teach responsibility via an active program in self-government. A careful assessment of treatment outcomes of these three types of programs demonstrated that there was no relationship between improvement in drinking and improvement in other areas of life. Successful treatment of alcoholism was not limited to fostering abstinence.

There is evidence that sometimes the emphasis on abstinence has been to the detriment of other aspects of the total gestalt which is the problem drinker's life organization. A follow-up study of forty-six ex-patients of the Cincinnati Alcoholism Clinic (an outpatient facility serving the indigent) bears on this point. All respondents had attended at least ten psychotherapy sessions, been rated as "improved," and were discharged at least eighteen months prior to the survey. At the time of follow-up approximately one-third of the group were abstainers, another third were normal drinkers, and a third were pathological drinkers. A critical finding was that in physical health, interpersonal and mental health, and vocational adjustment, there was no difference between the abstinent and normal drinkers. The researchers concluded that "ex-alcoholics now drinking in a non-pathological or normal fashion may be as well off in over-all 'life healthiness' as a comparable group of ex-alcoholics, and that over-all healthiness may not be a concomitant of abstinence."[147]

Numerous clinical reports have questioned the adequacy of abstinence as a criterion of successful treatment and have shown that abstinence may not represent an improvement in over-all health or life adjustment.[148] There is now evidence that alcoholics can develop and maintain "normal" drinking patterns. Incidence of such adjustment in the random samples studied thus far ranges from 4 per cent to 10 per cent.

A critical point here is that treatment programs, when they are successful at all, tend to produce successes whose characteristics reflect the agency's treatment philosophy. In other words, "the type of change in drinking patterns produced by a clinic may be significantly determined by the philosophy of the clinic." If addictive drinking is only one segment of a larger life organization, then changes in any of several elements may produce a new organization characterized by a different drinking pattern. Thus a variety of modes of drinking behavior may appear in an "improved" total life situation.[149]

Fitting treatment to patients. Another area where most rehabilitation programs fall short is matching the alcoholic with appropriate treatment. There are many kinds of alcoholics, many useful methods of treatment, and many forms of improvement. The role of treatment agent might be redefined as fitting the appropriate therapy to a patient.[150]

Most treatment evaluation studies have ignored the demographic and social characteristics of the alcoholic subjects. It has been known that there was great variability in the population of alcoholics, but somehow the practicing assumption continued to be that once one was involved in treatment it did not matter what kind of alcoholic he was. It is almost a truism that success is related to the characteristics of the alcoholic being treated. But there has been little success in identifying configurations of characteristics and linking them to the most appropriate form of treatment. One response to the variability among alcoholics has been the "shotgun approach," in which a facility combines a number of methods hoping that something will work. Sometimes these "ill-conceived combinations of treatment may be superfluous, confusing, or even destructive."[151]

Some research on social and psychological factors in the treatment of chronic alcoholism suggests that success rates may be improved if subjects have some choice about their treatment. Prognosis for treatment varies directly with the alcoholic's social and psychological stability. A comparative study by Kissin and his associates investigated the effects of allowing respondents some choice about their assignment to treatment programs. The amount of choice increased with the intensiveness of the treatment program offered.[152] For example, patients offered inpatient rehabilitation therapy were allowed to choose any other form of therapy if they rejected that form. However, drug therapy patients could only accept or reject drug therapy; no other programs were offered to them.

The study involved a comparison of success rates for three modes of treatment: drug therapy, psychotherapy plus adjunctive drug therapy, and inpatient rehabilitation ward therapy. The criterion for success was total or near total abstinence combined with "significant improvement" in social and occupational adjustments for at least six months before evaluation. Success rates were 5 per cent for a control group, 21 per cent for the drug therapy, 36 per cent for psychotherapy, and 15 per cent for the inpatient rehabilitation ward therapy.[153] The findings were that socially and psychologically stable individuals do best in psychotherapy, socially unstable but intellectually sophisticated patients do well in inpatient rehabilitation programs, and "socially intact" but less psychologically sophisticated alcoholics appear to do best in drug therapy.[154] Kissin, Platz, and Su concluded that social and psychological characteristics were sufficiently predictive of success to be taken into account in assigning patients. An ideal program would offer a variety of treatments, and clinicians would work to screen patients and route them into the kinds of treatment proved most successful with people like themselves. At the same time, choice should be maximized.

Other problems. It seems likely that much of the favorable results in the alcoholism treatment literature can be traced to an absence of careful controls. There is evidence that the more stringent the design of an evaluation study, the less favorable will be its conclusions. Stated differently, there has been a lot of sloppy evaluation, and sloppy evaluation tends to produce positive results. It is not enough for staff members of a program to feel that it "does some good" or for patients to give testimonials. Too often, evaluation studies are tacked on to a treatment program rather than being established as an integral part of the program. Usually this means that proper baseline measures cannot be obtained, proper assignment to control and experimental groups is impossible, and a variety of systematic biases remain uncontrolled.[155]

Let us emphasize the snail's pace of progress in program evaluation. In 1957, Gibbins and Armstrong pointed to a need for the careful study of changes in "total behavior" of patients following treatment of alcoholism.[156] They stressed that the variables studied should be objective and quantifiable because the judgments of success and failure in many so-called evaluative studies were linked to the values and attitudes of the investigators rather than to objective criteria. They also noted that the typical absence of data collection for periods preceding treatment cast into confusion the assessment of treatment impact. If pretreatment data were not available or if there were not suitable control groups, they said, it was technically impossible to demonstrate that change had taken place or to show the direction of that change. Other difficulties in evaluating the ef-

fects of treatment programs stem from the fact that most patients
have been exposed previously to other kinds of alcoholism therapy,
and many make use of other types of treatment after or at the
same time they are involved in the type of treatment being evaluated. Thus it is not surprising that the hypothesized relationship between duration of contact with a program and treatment "progress"
often does not appear.

Most of the rehabilitation programs we have reviewed require
some commitment and motivation on the part of the person being
treated. It is not enough that he be exposed to structured environ-
ments, aversive conditioning, insight therapy, or more "humane"
treatment. Unless he both desires to be rehabilitated and believes
that he can be rehabilitated, none of the treatment programs can
do much.

With a motivated client who thinks a program can help him, it
probably does not matter much what kind of treatment is given. If
he believes in it, and if those administering the treatment believe in
it, the results are likely to be as positive as would result from any
other treatment mode now available. In the field of human rehabilitation, thinking makes it so. If the art of rehabilitating skid row
men were more advanced, this assessment might require more
qualification. But given the state of scientific knowledge about the
multiproblem skid row man, it seems plain that more variation in
treatment outcome can be explained via differentials in patients'
motivations and expectations than can be accounted for by more
"external" factors.

This has been a lengthy chapter, and a brief summary is in order.
We began with a discussion of treatment for vagrancy: labor colonies, compulsory labor, and segregation or containment of vagrants were popular ideas in the late 1800's and early 1900's. In the
following decades there has been an increasing emphasis on interdisciplinary or "coordinated" programs, and a growing concern
with alcoholism as an attribute of the homeless.

Rehabilitation programs for the homeless usually have a low
funding priority, in part because the homeless men are thought to

have "little promise" in comparison to other segments of the community. There has been some community organization of homeless persons (and others) in single-room-occupancy buildings, and it has been proposed that alcoholics be paid to keep peace on skid row. Most hospitals and jails do not offer genuine treatment of alcoholism, and skid row missions serve only a select clientele.

Despite the wide acceptance of the disease concept of alcoholism, more alcoholics are treated by incarceration than by all other treatment modes combined. However, a new development may change this: Detoxification centers serve as substitutes for jails in several cities. Some problems in the detoxification center programs are inadequate funding and the dilemma between providing rehabilitation (a long-term process) and detoxification (a short-term goal).

Many treatment programs unintentionally *create* social barriers to abstinence, rather than surmounting them. Alcoholics Anonymous seems more effective than most programs because it circumvents the abstinence barrier by accepting drug dependence as a state of being, offers a course of action based on acceptance of that definition of the situation, and provides appropriate social controls.

Lack of critical evaluation is perhaps the greatest weakness of most alcoholism treatment programs. Another area where treatment programs often fail is in fitting patients to appropriate treatment. Too often an agency's standard regimen is prescribed for all clients, regardless of their individual experiences or needs. A better approach would provide a variety of possible treatment modes, and some choice would be available to the client.

Many of the favorable results reported in the alcoholism treatment literature can be traced to an absence of adequate controls in the experimental design. The more stringent the design of an evaluation study, the less favorable its conclusions tend to be. Most evidence suggests that costly programs may be no more effective than no programs at all. The proportion of alcoholics who are "cured" by themselves, without recourse to formal treatment, is often as high as that achieved by elaborate therapies and treatment programs. In fact, with a motivated client, the specific content of the treatment may have little effect on the outcome.

8 | Closing thoughts and pressing questions

We shall begin by reviewing two of the major themes developed in this book. They are the permanence of disaffiliation as an aspect of social life and the utility of "disaffiliation" and "defectiveness" as underlying dimensions basic to understanding skid row and its men. Then we shall consider the interplay of imputed defectiveness, powerlessness, and low self-esteem in impeding efforts at rehabilitation.

Disaffiliation and defectiveness

Strangers, outcasts, refugees, pilgrims, and mendicants are created as "natural" social consequences of social change, stratification, social mobility, conflict, and social control. Societies differ in their norms about treatment of strangers and acceptance of the disaffiliates created by social processes of their time and place, but one or more of these types of disaffiliate appear in all societies. Even if normal social processes do not produce "involuntary" disaffiliates, the spiritual or aesthetic benefits of voluntary disaffiliation are usually sufficient to produce a substantial number of vagrants, wanderers, or "drop outs."

In recent times the skid row man has been a particularly stig-

matized disaffiliate, and the combination of the effects of stigmatization and disaffiliation has made his "recovery" especially difficult.
That is not necessarily the case for other kinds of disaffiliation:
Migrants and refugees are much easier to incorporate into the social context than are chronic wanderers and alcoholics. Skid row
men may themselves prove easier to reaffiliate when they move
away from skid row and the social stigmatization that accompanies
life there. Whether they are on skid row or elsewhere may have little immediate bearing on their chances for reaffiliation, but in terms
of the personal costs accrued in interaction with others and in exposure to social controls which reinforce their imputed worthless-
ness, life off skid row—i.e., the dispersion of the homeless—would
seem most compatible with a positive prognosis for reaffiliation.
Thus, there may always be disaffiliates, but the peculiar social form
of skid row may be temporary.

The numerous classifications of the homeless have influenced
their treatment. If the underlying variable is seen as employment
status, for example, then "treatment" consists of attempts to find
jobs; if it is seen as alcoholism, then programs aim to keep men
sober. If it is seen as mobility, then "rehabilitation" may consist of
getting the men to settle down for a time. However, the problem
with treating these variables as the significant underlying traits of
the skid row resident is that most people who exhibit the "pathological" characteristics of unemployment, alcoholism, or mobility
are not homeless, do not live on skid row, and do not suffer the
unique stigmatization accorded the skid row man. The vast majority
of the unemployed, the alcoholics, and the migrants do not end up
living alone in cheap hotel rooms, sharing a special jargon, being
subjected to high probabilities of arrest, and suffering costs from
social interaction that eventually produce monumentally negative
self-images. One can argue that any of these conditions must be
combined with exposure to the skid row community before a man
is recruited to skid row. But saying that unemployment plus exposure to the subculture of skid row is what finally produces a skid
row man still misses the unique social definition of skid row, both

among its residents and in the rest of society, as the last resting place for social misfits, the "mile of forgotten men," the "bottom of the barrel."

Recognizing the importance of affiliations in generating "significant others," affirming identity, and creating means for controlling one's environment, we can see the importance of the dimension "disaffiliation." As long as a man has viable social ties, i.e., has other persons bound to him by reciprocal rights and obligations, his defectiveness is, at worst, only partial. But the more disaffiliated he becomes, and the more powerless, the less "needed" or "expected" or "obligated" he is, and the easier it is for the adjectives "lost," "forgotten," "passed by," and "surplus" to be applied to the self. With the passing of obligations go also rights, and the new self-definition is imprinted via stigmatization, victimization, and discrimination in interaction with others. If a man has visible stigma —marks of his being "damaged goods" visible to all—the impact on the self of his powerlessness and disaffiliation may be even greater.

We recognize that skid row men are multiproblem men, and that generalizing about their "basic problem" is risky. But time and again the far-reaching implications of their reputed defectiveness have surfaced. The police define them as all guilty, all abnormal; rehabilitation agents define them as hopeless and incurable; mission workers see them as wayward men too weak to change their ways; and other skid row men define them as untrustworthy, as misfits, as forgotten men. Morally, mentally, physically, they are defective; tubercular and alcoholic, with mangled or missing limbs, visible sores and scars, bandaged, propped up, or stretched out in the filth of the city sidewalk, their defectiveness is advertised to others and reaffirmed to themselves. Lodging house clerks, nurses, mission workers, and policemen have learned not to expect reform; relapse is the rule, and hopelessness the attitude. The past is locked away and better forgotten, the present is capricious and untrustworthy, and there is no future. The imputed defectiveness, validated in interaction and internalized, acts to prevent the establishment of new affiliations or the reactivation of old ones.

With the attenuation of his affiliations goes what little power the homeless man could command. The stranger, especially the aged, scarred, alcoholic, and deformed stranger, has no social margin. He may be free to come and go, subject always to the approval of the powerful affiliated ones about him. He is on the outside; their organizations and programs represent their interests, not his. The disaffiliate has no voice in their decisions about his treatment or his future.

Imputed defectiveness, powerlessness, and low self-esteem as deterrents to rehabilitation

The primary problem of the skid row man is not alcoholism. Nor is it advanced age, physical disability, and moral inferiority. Instead, the primary problem is that the combined weight of stigmatization which accompanies many different kinds of human defectiveness is focused upon a few men in a distinctive neighborhood. Disease, dirt, and drunkenness are elements of the stereotype of the skid row man. Poverty, sloth, and irresponsibility mark skid row, and it does not matter that some of these characteristics are only in the beholder's eye. The skid row man himself is one of the beholders, and his stereotypes about the row and its men are just as harsh as those of more respectable citizens. Skid row is where the degenerates, the dregs, and the defective settle, and the resident must fight a continual desperate battle to maintain enough self-esteem to live. He may stress little things which set him apart from other men, or continually remind himself that his past was different, that he is not a "bum" like many of those around him.

In *The Outsider* Colin Wilson began a chapter entitled "The Question of Identity" with this statement:

The outsider is not sure who he is. 'He has found an "I", but it is not his true "I".' His main business is to find his way back to himself.[1]

The skid row man, having found an "I" on skid row, hopes that the "I" he now possesses is *not* his own, and to the extent of that hope, he is rehabilitable. If he has never really "found himself" before coming to the row, the skid row identity may be particularly hard to shake, especially if the labeling process has been set into motion by the social control agents of skid row.

He may agree that "skid row is the lowest point in the status order of society."[2] If so, an aversion to stable social attachments to skid row men is understandable. If he reacts to putative membership in that lowest stratum by adopting one of the attitudes of skid row men which "neutralize" society's condemnation—condemning the condemners (everyone who is not a skid row man is a condemner, so everyone who is not a skid row man is contemptible in some other way), "taking" the condemners by demanding compensation for every contact with respectable society, or deceiving the condemners by telling them falsehoods[3]—he still has the problem of reacting to other skid row men. His rejection of societal values in an attempt to reduce his own dissonance and inflate the worth of the "I" which he finds himself does not mean he can accept the "insiders" of skid row. Stephen Crane's poem, in which the devil watcher is startled when one of the leaping, carousing devils calls him "brother," comes to mind.[4] The skid row man can protect himself from the respectables by rejecting them. If they judge him to be defective, then *their* standards are incorrect. But as he looks around himself at other skid row men, his own standards force him to reject many of his peers. He clings to the belief that he is not as "defective" as those about him.

The struggle to live when one is convinced he has "spoiled his goods" is dramatized in the statement of "Slim Lemert," a Los Angeles skid row man:

"As long as there is a cellar," Slim says, "there's going to be a rat in it. I'm the rat, I guess."

Lemert nurses his wine slowly at first, sipping half the glass meditatively, then suddenly gulps the rest all at once. "I'll tell you something very funny," he says. "I hate wine. I almost puke every time I drink it. But if I didn't stay drunk, the chances are I'd kill myself."[5]

Slim's problem is not alcoholism; it is that he has adopted some elements of the non-human stereotypes often applied to homeless men. Some people call them degenerates or "scum." Slim questions his own humanity. He calls himself a rat.

Another man who is not likely to make it off skid row is Larry, described in a Philadelphia newspaper article subtitled "Skid Row's People Need New Places and New Hopes." A rehabilitation agent who knew him said, "Larry hates it on Skid Row. And why shouldn't he? It's foul and dirty and grindingly uncomfortable. He drinks to forget it." Larry himself demonstrated the kind of fatalism we might expect from one whose defectiveness had been emphasized in a thousand different ways. When asked why he did not leave skid row, he said,

How can I? First of all, my clothes. They're dirty and lousy. If I got new clothes, they'd only be hand-me-downs or from second-hand stores.

And suppose I was asked where I live? Nobody is going to hire anybody for a decent job who gives a Vine St. address.

Hell, I'm a pretty good carpenter. But where am I going to get the money to buy the tools I need to report? Naw, I don't see any way out.[6]

In another portion of the article the journalist described skid row men in general: "They have a continuing sense of degradation which leaves them only when they drink." For those who do not defend themselves against the sense of degradation by seeking oblivion in alcohol, the stress of stigmatization can be relieved by careful attention to symbols which set one apart from other men. In fact one of the simplest and least expensive rehabilitation programs ever proposed is based upon acquisition of status symbols which lift a man above the "real" defectives on skid row. Its author was a Bowery man named Jim Lyons:

The way out of the Bowery has three touchstones, Jim has observed.

"First, a suit of decent clothes. That's number one. Second, a wrist watch. A watch lifts a man above the bums. No bum has a watch. A man looks at his own watch and realizes he is no longer an all-out Bowery stiff. Then comes the third—a ring for his finger."

Jim glanced at his own hand.

"A ring," he said, "it's like a badge. If a man is wearing a ring he can look at it and know he's three steps from being a bum; suit, watch, then ring."

. . .

"If they only had the sense to blow, get to hell out, when they buy the ring," he said. "At that point they're on the way back. They should get uptown fast! I tell them that, but they try to come back—all the way—*here*. It can't be done."[7]

Skid row men see others who try to escape fail, and their own hopes of ever getting away wane. Every personal failure adds another increment of stigmatization as the "chronic" or "repeater" label sinks deeper. Alcohol is one way out. Death is another. Both permit a man to escape his sense of defectiveness.

It is said that healthy wolves will turn upon one of their pack who is sick and destroy him. Similarly, tropical fish attack and kill diseased fish among them. Humans are different because the diseased one cooperates in his own destruction. The greater the severity of their imputed defects, the closer the human reaction to that of the wolf pack, and the more willing the "defective" to add self-destructive psychological forces to those that come from without. The self-fulfilling prophecy could be halted if someone could convince him he was not irrevocably defective. But that requires treatment agents and fellow citizens who do not believe it.

As long as the homeless hear such labels as "dehumanized," "subhuman," "derelict," with their connotation of finality and unredeemable defectiveness, the men of skid row will pay the costs in self-hate and the public will continue to believe the experts' prognoses for the "hopeless" men. As it now stands, even sympathetic workers and writers sometimes cannot help likening homeless men to animals. Thus,

I began to think they never had an original thought or noble moment. Everything about them—their faces, their bodies, their minds, their souls—was stunted and soiled. They lacked the ability even to *experience* their lives as real. Harry and Al were professional survivors. They saw only what was directly in front of them, they asked no questions, felt no anger, demanded no love; they just made do, just kept body and soul together. They reminded me of a couple of antique cockroaches, those marvelous insects that no amount of civilization can kill. Cockroaches survive everything; and so had Harry and Al.[8]

Most of us are familiar with the story, "The Frog Prince," in which a princess, finally induced to kiss a frog, finds him instantly transformed into a handsome prince. The frog, treated to a human form of communication, a kiss, becomes human. The particular content of the communication is unimportant, provided it meets the requirements set by the spell caster.

In contrast to the frog, the "spell" of the homeless man is almost always a long time coming. Typically, it is a gradual metamorphosis that creates a prisoner before the man is aware, and awareness usually comes too late for him to reverse the process. Part frog, people begin treating him as whole frog, and the "enchantment" is completed as he disbelieves his mirror and self-knowledge and instead comes to believe the message sent by those who treat him as a frog. His mirror lies; he is frog; the papers, the clerks, the policemen, and all the other men react to him as frog; the rehabilitation agents, supposedly "frog changers," know from experience that only one in a thousand frogs are princes, and so they treat all frogs as frogs.

In fact, the enchantment *can* be lifted, but it is a slow process, requiring the cooperation of the frog himself, his intense belief that he is not a frog after all, coupled with being treated by others as human. There are no magic potions; neither aversion treatments, sudden psychiatric insights, employment opportunities, nor simple geographic transfers can work the disenchantment. He must acquire human affiliations, communicate and be received as a human, not a discard. Even so, if he had been frog too long, the damage to self-image may be too great. His eyes, trained to translate the humanoid image to frog, see frog; he acts frog, and others come to see frog.

The sociological approach to homelessness, only fleetingly tried and then typically as an adjunct to other "core" forms of treatment, would consist in changing the definition of the situation. In brief, it would mean convincing the man of his "non-frog-ness," and confirming his manhood via appropriate activity, interaction, and respect. All this, of course, in an atmosphere where "disenchantment" was defined as normal.

Some questions for further study

The questions below represent, in my view, the most fertile areas for future studies of homelessness and skid row. To some extent, this is a personal statement of the directions I think future research on homelessness ought to take. I have tried to include questions basic to understanding and rehabilitating skid row men, to assessing more accurately the relationships between skid row and the rest of society, and to understanding what things further analysis of homelessness can tell us about human society in general.

1. To what extent is the disaffiliation of the homeless man voluntary, and to what degree does the claim of voluntary disaffiliation represent a protective rationalization for the experience of rejection?

2. How final is the status of skid row man? How many men have spent a portion of their life on skid row, escaped, and been "redeemed," acquiring new social margin and new affiliations? We know there is a great deal of mobility on and off skid row, but the degree to which it represents upward mobility out of disaffiliation and impoverishment is not known.

3. What are the personal consequences perceived by the skid row man of living "in dispersion," off skid row, rather than on it?

4. What functions do skid row facilities serve for constituencies other than skid row men, and to what extent do these external considerations supersede the supposed primary objective of delivering services to clients? For example, what are the functions for a religious organization of running a "skid row mission" above and beyond the simple delivery of succor to the needy homeless? How much of the activity of the mission organization actually sustains the charity for which it presumably exists?

5. How effective are the various service organizations of skid row, as rated by the men who live there? How effective are they by other criteria? What might be done to make them more effective?

6. What is the future of skid row in the United States? Will it prove to have been merely a temporary phenomenon of the late nineteenth and twentieth centuries, or is the "single-man slum" to be a permanent fixture of urban society?

7. What can be done to change the negative image of skid row itself? As long as proponents of alcoholism programs and seekers of public support for the disease concept make the distinction between the "good" alcoholic who has a disease and the "bad" skid row alcoholic who cannot be helped, efforts to find just how redeemable the skid row man is are unlikely to gather much support.

8. How can the personal costs of stigmatization as a skid row man be reduced, or better still, how could the stigmatization be avoided?

9. How much does the public at large know about skid row and its men? What are the components of the stereotypes held, and how are they transmitted and reinforced?

10. What kind of activities might reverse the "self-fulfilling prophecy" which brings the skid row man to view himself as defective, worn out, diseased, and useless? How could contingencies in the skid row setting be restructured to enhance rather than depress the men's self-esteem?

11. How frequently does a loss in self-esteem accompany the move to skid row and participation in its institutions?

12. How do personal perspectives change with continued residence on skid row? Curtin has noted that during her stay in a hotel where homeless men lived, ". . . the longer I stayed around the hotel, the more convinced I became that nobody cared."[9]

13. To what extent are the homeless a minority group? A thorough analysis of their relationships with others, using the theoretical perspectives of majority-minority relations, might be enlightening.

14. What might be done to minimize the friction between the

agents of social control and their clients from skid row? Since many of the problems seem to stem from contradictory definitions of the situation, how might both parties be better prepared for the type of interaction they will experience and the accompanying stresses?

15. To what extent do experts' definitions of the situation tend to perpetuate rather than ameliorate the problems?

16. In terms of practical costs to society as well as personal costs to homeless men (via denying their present worth and affirming their status as deviants in attempting to rehabilitate or resocialize them), might it not be better to 1. leave them alone or 2. provide "no-strings-attached" sustenance and medical care in lieu of the expensive existing social control programs whose utility *for the homeless man* is open to serious question? Under this plan "re-formation" would be left to the men themselves and to organizations in the wider society whose function is the socialization of adults who seek it.

17. If the skid row men had a say in the kind of facilities and treatment available to them, what would they choose? What would be the effects of giving them, as a group, some say in the direction of the changes now, for the most part, imposed upon them? To what extent would they be willing to participate in such decision making, if it were made easy for them?

18. How can alcoholism rehabilitation programs be restructured to allow a maximum of choice to the client, and to permit systematic evaluation so that ineffective programs can be identified?

19. How can ineffective programs which for traditional, professional, or other reasons have been instituted and maintained, be shut down entirely or replaced with more effective programs?

20. Is it cheaper to society to allow men to "vegetate" comfortably than to insist on tying participation in rehabilitation programs to their lodging and food? Are the "rehabilitation" rates for facilities which merely provide sustenance and voluntary recreation, counseling, and medical attention lower than for programs which attempt to "remake" the men?

21. How can skid row men be motivated to establish affiliations,

to exert influence effectively, and thereby to increase their control over their social and physical environment?

22. How might rehabilitation agencies be restructured to avoid the sense of continual failure, or even to produce enough legitimate "successes" so that both the social control agents and the homeless men they serve could know that "redemption" was more than an outside possibility?

Notes

Chapter 1

1. Larry Van Gelder, "The Bowery: Tragedy in the Rain," *New York Herald Tribune,* December 15, 1966, p. 29.
2. Charles Wright, "Men's Municipal Shelter: Life Under the Underside," *The Village Voice,* June 20, 1968, pp. 20, 22.
3. "Relief Problems of Bowery Rising," *New York Times,* November 3, 1964, p. 33.
4. George Nash, *The Habitats of Homeless Men in Manhattan,* New York: Columbia University, Bureau of Applied Social Research, 1964, p. D-16.
5. David McReynolds, "The Bowery: A Ghetto Without a Constituency," *The Village Voice,* December 5, 1968, p. 26.
6. Arthur Steuer, "A Dollar a Bed," *New York Herald Tribune,* September 20, 1964, pp. 15-16.
7. Patricia Nash, *The Methodology of the Study of Bowery Lodging Houses,* New York: Columbia University, Bureau of Applied Research, 1964, p. 30.
8. *Ibid.* p. 34.

Chapter 2

1. Theodore Caplow, Howard M. Bahr, and David Sternberg, "Homelessness," in David Sills, ed., *International Encyclopedia of the Social Sciences,* New York: Macmillan, 1968, Vol. 6, pp. 494-99.
2. Elfan Rees, "The Refugee and the United Nations," *International Conciliation,* 492 (June 1953), p. 313.
3. Gillin remarks that "begging is a phenomenon of civil, not of savage, societies," noting that early human societies had no beggars. J. L. Gillin, "Vagrancy and Begging," *American Journal of Sociology,* 35 (No-

vember 1929), p. 424. Vexliard also asserts that begging and vagrancy did not exist in primitive, preliterate societies, nor in ancient societies previous to the urban civilization of the city-states and the institution of private property. Alexandre Vexliard, *Introduction a la sociologie du vagabondage*, Paris: Librairie Marcel Riviere et Cie, 1956, p. 9.

4. Harlan W. Gilmore, *The Beggar*, Chapel Hill: University of North Carolina Press, 1940, p. 7.

5. Homer, *The Odyssey*, Ennis Rees, trans., New York: Random House, 1960, p. 290.

6. Gillin, *loc. cit.* p. 425.

7. Vexliard, *op. cit.* p. 28.

8. Gillin, *loc. cit.* p. 426; see also John Cooke, "Vagrants, Beggars, and Tramps," *Quarterly Review*, 209 (October 1908), pp. 389-90.

9. Gilmore, *op. cit.* pp. 13-14.

10. *Ibid.* pp. 18-22.

11. Homer, *op. cit.* pp. 238, 293.

12. Matthew, 6:19; Luke, 9:58.

13. Philip O'Connor, *Britain in the Sixties: Vagrancy*, Baltimore: Penguin Books, 1963, p. 22.

14. Gilmore, *op. cit.* pp. 16-17. For an extensive discussion of the influence of religion in English wandering life of the Middle Ages, see J. J. Jusserand, *English Wayfaring Life in the Middle Ages,* New York: Putnam, 1950, 4th ed. A comprehensive survey of the orders of St. Francis is Alexandre Masseron and Marion A. Habig, *The Franciscans*, Chicago: Franciscan Herald Press, 1959.

15. Daisetz Teitaro Suzuki, *Essays in Zen Buddhism,* New York: Grove Press, 1949, pp. 351-52. See also Albert Edwards, "The Beggars of Mogador," *The Outlook*, 101 (August 24, 1912), p. 931.

16. Karl Ludvig Reichelt, *Truth and Tradition in Chinese Buddhism,* Shanghai: Commercial Press, 1927, p. 228.

17. Edward J. Thomas, *The History of Buddhist Thought,* London: Kegan Paul, Trench, Trubner; New York: Alfred A. Knopf, 1933, p. 11.

18. Reichelt, *op. cit.,* pp. 231-33.

19. Gideon Sjoberg, *The Preindustrial City*, Glencoe: Free Press, 1960, pp. 258-59.

20. *Ibid.* p. 259.

21. *Ibid.* pp. 133-35.

22. *Ibid.* p. 140.

23. *Ibid.* pp. 158, 159.

24. *Ibid.* p. 160.

25. *Ibid.* p. 160.

26. *Ibid.* p. 137.

27. Jerome K. Myers and Bertram H. Roberts, *Family and Class Dynamics in Mental Illness,* New York: John Wiley, 1959, p. 172.

28. *Ibid.* pp. 174, 176.

29. *Ibid.* pp. 184-85.

30. Ephraim Harold Mizruchi, *Success and Opportunity*, New York: Free Press of Glencoe, 1964, pp. 112-13; Genevieve Knupfer, "Portrait of the Underdog," *Public Opinion Quarterly*, 11 (Spring 1947), pp. 103-14. Reprinted in Reinhard Bendix and Seymour Martin Lipset, *Class Status and Power*, Glencoe: The Free Press, 1953, pp. 255-63.
31. *Ibid.* p. 256.
32. Albert K. Cohen and Harold M. Hodge, Jr., "Characteristics of the Lower-Blue-Collar-Class," *Social Problems*, 10 (Spring 1963), p. 315.
33. *Ibid.* pp. 316-17.
34. Mizruchi, *op. cit.* p. 112; See also August B. Hollingshead, *Social Class and Mental Illness*, New York: John Wiley, 1958, p. 122.
35. Cohen and Hodge, *loc. cit.* pp. 323-24.
36. Hollingshead, *op. cit.* p. 130.
37. Nechama Tec and Ruth Granick, "Social Isolation and Difficulties in Social Interaction of Residents of a Home for Aged," *Social Problems*, 7 (Winter 1959-60), pp. 226-32.
38. Robert S. Lynd and Helen M. Lynd, *Middletown in Transition: A Study in Cultural Conflicts*, New York: Harcourt, Brace, 1937, p. 467.
39. Malcolm J. Proudfoot, *European Refugees, 1939-1952*, London: Faber and Faber, 1957, pp. 53, 446. John Hope Simpson, *The Refugee Problem*, Oxford, England: Clarendon Press, 1939, pp. 3-4.
40. K. C. Cirtautas, *The Refugee: A Psychological Study*, Boston: Meador, 1957, pp. 29-39.
41. Elfan Rees, *loc. cit.* pp. 277-78.
42. Margaret Mary Wood, *Paths of Loneliness*, New York: Columbia University Press, 1953, p. 27.
43. Henry Mayhew, *London Labor and the London Poor*, New York: Harper and Brothers, 1851, p. 438.
44. Sidney D. Gamble and John Stewart Burgess, *Peking: A Social Survey*, New York: George H. Doran, 1921.
45. Madge C. Jenison, "Germany's Tramp Workmen," *Harper's Weekly*, 55 (October 14, 1911), p. 15.
46. C. J. Ribton-Turner, *A History of Vagrants and Vagrancy and Beggars and Begging*, London: Chapman and Hall, 1887, p. 315.
47. See Louisa R. Shotwell, *The Harvesters*, Garden City: Doubleday, 1961.
48. Frances Jerome Woods, *Cultural Values of American Ethnic Groups*, New York: Harper and Brothers, 1956, p. 174.
49. U.S. Department of Labor, *Farm Labor Fact Book*, U.S. Government Printing Office, 1959, p. 110.
50. Shotwell, *op. cit.* pp. 35, 37.
51. Noel P. Gist and Sylvia Fleis Fava, *Urban Society*, New York: Thomas Y. Crowell, 1964, p. 368.
52. See, for example, Wallace's designation of homeless men as those who participate in the institutions of skid row. Samuel E. Wallace, *Skid Row as a Way of Life*, Totowa, N.J.: Bedminster Press, 1965.
53. Caplow *et al.*, *op. cit.* p. 494; see also Howard M. Bahr, ed., *Disaffiliated*

Man: Essays and Bibliography on Skid Row, Vagrancy, and Outsiders, Toronto: University of Toronto Press, 1970, pp. 39-50.

54. William F. Gleason, *The Liquid Cross of Skid Row,* Milwaukee: Bruce, 1966, p. 137.

55. Floyd Hunter, *Community Power Structure: A Study of Decision Makers,* Chapel Hill: University of North Carolina Press, 1953, p. 80; Amos H. Hawley, "Community Power and Urban Renewal Success," *American Journal of Sociology,* 68 (January 1963), p. 422; Robert M. MacIver, *Power Transformed,* New York: Macmillan, 1964, p. 110; Hans Gerth and C. Wright Mills, trans., *From Max Weber: Essays in Sociology,* New York: Oxford University Press, 1946, p. 180; C. Wright Mills, *The Power Elite,* New York: Oxford University Press, 1959, p. 9; Katherine Organski and A. F. K. Organski, *Population and World Power,* New York: Alfred A. Knopf, 1961, p. 9.

56. Gerth and Mills, *op. cit.* pp. 180-81; MacIver, *op. cit.* p. 81.

57. Hawley, *loc. cit.* p. 423.

58. *Ibid.*; Robert Presthus, *Men at the Top,* New York: Oxford University Press, 1964, pp. 6-7.

59. Ernest A. T. Barth and Baha Abu-Laban, "Power Structure and the Negro Sub-Community," *American Sociological Review,* 24 (February 1959), p. 74.

60. Lee E. Doerries, "Purpose in Life and Social Participation," *Journal of Individual Psychology,* 26 (May 1970), pp. 50-53.

61. Robert E. Park, "The Mind of the Hobo: Reflections Upon the Relation Between Mentality and Locomotion," in Robert E. Park, Ernest W. Burgess, and Roderick D. McKenzie, *The City,* Chicago: University of Chicago Press, 1925, pp. 156-60.

62. Arthur Bonner, *Jerry McAuley and His Mission,* Neptune, N.J.: Loizeaux Brothers, 1967, p. 11.

63. Logan L. Thomas, "Report on the Greater New York Gospel Mission," Research Bureau, Welfare Council of New York City, September, 1931, pp. 4-5.

64. *Ibid.* p. 5.

65. Bonner, *op. cit.* p. 43.

66. Donald J. Bogue, *Skid Row in American Cities,* Chicago: Community and Family Center, University of Chicago, 1963, p. 1.

67. Wallace, *op. cit.* pp. 96-97.

68. Leonard U. Blumberg, Thomas E. Shipley, Jr., and Joseph O. Moor, Jr., "The Skid Row Man and the Skid Row Status Community," *Quarterly Journal of Studies on Alcohol,* 32 (December 1971), p. 912.

69. *Ibid.* pp. 909-29.

70. Bonner, *op. cit.* p. 102.

71. James F. Rooney, "Societal Forces and the Unattached Male: An Historical Review," in Bahr, ed., *Disaffiliated Man,* p. 18.

72. Wallace, *op. cit.* pp. 13-25; Rooney, *op. cit.* pp. 28-34. For other histories of skid row neighborhoods see Elmer Bendiner, *The Bowery*

Man, New York: Thomas Nelson and Sons, 1961; Alvin F. Harlow, *Old Bowery Days,* New York: D. Appleton, 1931; and portions of Kenneth Allsop, *Hard Travellin': The Hobo and His History,* New York: New American Library, 1968. See also the journalistic, historical, and literary accounts cited in Bahr, ed., *Disaffiliated Man,* pp. 281-317.
73. Wallace, *op. cit.* p. 25; Rooney, *op. cit.* p. 34.
74. Earl Rubington, "The Changing Skid Row Scene," *Quarterly Journal of Studies on Alcohol,* 32 (March 1971), pp. 131-34.
75. *Ibid.* p. 133.

Chapter 3
1. Leonard Blumberg and Thomas E. Shipley, Jr., review of James P. Spradley *You Owe Yourself a Drunk* and Jacqueline P. Wiseman, *Stations of the Lost, American Journal of Sociology,* 76 (March 1971), p. 962.
2. Samuel E. Wallace, *Skid Row as a Way of Life,* Totowa, N.J.: Bedminster Press, 1965, p. 130.
3. Howard M. Bahr, "Homelessness, Disaffiliation, and Retreatism," in Howard M. Bahr, ed., *Disaffiliated Man: Essays and Bibliography on Skid Row, Vagrancy, and Outsiders,* Toronto: University of Toronto Press, 1970, p. 46.
4. Lewis Mumford, *The Culture of Cities,* New York: Harcourt, Brace, 1938, p. 29.
5. Barnard L. Collier, "Down and Out on the Bowery: How it Feels," *New York,* May 12, 1969, p. 26.
6. *Ibid.*
7. Mrs. Cecil Chesterton, *In Darkest London,* London: Stanley Paul, 1920, pp. 72-73.
8. Joan K. Jackson and Ralph Connor, "The Skid Road Alcoholic," *Quarterly Journal of Studies on Alcohol,* 14 (September 1953), p. 468.
9. *Ibid.* p. 478.
10. Robert A. Scott, "The Construction of Conceptions of Stigma by Professional Experts," in Jack D. Douglas, ed., *Deviance and Respectability: The Social Construction of Moral Meanings,* New York: Basic Books, 1970, pp. 255-90.
11. *Ibid.* p. 268.
12. *Ibid.* p. 273.
13. *Ibid.* p. 277.
14. *Ibid.* p. 280.
15. *Ibid.* pp. 284-85.
16. Jacqueline P. Wiseman, "Benefactors, Beneficiaries, Compassion, Gratitude and Trust: Forms of Social Relationship Between the Helper and the Helped," *Stations of the Lost: The Treatment of Skid Row Alcoholics,* Englewood Cliffs, N.J.: Prentice-Hall, 1970, pp. 239-68.
17. *Ibid.* p. 268.

18. Stanley K. Henshaw, *Camp LaGuardia: A Voluntary Total Institution for Homeless Men,* New York: Bureau of Applied Social Research, Columbia University, 1968, pp. 153-59.

19. David J. Pittman and Duff G. Gillespie, "Social Policy as Deviancy Reinforcement: The Case of the Public Intoxication Offender," in David J. Pittman, ed., *Alcoholism,* New York: Harper and Row, 1967, p. 117.

20. Wiseman, *op. cit.* pp. 133-42, 147-54.

21. *Ibid.* pp. 134-35.

22. *Ibid.* p. 150.

23. *Ibid.* p. 154.

24. Kenneth Allsop, *Hard Travellin': The Hobo and His History,* New York: New American Library, p. 416.

25. Margaret B. Bailey and Estelle Fuchs, "Alcoholism and the Social Worker," *Social Work,* 5 (October 1960), pp. 15-16.

26. *Ibid.* p. 18.

27. Margaret B. Bailey, "Attitudes toward Alcoholism Before and After a Training Program for Social Caseworkers," *Quarterly Journal of Studies on Alcohol,* 31 (September 1970), p. 674.

28. *Ibid.* p. 674.

29. Irving Wolf, Morris E. Chafetz, Howard T. Blane and Marjorie J. Hill, "Social Factors in the Diagnosis of Alcoholism," *Quarterly Journal of Studies on Alcohol,* 26 (March 1965), pp. 72-79.

30. Paul Devenyi, "Medical Treatment and Study of Alcoholism," *Addictions,* 15 (Winter 1968), pp. 2-3. Emphasis added.

31. Philip O'Connor, *Britain in the Sixties: Vagrancy,* Baltimore: Penguin Books, 1963, p. 150.

32. *Ibid.* p. 160.

33. *Ibid.* p. 168.

34. *Ibid.* p. 175.

35. *Ibid.* pp. 177-79.

36. *Ibid.* pp. 184-85.

37. *Ibid.* pp. 185-86.

38. "Pullman Girl Describes Chicago Experiences," *The Pullman Herald,* December 7, 1967, p. 12.

39. McCandlish Phillips, "Street Beggars Called Blot on City," *New York Times,* November 27, 1964, p. 37.

40. Emanuel Perlmutter, "IRT to Abandon 42nd St. Arcade, Called Breeding Place of Crime," *New York Times,* January 22, 1964, p. 39.

41. Thomas Furey, "Wave of Bums Sweeps Over Parks, Streets," *New York World Telegram and Sun,* November 1, 1961, pp. 1, 3.

42. "Skid Row Cleanup," *Wall Street Journal,* February 14, 1967, pp. 1, 17.

43. McCandlish Phillips, "Bus Terminal at Night: A Derelict's Haven," *New York Times,* January 8, 1967, p. 1.

44. *Ibid.* p. 65.

45. Helen Sutton, " 'House of Horrors' on Way Out," *New York Journal-American,* September 3, 1964, p. 2.
46. " 'Village' Angered by Rising Number of Derelicts in Washington Square," *New York Times,* September 21, 1964, p. 33.
47. "Park Derelicts Worry Officials," *New York Times,* January 13, 1965, p. 29.
48. "Park Patrols to Get Plainclothes Details and More Scooters," *New York Times,* February 8, 1965, p. 27.
49. *New York Times,* May 7, 1967, p. 13.
50. J. Anthony Lukas, "Security Widened at Soviet Mission After Arrest," *New York Times,* June 22, 1967, pp. 1, 14.
51. "Mr. Z.," *Newsweek,* June 12, 1967, p. 33.
52. Herbert R. Mayes, "Trade Winds," *Saturday Review,* March 9, 1968, p. 16.
53. The questionnaire was designed and distributed by George Nash. Martha Gershun analyzed the data and prepared the unpublished memorandum for the Homelessness Project conducted at the Bureau of Applied Social Research. The present summary is based on the memorandum.
54. H. J. Wahler, "Winning and Losing in Life: A Survey of Opinions about Causes," *Mental Hygiene,* 55 (January 1971), pp. 91-95.
55. *Ibid.* pp. 94-95.
56. *The New Yorker Album, 1925-1950,* New York: Harper, 1951.
57. *The New Yorker,* 37 (March 11, 1961), p. 138.
58. *The New Yorker,* 38 (November 3, 1962), p. 111.
59. *The Saturday Evening Post,* 232 (April 15, 1961), p. 117.
60. *The New Yorker,* 38 (September 1, 1962), p. 38.
61. *The New Yorker 1950-1955 Album,* New York: Harper & Brothers, 1955.
62. *The New Yorker,* 38 (October 13, 1962), p. 57.
63. *The New Yorker,* 42 (August 27, 1966), p. 31.
64. *Saturday Review,* 50 (March 4, 1967), p. 18.
65. *The New Yorker 1950-1955 Album,* New York: Harper & Brothers, 1955.
66. *The New Yorker,* 38 (May 12, 1962), p. 36.
67. *The New Yorker 1950-1955 Album,* New York: Harper & Brothers, 1955.
68. *The New Yorker,* 38 (September 22, 1962), p. 35.
69. Morrie Brickman, "The Small Society," *Seattle Post Intelligencer,* November 23, 1966, p. 6.
70. *The New Yorker,* 37 (April 15, 1961), p. 46.
71. *The New Yorker,* 38 (November 17, 1962), p. 47.
72. *The New Yorker,* 38 (May 19, 1962), pp. 44-45.
73. *The New Yorker 1950-1955 Album,* New York: Harper & Brothers, 1955.
74. *Saturday Evening Post,* 232 (March 19, 1960), p. 42.

75. *The New Yorker 1950-1955 Album,* New York: Harper & Brothers, 1955; *The New Yorker,* 39 (April 6, 1963), p. 44.
76. *The New Yorker,* 42 (June 18, 1966), p. 36.
77. *The New Yorker,* 38 (August 25, 1962), p. 26.
78. *The New Yorker,* 37 (March 18, 1961), p. 36.
79. *Saturday Evening Post,* 234 (January 28, 1961), p. 84.
80. *The New Yorker,* 39 (June 1, 1963), p. 27.
81. *The New Yorker,* 39 (August 31, 1963), p. 29.
82. *The New Yorker 1950-1955 Album,* New York: Harper & Brothers, 1955.
83. *The New Yorker,* 39 (March 2, 1963), p. 39.
84. *The New Yorker 1950-1955 Album,* New York: Harper & Brothers, 1955.
85. *The New Yorker,* 37 (February 18, 1961), p. 43.
86. *The New Yorker,* 38 (June 2, 1962), pp. 36-37.
87. *The New Yorker,* 38 (September 29, 1962), p. 35.
88. *The New Yorker 1950-1955 Album,* New York: Harper & Brothers, 1955.
89. *The New Yorker,* 38 (July 28, 1962), p. 27.
90. *The New Yorker 1950-1955 Album,* New York: Harper & Brothers, 1955.
91. *Saturday Evening Post,* 232 (February 20, 1960), p. 40.
92. *Saturday Evening Post,* 232 (January 23, 1960), p. 46.
93. *The New Yorker,* 42 (April 30, 1966), p. 39.
94. *The New Yorker,* 43 (February 18, 1967), p. 150.
95. *The New Yorker,* 39 (June 22, 1963), p. 26.
96. *The New Yorker 1950-1955 Album,* New York: Harper & Brothers, 1955.
97. *The New Yorker,* 42 (June 4, 1966), p. 142.
98. *The New Yorker,* 42 (May 7, 1966), p. 131.
99. *The New Yorker,* 39 (September 14, 1963), p. 169.
100. *The New Yorker,* 37 (August 12, 1961), p. 29.
101. *Saturday Review,* 49 (August 6, 1966), p. 4.
102. Wallace, *op. cit.* p. 130.
103. Ruth Fox, "Alcoholism in 1966. (Editor's Notebook)," *American Journal of Psychiatry,* 123 (September, 1966), pp. 337-38.
104. Paul W. Haberman and Jill Sheinberg, "Public Attitudes Toward Alcoholism as an Illness," *American Journal of Public Health,* 59 (July 1969), pp. 1210-11.
105. *Ibid.* pp. 1211-12.
106. *Ibid.* pp. 1213-15.
107. Gerald Globetti, "Social Acceptance of the Recovered Alcoholic," *Inventory: A Quarterly Journal on Alcohol and Alcoholism,* 18 (October-December 1968), p. 30.
108. Arnold S. Linsky, "The Changing Public Views of Alcoholism," *Quarterly Journal of Studies on Alcohol,* 31 (September 1970), pp. 694-95.

109. *Ibid.* p. 697.
110. *Ibid.* p. 701.
111. *Ibid.*
112. Thomas S. Szasz, "Alcoholism: A Socio-Ethical Perspective," *Washburn Law Journal,* 6 (1967), pp. 255-68.
113. *Ibid.* p. 260. In a recent novel Saul Bellow deals with the labeling phenomenon in a similar vein: "And I'm convinced that knowing the names of things braces people up. I've gone to shrinkers for years, and have they cured me of anything? They have not. They have put labels on my troubles, though, which sound like knowledge. It's a great comfort, and worth the money. You say, 'I'm manic.' Or you say, 'I'm a reactive-depressive.' You say about a social problem, 'It's colonialism.' Then the dullest brain has internal fireworks, and the sparks drive you out of your skull. It's divine. You think you're a new man. Well, the way to wealth and power is to latch on to this. When you set up a new enterprise, you redescribe the phenomena and create a feeling that we're getting somewhere." Saul Bellow, *Mr. Sammler's Planet,* New York: Fawcett World Library, 1970, p. 92.
114. Szasz, *loc. cit.* p. 262.
115. *Ibid.* p. 268.
116. Linsky, *loc. cit.* p. 703.

Chapter 4

1. Donald J. Bogue, *Skid Row in American Cities,* Chicago: Community and Family Study Center, University of Chicago, 1963, p. 2.
2. Leonard U. Blumberg *et al., The Men on Skid Row,* Philadelphia: Department of Psychiatry, Temple University School of Medicine, 1960, p. 41.
3. Howard M. Bahr, *Homelessness and Disaffiliation,* New York: Bureau of Applied Social Research, Columbia University, p. 409.
4. National Assistance Board, *Homeless Single Persons,* London: Her Majesty's Stationery Office, 1966, pp. 50, 93, 114, 154.
5. Blumberg *et al., op. cit.* p. 35; Bahr, *op. cit.* pp. 89, 306.
6. Bogue, *op. cit.* p. 109.
7. Blumberg *et al., op. cit.* p. 36; Theodore Caplow, Keith A. Lovald, and Samuel E. Wallace, *A General Report on the Problem of Relocating the Population of the Lower Loop Redevelopment Area,* Minneapolis: Minneapolis Housing and Redevelopment Authority, 1958, p. 72.
8. Alice Willard Solenberger, *One Thousand Homeless Men,* New York: Charities Publication Committee, 1911, p. 22.
9. National Assistance Board, *op. cit.* pp. 107, 114, 153.
10. Blumberg *et al., op. cit.* p. 35; Caplow *et al., op. cit.* p. 73; Bogue, *op. cit.* p. 108.
11. Bogue, *op. cit.* p. 371.
12. *Ibid.* pp. 368-71; Bahr, *op. cit.* pp. 198-99.

13. Bahr, *op. cit.* pp. 199-200.
14. Caplow *et al., op. cit.* pp. 99-100.
15. Bogue, *op. cit.* p. 10.
16. Blumberg, *op. cit.* pp. 73-76.
17. *Ibid.* p. 78.
18. Bahr, *op. cit.* pp. 89-90, 307.
19. Bert Shulimson and Kate Clair, "A Social Survey of the Federal-Anderson Project Area," Pittsburgh: Community Services Section, Comprehensive Planning Division, Department of City Planning, Pittsburgh, Pennsylvania, November 1965, pp. 3, 6-7; Bogue, *op. cit.* p. 102.
20. Samuel E. Wallace, *Skid Row as a Way of Life,* Totowa, N.J.: Bedminster Press, 1965, pp. 86-87.
21. James P. Spradley, *You Owe Yourself a Drunk: An Ethnography of Urban Nomads,* Boston: Little, Brown and Company, 1970, p. 256.
22. Nels Anderson, *Men on the Move,* Chicago: University of Chicago Press, 1940; Kenneth Allsop, *Hard Travellin': The Hobo and His History,* New York: New American Library, 1967. See also works cited in "Employment and Unemployment" and "Skid Row and its Men," Howard M. Bahr, ed., *Disaffiliated Man: Essays and Bibliography on Skid Row, Vagrancy, and Outsiders,* Toronto: University of Toronto Press, 1970, pp. 94-143, 318-39.
23. Howard M. Bahr, "The Gradual Disappearance of Skid Row," *Social Problems,* 15 (Summer 1967), p. 43.
24. Western Real Estate Research, *Analysis of the Sacramento Labor Market Area,* Sacramento: Redevelopment Agency of the City of Sacramento, 1957.
25. Bogue, *op. cit.* pp. 176-82.
26. *Ibid.* pp. 179-80.
27. *Ibid.* p. 188.
28. National Assistance Board, *op. cit.* pp. 52-53, 90-91, 121-22, 156-57.
29. Bogue, *op. cit.* p. 197.
30. Solenberger, *op. cit.* pp. 36, 38, 44.
31. See Solenberger, *op. cit.* pp. 88-111, in which she devoted an entire chapter to "The Insane, Feeble-minded, and Epileptic."
32. *Ibid.* pp. 88-89.
33. Eric Hoffer, *The Ordeal of Change,* New York: Harper and Row, 1964, pp. 139-40.
34. *Ibid.* p. 141.
35. *Ibid.* pp. 142-43.
36. *Ibid.* p. 148.
37. James F. Rooney, "Societal Forces and the Unattached Male: An Historical Review," in Bahr, ed., *Disaffiliated Man,* p. 33.
38. *Ibid.* p. 34.
39. F. E. Feeney, D. F. Mindlin, V. H. Minear, and E. E. Short, "The Challenge of the Skid Row Alcoholic: A Social, Psychological and Psychiatric Comparison of Chronically Jailed Alcoholics and Cooperative Al-

coholic Clinic Patients," *Quarterly Journal of Studies on Alcohol,* 16 (December 1955), pp. 658-59.

40. *Ibid.* p. 661.
41. *Ibid.* p. 658.
42. Edwin H. Sutherland and Harvey J. Locke, *Twenty Thousand Homeless Men,* Chicago: J. B. Lippincott, 1936, pp. 42-43.
43. Bogue, *op. cit.* pp. 199-223.
44. *Ibid.* p. 214.
45. Blumberg *et al., op. cit.* pp. 89, 91.
46. Caplow, Lovald, and Wallace, *op. cit.* pp. 170, 173.
47. Feeney *et al., op. cit.* p. 658.
48. Bogue, *op. cit.* p. 207.
49. Blumberg *et al., op. cit.* p. 89; Caplow *et al., op. cit.* p. 170.
50. William F. Gleason, *The Liquid Cross of Skid Row,* Milwaukee: Bruce, p. 38.
51. See, for example, much of Bogue's *Skid Row in American Cities.* His fivefold drinking classification (teetotaler, light drinker, moderate drinker, heavy drinker, and alcoholic derelict) is applied throughout the book, and his sections on "Extent of Problem Drinking and Alcoholic Dereliction on Skid Row" (pp. 90-93) and a chapter "Drinking Behavior" (pp. 272-304) are especially relevant. See also "The Bars," in Wallace, *op. cit.* pp. 69-76; David J. Pittman and C. Wayne Gordon, *Revolving Door: A Study of the Chronic Police Case Inebriate,* Glencoe: Free Press, 1958, pp. 59-77; Earl Rubington, "The Bottle Gang," *Quarterly Journal of Studies on Alcohol,* 29 (December 1968), pp. 943-55; James F. Rooney, "Group Processes Among Skid Row Winos," *Quarterly Journal of Studies on Alcohol,* 22 (September 1961), pp. 444-60; Joan K. Jackson and Ralph Connor, "The Skid Road Alcoholic," *Quarterly Journal of Studies on Alcohol,* 14 (September 1953), pp. 468-86; W. Jack Peterson and Milton A. Maxwell, "The Skid Road 'Wino'," *Social Problems,* 5 (Spring 1958), pp. 308-16; Robert Straus and Raymond G. McCarthy, "Nonaddictive Pathological Drinking Patterns of Homeless Men," *Quarterly Journal of Studies on Alcohol,* 12 (December 1951), pp. 601-11; Robert Straus, "Alcohol and the Homeless Man," *Quarterly Journal of Studies on Alcohol,* 7 (December 1946), pp. 360-404; Richard F. Docter, "Drinking Practices of Skid Row Alcoholics," *Quarterly Journal of Studies on Alcohol,* 28 (December 1967), pp. 700-708.
52. Figures for the Bowery, Camp LaGuardia, Philadelphia, Chicago, and Minneapolis are reported in Howard M. Bahr, "Lifetime Affiliation Patterns of Early- and Late-Onset Heavy Drinkers on Skid Row," *Quarterly Journal of Studies on Alcohol,* 30 (September 1969), pp. 649-50.
53. Stanley K. Henshaw, *Camp LaGuardia: A Voluntary Total Institution for Homeless Men,* New York: Bureau of Applied Social Research, Columbia University, 1968, p. 130.
54. Bahr, *Homelessness and Disaffiliation,* pp. 266-67.

55. Elmer Bendiner, *The Bowery Man,* New York: Thomas Nelson and Sons, 1961, p. 90.
56. Western Real Estate Research, *op. cit.* Table P-2.
57. Jacqueline P. Wiseman, *Stations of the Lost: The Treatment of Skid Row Alcoholics,* Englewood Cliffs, N.J.: Prentice-Hall, 1970, p. 290; Bogue, *op. cit.* pp. 106-8.
58. Bahr, *Homelessness and Disaffiliation,* pp. 86-87, 302.
59. James F. Rooney, "The Shortage of Negroes on Skid Row," unpublished manuscript.
60. Bogue, *op. cit.* p. 108; Caplow *et al., op. cit.* p. 25; Blumberg *et al.,* p. 11; and Bahr, *Homelessness and Disaffiliation,* pp. 87-88, 303.
61. Bahr, *Homelessness and Disaffiliation,* pp. 72-73.
62. Bahr, *Homelessness and Disaffiliation,* pp. 75-77, 297.
63. Bogue, *op. cit.* pp. 232-33.
64. Pittman and Gordon, *loc. cit.* pp. 24, 27.
65. Blumberg *et al., op. cit.* pp. 23-24.
66. Caplow *et al., op. cit.* pp. 79-82.
67. Bogue, *op. cit.* p. 110.
68. Bahr, *Homelessness and Disaffiliation,* pp. 98, 308.
69. John C. Hotten, trans., *The Book of Vagabonds and Beggars: With a Vocabulary of their Language* (*Liber Vagatorium*), Martin Luther, ed., in 1528, London: John Camden Hotten, 1860.
70. Nels Anderson, *The Hobo: The Sociology of the Homeless Man,* Chicago: University of Chicago Press, 1923, pp. 87, 89.
71. *Ibid.* pp. 93-94.
72. *Ibid.* p. 98.
73. *Ibid.* pp. 102-3.
74. Bogue, *op. cit.* pp. 48-49.
75. *Ibid.* pp. 96-99.
76. Jackson and Connor, *loc. cit.* pp. 469-70.
77. Boris M. Levinson, "The Homeless Man: A Psychological Enigma," *Mental Hygiene,* 47 (October 1963), p. 596.
78. *Ibid.* pp. 597-98.
79. *Ibid.* p. 597.
80. *Ibid.* p. 599.
81. Spradley, *op. cit.* pp. 65-70, 79.
82. *Ibid.* pp. 71-78.
83. *Ibid.* pp. 81-92.
84. Wallace, *op. cit.* pp. 180-81, 187-88.
85. *Ibid.* pp. 198-99.
86. *Ibid.* pp. 201-2.
87. Samuel E. Wallace, "The Road to Skid Row," *Social Problems,* 16 (Summer 1968), pp. 92-105.
88. Bahr, ed., *Disaffiliated Man,* p. 41.
89. *Ibid.* pp. 41-42.

Chapter 5

1. George Nash and Patricia Nash, *A Preliminary Estimate of the Population and Housing of the Bowery in New York City,* New York: Bureau of Applied Social Research, Columbia University, 1964.

2. Samuel E. Wallace, *Skid Row as a Way of Life,* Totowa, N.J.: Bedminster Press, 1965, pp. 32-46.

3. Patricia Nash, "Homeless Men at Home," Bureau of Applied Social Research, Columbia University, 1965, pp. 37-38. An unpublished memorandum on the homelessness project.

4. Theodore Caplow, Keith A. Lovald, and Samuel E. Wallace, *A General Report on the Problem of Relocating the Population of the Lower Loop Redevelopment Area,* Minneapolis: Minneapolis Housing and Redevelopment Authority, 1958, p. 133.

5. Donald J. Bogue, *Skid Row in American Cities,* Chicago: University of Chicago Community and Family Study Center, 1963, pp. 135, 138, 142-43.

6. Leonard U. Blumberg *et al., The Men on Skid Row,* Philadelphia: Department of Psychiatry, Temple University School of Medicine, 1960, pp. 157, 159, 161-65.

7. Nash, *op. cit.*

8. Elmer Bendiner, *The Bowery Man,* New York: Thomas Nelson and Sons, 1961, pp. 23-24.

9. Bogue's list of agencies in Chicago that help homeless men included eleven religious organizations, a few of which were only casework or referral agencies. Most were gospel missions. The eleven were the Cathedral Shelter, the Catholic Charities of Chicago, the Chicago Christian Industrial League, the Chicago Gospel Mission, the Chicago United Mission, the Lutheran Home Rescue Mission, the Olive Branch Mission, the Pacific Garden Mission, the Salvation Army Harbor Light Center, the Salvation Army Men's Social Service Center, and the Sunshine Gospel Mission. See Bogue, *op. cit.* pp. 424-38.

10. See Wallace, *op. cit.* pp. 49-67; Bogue, *op. cit.* pp. 418-38; Bendiner, *op. cit.* pp. 104-17; Jacqueline P. Wiseman, *Stations of the Lost: The Treatment of Skid Row Alcoholics,* Englewood Cliffs, N.J.: Prentice-Hall, 1970, pp. 167-214; Nels Anderson, *Men on the Move,* Chicago: University of Chicago Press, 1940, pp. 250-62; Howard John Clinebell, Jr., "Some Religious Approaches to the Problem of Alcoholism," Columbia University, 1954, unpublished doctoral dissertation; Melvin G. Larson, *Skid Row Stopgap: The Memphis Story,* Wheaton, Illinois: Van Kempen Press, 1950; Arthur Bonner, *Jerry McAuley and his Mission,* Neptune, New Jersey: Loizeaux Brothers, 1967; Tom Kromer, *Waiting for Nothing,* New York: Alfred A. Knopf, 1935.

11. Wiseman, *op. cit.* p. 172.

12. *Ibid.* pp. 191-205.

13. Bonner, *op. cit.* p. 114.

14. Bogue, *op. cit.* p. 432.

15. Wiseman, *op. cit.* p. 187.

16. Kromer, *op. cit.* pp. 178-84.

17. Bendiner, *op. cit.* p. 39.

18. George Nash, "Bowery Bars," Bureau of Applied Social Research, Columbia University, 1964, an unpublished memorandum written for the Bowery Project; Matthew P. Dumont, "Tavern Culture, The Sustenance of Homeless Men," *American Journal of Orthopsychiatry,* 37 (October 1967), pp. 938-45. See also Sherri Cavan, *Liquor License: An Ethnography of Bar Behavior,* Chicago: Aldine, 1966; Boyd Macrary, "The Tavern and the Community," *Quarterly Journal of Studies on Alcohol,* 13 (December 1952), pp. 609-37. For historical perspective, two papers about the social functions of Chicago saloons are of interest. See Royal L. Melendy, "The Saloon in Chicago," *American Journal of Sociology,* 6 (November 1900 and January 1901), pp. 289-306, 433-64; E. C. Moore, "Social Value of the Saloon," *American Journal of Sociology,* 3 (July 1897), pp. 1-12.

19. George Nash, *op. cit.* pp. 41-45; Dumont, *op. cit.* pp. 12-14.

20. Bogue, *op. cit.* pp. 273-78.

21. Dumont, *op. cit.* p. 941.

22. G. Nash, *op. cit.* p. 50.

23. *Ibid.* p. 51. See Kromer, *op. cit.* pp. 59-74 for a first-person account of the exchange between homeless man and homosexual.

24. G. Nash, *op. cit.* p. 55.

25. *Ibid.* pp. 148-50.

26. A New York reporter passed as a homeless man for a day and reported his experiences with employment agencies and jobs in, Barnard Collier, "Down and Out on the Bowery: How it Feels," *New York,* May 12, 1969, pp. 24-29; information about working for Labor-Aides is drawn from George Nash, "A Spot Job Center," Bowery Project, Bureau of Applied Social Research, Columbia University, 1964, unpublished project memorandum.

27. Wallace, *op. cit.* pp. 84-86.

28. *Ibid.* pp. 109-21.

29. Collier, *loc. cit.* p. 26.

30. Edmund G. Love, *Subways Are for Sleeping,* New York: Harcourt-Brace, 1956.

31. New York *Journal-American,* December 24, 1961.

32. George Nash, *The Habitats of Homeless Men in Manhattan,* New York: Bureau of Applied Social Research, Columbia University, 1964, p. E-44.

33. *Ibid.* p. E-46.

34. *Ibid.* pp. E-45–E-47.

35. Marlene Nadle, "A Little Light at the Bottom of the Stairs," *The Village Voice,* Thursday, March 2, 1967, p. 1.

36. James F. Rooney, "Group Processes Among Skid Row Winos," *Quar-*

terly Journal of Studies on Alcohol, 22 (September 1961), pp. 444-60.

37. *Ibid.* pp. 449-50.

38. *Ibid.* p. 451.

39. *Ibid.* p. 453.

40. *Ibid.* p. 459.

41. *Ibid.* p. 453.

42. *Ibid.* p. 456.

43. *Ibid.* p. 457.

44. William F. Gleason, *The Liquid Cross of Skid Row,* Milwaukee: Bruce Publishing, 1966, p. 176.

45. Joan K. Jackson and Ralph Connor, "The Skid Road Alcoholic," *Quarterly Journal of Studies on Alcohol,* 14 (September 1953), p. 475.

46. William Jack Peterson, "The Culture of the Skid Road Wino," State College of Washington, 1955, p. 83, unpublished master's thesis.

47. W. Jack Peterson and Milton A. Maxwell, "The Skid Road 'Wino'," *Social Problems,* 5 (Spring 1958), p. 309.

48. *Ibid.* p. 311.

49. *Ibid.* pp. 313-14.

50. Earl Rubington, "The Bottle Gang," *Quarterly Journal of Studies on Alcohol,* 29 (December 1968), pp. 943-55.

51. *Ibid.* pp. 947-48.

52. *Ibid.* pp. 952-54.

53. Gleason, *op. cit.* pp. 176-77.

54. Jackson and Connor, *loc. cit.* p. 473.

55. Wallace, *op. cit.* pp. 184-85.

56. *Ibid.* p. 185.

57. *Ibid.* p. 184.

58. Bogue, *op. cit.* p. 273.

59. See Sherri Cavan's discussion of bar sociability in Cavan, *op. cit.* pp. 49-66. Also see Erving Goffman, *Behavior in Public Places,* New York: Free Press, 1963, pp. 131-32.

60. Cavan, *op. cit.* pp. 49-66.

61. George Nash, "Bowery Bars," Bowery Project, Bureau of Applied Social Research, Columbia University, 1964, pp. 20-21, unpublished project memorandum.

62. Theodore Caplow, transcript of Homelessness Project staff meeting, Bureau of Applied Research, February 25, 1965.

63. Bogue, *op. cit.* pp. 143-44.

64. *Ibid.* p. 144.

65. *Ibid.* p. 148.

66. *Ibid.* p. 153.

67. Western Real Estate Research, *Analysis of the Sacramento Labor Market Area,* Sacramento: Redevelopment Agency of the City of Sacramento, 1957, p. P-7.

68. Blumberg *et al., op. cit.* p. 39.

69. Patricia Nash, "Homeless Men at Home," Bowery Project, Bureau of Applied Social Research, Columbia University, 1965, pp. 34, 37-39, unpublished project memorandum.
70. *Ibid.* p. 39.
71. G. Nash, *The Habitats of Homeless Men in Manhattan,* p. A-10.
72. Stanley K. Henshaw, *Camp LaGuardia: A Voluntary Total Institution for Homeless Men,* New York: Columbia University, Bureau of Applied Social Research, 1968, p. 113.
73. Wiseman, *op. cit.* p. 28.
74. *Ibid.* p. 39.
75. Jackson and Connor, *loc. cit.* p. 474.
76. James F. Rooney, "Race Relations on Skid Row," unpublished manuscript.
77. *Ibid.*
78. *Ibid.* p. 9.
79. Gleason, *op. cit.* p. 36.
80. Rooney, "Race Relations on Skid Row," p. 16.
81. Keith Arthur Lovald, "From Hobohemia to Skid Row: The Changing Community of the Homeless Man," University of Minnesota, 1960, p. 426, unpublished doctoral dissertation.
82. Rooney, "Race Relations on Skid Row," p. 20.
83. *Ibid.* pp. 31-32.
84. Wiseman, *op. cit.* p. 29.
85. G. Nash, *Habitats of Homeless Men in Manhattan,* p. E-40.
86. Bendiner, *op. cit.* pp. 27-28.

Chapter 6

1. M. J. Cramer, "A Survey of the Backgrounds and Attitudes of 100 Inmates of the Massachusetts Correctional Institution for Women at Framingham, Massachusetts," Report to the division of legal medicine, Office of the Commissioner on Alcoholism, and the Department of Corrections, 1969 (mimeographed). See also M. J. Cramer and Edward Blacker, "Early and Late Problem Drinkers Among Female Prisoners," *Journal of Health and Human Behavior,* 4 (Winter 1963), pp. 282-90; Cramer and Blacker, "Social Class and Drinking Experience of Female Drunkenness Offenders," *Journal of Health and Human Behavior,* 7 (Winter 1966), pp. 276-83.
2. A. Geracimos, "Where Do the Ladies Go? Distaff on Skid Row," *The Village Voice* (June 15, 1967), pp. 17, 40.
3. Margery Haring, *Out of Community: A Report on the Homeless People Project,* New York: Quaker Project on Community Conflict, 1967.
4. Theodore Caplow, Keith A. Lovald, and Samuel E. Wallace, *A General Report on the Problem of Relocating the Population of the Lower Loop Redevelopment Area,* Minneapolis: The Minneapolis Housing and Redevelopment Authority, 1958, p. 21.

5. Leonard U. Blumberg *et al.*, *The Men on Skid Row*, Philadelphia: Department of Psychiatry, Temple University School of Medicine, 1960.

6. Donald J. Bogue, *Skid Row in American Cities*, Chicago: Community and Family Study Center, University of Chicago, 1963, p. 14.

7. President's Commission on Law Enforcement and Administration of Justice, *Task Force Report: Drunkenness*, Washington: U.S. Government Printing Office, 1967; Chicago Committee on Alcoholism, "Survey of Alcoholism," *Quarterly Journal of Studies on Alcohol*, 16 (December 1955), p. 619.

8. The critical foci in defining homelessness are not "area of residence" or "economic status," but rather family and kinship ties, friendship constellations, and organizational participation. See Howard M. Bahr, *Homelessness and Disaffiliation*, New York: Columbia University, Bureau of Applied Social Research, 1968; and *Disaffiliated Man: Essays and Bibliography on Skid Row, Vagrancy, and Outsiders*, Toronto: University of Toronto Press, 1970. Several investigators have implied that homeless people exist off skid row but have confined their observations to skid row itself. See Bogue, *op. cit.*; Alice Willard Solenberger, *One Thousand Homeless Men: A Study of Original Records*, New York: Russell Sage Foundation, 1911.

9. Edith Lisansky, "Alcoholism in Women: Social and Psychological Concommitants," *Quarterly Journal of Studies on Alcohol*, 18 (December 1957), pp. 588-623.

10. B. Rosenbaum, "Married Women Alcoholics at the Washingtonian Hospital," Boston University School of Social Work, 1956, unpublished masters thesis; Cramer, *op. cit.*; T. Fort and Austin Porterfield, "Some Backgrounds and Types of Alcoholism Among Women," *Journal of Health and Human Behavior*, 2 (Winter 1961), pp. 283-92; Cramer and Blacker, "Early and Late Problem Drinkers Among Female Prisoners," pp. 276-83; M. W. Johnson, J. C. DeVries, and M. J. Houghton, "The Female Alcoholic," *Nursing Research*, 15 (September 1966), pp. 343-47; Barry A. Kinsey, *The Female Alcoholic: A Social Psychological Study*, Springfield, Illinois: Charles C Thomas, 1966. Surveys of drinking patterns of females include, J. W. Riley and C. F. Marden, "The Social Pattern of Alcoholic Drinking," *Quarterly Journal of Studies on Alcohol*, 8 (September 1947), pp. 265-73; J. W. Riley, C. F. Marden, and M. Lifshitz, "The Motivational Pattern of Drinking Based on the Verbal Responses of a Cross Section Sample of Users of Alcoholic Beverages," *Quarterly Journal of Studies on Alcohol*, 9 (June 1948), pp. 353-62; Harold A. Mulford, "Drinking and Deviant Drinking, U.S.A., 1963," *Quarterly Journal of Studies on Alcohol*, 25 (December 1964), pp. 634-43.

11. Illustrative examples of comparative research are the works of K. W. Wanberg and J. L. Horn, "Alcoholic Symptom Patterns of Men and Women: A Comparative Study," *Quarterly Journal of Studies on Alcohol*, 31 (March 1970), pp. 40-61; M. F. Newman and J. R. Hilgard,

"Alcoholism in Men Sometimes an Alternative to Schizophrenia in Women?" *Psychiatry Digest,* 28 (July 1967), pp. 33-37; G. Winokur and P. J. Clayton, "Family History Studies: Comparison of Male and Female Alcoholics," *Quarterly Journal of Studies on Alcohol,* 29 (December 1968), pp. 885-91.

12. Lisansky, *loc. cit.*

13. H. Massot and D. Massot, "Alcoolisme Feminin: Donnes Statistiques et Psychopathologuiques," *Journal of Medical Lyon,* 37 (1956), pp. 265-69.

14. H. P. Wood and E. L. Duffy, "Psychological Factors in Alcoholic Women," *American Journal of Psychiatry,* 123 (September 1966), pp. 341-45.

15. Manfred Bleuler, "Familial and Personal Backgrounds of Chronic Alcoholics," in Oskar Diethelm, ed., *Etiology of Chronic Alcoholism,* Springfield, Illinois: Charles C Thomas, 1955, pp. 110-66; Giorgio Lolli, "Alcoholism in Women," *The Connecticut Review of Alcoholism,* 5 (1953), pp. 9-11; P. Berner and W. Solms (*Quarterly Journal of Studies on Alcohol,* 15 (1954), p. 15.) Abstract of "Alkoholismus bei Frauen," *Wien Z. Nervenheilk* (1954), pp. 430-32; Rosenbaum, *op. cit.* pp. 79-89; R. J. Van Amberg, "A Study of 50 Women Patients Hospitalized for Alcohol Addiction," *Diseases of the Nervous System,* 4 (1943), pp. 246-51.

16. Cramer and Blacker, "Early and Late Problem Drinkers Among Female Prisoners."

17. Kinsey, *op. cit.*

18. R. Gordon Bell, "Alcohol and Loneliness," *Journal of Social Therapy,* 2 (June 1956), pp. 171-81.

19. Kinsey, *op. cit.* pp. 94-95.

20. Cramer and Blacker, "Early and Late Problem Drinkers Among Female Prisoners"; Wood and Duffy, *loc. cit.;* M. J. Sherfey, "Psychopathology and Character Structure in Chronic Alcoholism," in Oskar Diethelm, ed., *Etiology of Chronic Alcoholism*; J. H. Wall, "A Study of Alcoholism in Women," *American Journal of Psychiatry,* 93 (January 1937), pp. 943-55.

21. Johnson *et al., loc. cit.*

22. A number of interesting studies have evaluated the relationship between alcoholic offspring and family background. Notable among these are investigations by C. Amark ["A Study in Alcoholism: Clinical Social-Psychiatric and Genetic Investigation," *Acta Psychiatric Neurology,* 70 (Scandinavian supplement), pp. 1-283] who compared brothers and sisters of male alcoholics to the general population; and L. Kaij ["Studies on the Etiology and Sequels of Abuse of Alcohol," University of Lund, 1960, unpublished Ph.D. dissertation], who examined identical and fraternal twins with reference to a genetic background of alcoholism. Findings in both studies support the claim that alcoholism tends to run in family lines.

23. Joseph Mayer and M. Green, "Group Therapy of Alcoholic Women Ex-Prisoners," *Quarterly Journal of Studies on Alcohol,* 28 (September 1967), pp. 493-504; and B. Rosenbaum, "Married Women Alcoholics at the Washingtonian Hospital," *Quarterly Journal of Studies on Alcohol,* 19 (March 1958), pp. 79-89.

24. Kinsey, *op. cit.*

25. Massot and Massot, *loc. cit.;* Lolli, *loc. cit.;* Lisansky, *loc. cit.*

26. Wood and Duffy, *loc. cit.*

27. Lisansky, *loc. cit.;* Rosenbaum, *op. cit.* (1956); Lolli, *loc. cit.*

28. Kinsey, *op. cit.*

29. *Ibid.* pp. 85-88.

30. Rosenbaum, *loc. cit.* (1958).

31. Lisansky, *loc. cit.*

32. Kinsey, *op. cit.*

33. Rosenbaum, *loc. cit.* (1958).

34. E. M. Jellinek, "Phases in the Drinking History of Alcoholics. Analysis of a Survey Conducted by the Official Organ of Alcoholics Anonymous," *Quarterly Journal of Studies on Alcohol,* 7 (March 1946), pp. 1-88.

35. Albert D. Ullman, "Sex Differences in the First Drinking Experience," *Quarterly Journal of Studies on Alcohol,* 18 (June 1957), pp. 229-39.

36. Cramer, *op. cit.*

37. Lisansky, *loc. cit.*

38. E. M. Hughes, "Problem Alcoholics in a State Mental Hospital and on Parole," *Journal of Psychopathology,* 6 (1945), pp. 551-70.

39. Albert D. Ullman, "The First Drinking Experience of Addictive and 'Normal' Drinkers," *Quarterly Journal of Studies on Alcohol,* 14 (March 1953), pp. 181-91.

40. Kinsey, *op. cit.* p. 81.

41. Cramer and Blacker, "Social Class and Drinking Experience of Female Drunkenness Offenders."

42. E. H. Fort, "A Preliminary Study of Social Factors in the Alcoholism of Women," Texas Christian University (1949), unpublished M.A. thesis.

43. Wall, *op. cit.*

44. Lolli, *loc. cit.* pp. 9-11.

45. Rosenbaum, *loc. cit.* (1958).

46. M. W. Johnson, "Physicians' Views on Alcoholism: With Special Reference to Alcoholism in Women," *Nebraska State Medical Journal,* 50 (July 1965), pp. 378-84.

47. Benjamin Karpman, *Alcoholism in Women,* Washington, D.C.: Linacre Press (1956), p. vii.

48. *Ibid.* p. vii; see also Lolli, *loc. cit.* pp. 9-11; G. Deshaies, "L'alcoolisme de la Femme," *Review Alcoolisme,* 9 (1963), pp. 235-47.

49. Edith Lisansky, "The Woman Alcoholic," *Annals of the American Academy of Political and Social Science,* 315 (January 1958), pp. 73-81.

50. Joan Curlee, "Women Alcoholics," *Federal Probation,* 32 (March 1968), pp. 16-20. Kinsey, *op. cit.;* Joseph Hirsh, "Women and Alcoholism," in W. C. Bier, ed., *Problems in Addiction,* New York: Fordham University Press, 1962. W. Schmidt and J. DeLint ["Mortality Experience of Male and Female Patients," *Quarterly Journal of Studies on Alcohol Supplement A* (March 1969), pp. 112-18] report that clinicians are more likely to diagnose alcoholism as a severe psychopathology for women than for men. Wolfgang Schmidt, Reginald Smart, and Marcia Moss [*Social Class and the Treatment of Alcoholism: An Investigation of Social Class as a Determinant of Diagnosis, Prognosis, and Therapy,* Toronto: University of Toronto Press (1968)] also have documented the importance of social class as a factor in the diagnosis of alcoholism.

51. Horn and Wanberg, *loc. cit.;* K. Wanberg and J. Knapp, "Differences in Drinking Symptoms and Behavior of Men and Women Alcoholics," *British Journal of Addiction* 64 (1970), pp. 347-55; Lisansky, "Alcoholism in Women"; Lisansky, "The Woman Alcoholic"; Kinsey, *op. cit.*

52. Cramer and Blacker, "Social Class and Drinking Experience of Female Drunkenness Offenders."

53. Lisansky, "Alcoholism in Women: Social and Psychological Concommitants."

54. Wall, *loc. cit.*

55. Lisansky, "Alcoholism in Women: Social and Psychological Concommitants."

56. Kinsey, *op. cit.*

57. K. Abraham, "The Psychological Relations Between Sexuality and Alcoholism," in K. Abraham, ed., *Selected Papers,* London: Hogarth Press, 1927; O. Fenichel, *The Psychoanalytic Theory of Neurosis,* New York: Norton, 1945.

58. Horn and Wanberg, *loc. cit.;* Wanberg and Knapp, *loc. cit.*

59. Kinsey, *op. cit.*

60. Fort, *op. cit.*

61. Johnson, *et al., loc. cit.*

62. *Ibid.*

63. Cramer and Blacker, "Early and Late Problem Drinkers Among Female Prisoners."

64. Rosenbaum, *op. cit.* (1958); Kinsey, *op. cit.*

65. Robert MacIver, *The Ramparts We Guard,* New York: Macmillan, 1950, p. 18.

66. Richard Jessor, Theodore D. Graves, Robert C. Hanson, and Shirley L. Jessor, *Society, Personality, and Deviant Behavior,* New York: Holt, Rinehart, and Winston, 1968; P. Park, "Problem Drinking and Role Deviation," in D. Pittman and C. Snyder, eds., *Society, Culture, and Drinking Patterns,* New York: John Wiley and Sons, 1962, pp. 431-54.

67. Fictitious names have been used.

Chapter 7

1. William Harbutt Dawson, *The Vagrancy Problem,* London: P. S. King and Son, 1910; Robert Menzies Fergusson, *The Vagrant: What to do with Him,* London: James Nisbet, 1911; Edmond Kelly, *The Elimination of the Tramp,* New York: G. P. Putnam's Sons, 1908; *The Unemployables,* London: P. S. King and Son, 1907.

2. John J. McCook, "The Tramp Problem: What It Is and What to do With It," *Proceedings of the Twenty-Second National Conference of Charities and Correction* (1895), pp. 288-301.

3. Edward Devine, "The Shifting and Floating City Population," *Annals of the American Academy of Political and Social Science,* 10 (September 1897), pp. 149-64.

4. Jason F. Jackson, "The Rural Tramp," *Proceedings of the Thirtieth National Conference of Charities and Correction* (1903), pp. 401-4.

5. Louis Paulian, *Paris qui mendie: Mal et remedi,* Paris: Ollendorf, 1893.

6. Levi L. Barbour, "Vagrancy," *Proceedings of the Eighth Annual Conference of Charities and Correction* (1881), pp. 131-38; Charles Rolleston, "Mischievous Charity," *Westminster Review,* 163 (February 1905), pp. 148-55; "Social Parasites," *Westminster Review,* 162 (December 1904), pp. 623-32.

7. Kelly, *The Unemployables.*

8. Alice C. Willard, "Reinstatement of Vagrants Through Municipal Lodging Houses," *Proceedings of the National Conference of Charities and Correction* (1903), pp. 404-11.

9. Paulian, *op. cit.*

10. Glenn H. Johnson, *Relief and Health Problems of a Selected Group of Non-Family Men,* Chicago: University of Chicago Press, 1937.

11. William J. Plunkert, "Skid Row Can Be Eliminated," *Federal Probation,* 25 (June 1961), pp. 41-44.

12. Eugene Bertram Willard, "Psychopathic Vagrancy," *Welfare Magazine,* 19 (May 1928), pp. 565-73.

13. Jonathan Weiss, "The Law and the Poor," *Journal of Social Issues,* 26 (Number 3, 1970), pp. 59, 60-61.

14. *Ibid.* pp. 60-65.

15. See Geoffrey C. Hazard, Jr., "Legal Problems Peculiar to the Poor," *Journal of Social Issues,* 26 (Number 3, 1970), pp. 47-58.

16. Burr C. Hollister, "Alcoholics and Public Drunkenness: The Emerging Retreat from Punishment," *Crime and Delinquency,* 16 (July 1970), p. 242.

17. Richard J. Driver, "The United States Supreme Court and the Chronic Drunkenness Offender," *Quarterly Journal of Studies on Alcohol,* 30 (March 1969), pp. 165-73.

18. See for example, *ibid.*; Hollister, *loc. cit.*; and, with respect to the problems of attempting to link legal reform with the disease concept of alcoholism, Herbert Fingarette, "The Perils of Powell: In Search of a Factual Foundation for the Disease Concept of Alcoholism," *Harvard*

Law Review, 83 (February 1970), pp. 793-812. For a discussion of Canadian legislation relevant to the treatment of chronic alcoholism, see R. F. Reid, "Alcohol: Problems and Recent Legislation," *University of Toronto Law Journal,* 18 Number 1 (1968), pp. 87-97.

19. Hollister, *loc. cit.* pp. 243-46.

20. Federal Bureau of Investigation, *Crime in the United States: Uniform Crime Reports—1969,* Washington, D.C.: U.S. Government Printing Office, 1970, pp. 111, 122.

21. Jacqueline P. Wiseman, *Stations of the Lost: The Treatment of Skid Row Alcoholics,* Englewood Cliffs, N.J.: Prentice-Hall, 1970, p. 65.

22. The President's Commission on Law Enforcement and Administration of Justice, *Task Force Report: Drunkenness,* Washington, D.C.: U.S. Government Printing Office, 1967, p. 1; Wiseman, *op. cit.* p. 65.

23. The President's Commission on Law Enforcement and Administration of Justice, *op. cit.* p. 1.

24. James P. Spradley, *You Owe Yourself a Drunk,* Boston: Little, Brown, and Company, 1970, p. 11.

25. The President's Commission on Law Enforcement and Administration of Justice, *op. cit.* p. 2.

26. Egon Bittner, "The Police in Skid-Row: A Study of Peace Keeping," *American Sociological Review,* 32 (October 1967), pp. 699-715.

27. *Ibid.* p. 704.

28. *Ibid.* p. 705.

29. *Ibid.* pp. 705-6.

30. *Ibid.* p. 706.

31. *Ibid.* p. 707.

32. *Ibid.* p. 708.

33. *Ibid.* p. 709.

34. *Ibid.* p. 710.

35. *Ibid.* p. 711.

36. *Ibid.* p. 713.

37. *Ibid.*

38. *Ibid.* p. 714.

39. P. J. Giffen, "The Revolving Door: A Functional Interpretation," *The Canadian Review of Sociology and Anthropology,* 3 (August 1966), p. 155.

40. *Ibid.* p. 156.

41. Wiseman, *op. cit.* p. 88.

42. *Ibid.* pp. 86-100.

43. *Ibid.* p. 100.

44. David J. Pittman and C. Wayne Gordon, *Revolving Door: A Study of the Chronic Police Case Inebriate,* Glencoe: Free Press, 1958, p. 42.

45. The President's Commission on Law Enforcement and Administration of Justice, *op. cit.* p. 3.

46. Spradley, *op. cit.*

47. *Ibid.* p. 128. Emphasis added.

48. *Ibid.* p. 133.
49. *Ibid.* pp. 133-39.
50. James P. Spradley, "The Moral Career of a Bum," *Trans-Action,* 7 (May 1970), p. 19; see Spradley, *You Owe Yourself a Drunk,* p. 149, for a slightly different wording.
51. *Ibid.* pp. 191-92.
52. Spradley, "The Moral Career of a Bum," p. 29.
53. Giffen, *loc. cit.* p. 156.
54. *Ibid.* p. 159.
55. *Ibid.*
56. The President's Commission on Law Enforcement and Administration of Justice, *op. cit.* p. 3.
57. Eva Maria Blum and Richard H. Blum, *Alcoholism: Modern Psychological Approaches to Treatment,* San Francisco: Jossey-Bass, 1967.
58. *Ibid.* p. 314.
59. Greater Philadelphia Movement, "What to Do About the Men on Skid Row: Report of the Greater Philadelphia Movement to the Redevelopment Authority of the City of Philadelphia," January 1961, p. 7.
60. *Ibid.* p. 11.
61. Blum and Blum, *op. cit.* pp. 236-38.
62. *Ibid.* p. 237.
63. *Ibid.* p. 236.
64. James F. Rooney, "Societal Forces and the Unattached Male: An Historical Review," in Howard M. Bahr, ed., *Disaffiliated Man: Essays and Bibliography on Skid Row, Vagrancy, and Outsiders,* Toronto: University of Toronto Press, 1970, pp. 31-34.
65. Joan Shapiro, "The Slum Hotel: An Arena for Group Work with Urban Rejects," Dallas, Texas, May 24, 1967, a paper presented at the National Conference on Social Welfare; see also "The World of 207," New York: New York City Housing and Redevelopment Board, February, 1966 (mimeographed).
66. Joan Shapiro, "Single-Room Occupancy: Community of the Alone," *Social Work,* 11 (October 1966), pp. 24-33.
67. Joan Shapiro, "Charismatic Leaders Among Slum Hotel Residents," a paper read at the New York District Branches Divisional Meeting of the American Psychiatric Association, in New York City, November 17, 1967.
68. Earl Rubington, "Alcoholic Control on Skid Row," *Crime and Delinquency* (October 1967), pp. 531-37.
69. Blum and Blum, *op. cit.* pp. 159, 236.
70. Wiseman, *op. cit.*; see also Lawrence Katz, "The Salvation Army Men's Social Service Center: I. Program," *Quarterly Journal of Studies on Alcohol,* 25 (June 1964), pp. 324-32; "The Salvation Army Men's Social Service Center: II. Results," *Quarterly Journal of Studies on Alcohol,* 27 (March 1966), pp. 636-47. Katz states that admission to the Centers depends on a potential client's willingness to take part in the

therapy programs and on his having an identifiable and treatable handicap.

71. Wiseman, *op. cit.* pp. 171-81.

72. Katz, "The Salvation Army Men's Social Service Center: II. Results."

73. Wilfred Boothroyd, Gordon Bell, G. H. Ettinger, William Hall, Irwin Hilliard, Ian MacDonald, and J. L. Silversides, "Medical Care of the Alcoholic Patient," *The Canadian Medical Association Journal,* 95 (August 27, 1966), pp. 407-9.

74. Richard Bates, "The Sparrow Hospital Program," *Inventory: A Quarterly Journal on Alcohol and Alcoholism,* 17 (January-March 1968), pp. 21-25.

75. *Ibid.* p. 25.

76. Richard C. Bates, "Medical Treatment of Alcoholism," *Inventory: A Quarterly Journal on Alcohol and Alcoholism,* 17 (January-March 1968), pp. 16-19, 25. For descriptions of alcoholism treatment programs in other general hospitals, see, for example, Anthony J. Matkom, "An Alcoholic Treatment Center in a General Hospital," *Quarterly Journal of Studies on Alcohol,* 30 (June 1969), pp. 453-57; Jack D. Gordon, "The Alcoholic Patient," *Hospitals,* 44 (May 16, 1970), pp. 63-64; James H. Dunn and Margaret L. Clay, "Physicians Look at a General Hospital Alcoholism Service," *Quarterly Journal of Studies on Alcohol,* 32 (March 1971), pp. 162-67. A caution that emergency hospital care may simply produce another kind of "revolving door" is given in Abraham Gelperin and Eve Arlin Gelperin, "The Inebriate in the Emergency Room," *American Journal of Nursing,* 70 (July 1970), pp. 1494-97. They plead for a comprehensive community-based program, not merely a hospital program.

77. William P. Rohan, "A Follow-up Study of Hospitalized Problem Drinkers," *Diseases of the Nervous System,* 31 (April 1970), p. 5.

78. *Ibid.* pp. 5-6.

79. *Ibid.* p. 2.

80. Blum and Blum, *op. cit.* pp. 152-53.

81. Wiseman, *op. cit.* pp. 129-47.

82. *Ibid.* p. 147.

83. Charles H. McCaghy, James K. Skipper, Jr., and James D. Bruce, "Evaluation of a Short-Term Treatment Program for Potential Chronic Police Case Inebriates," a report of research supported by the State of Ohio Department of Health Research Project Grant No. 29-R-67, July 1970 (mimeographed).

84. *Ibid.* p. 11.

85. *Ibid.* p. 32.

86. *Ibid.* pp. 39-40.

87. *Ibid.* p. 40.

88. The description of Camp LaGuardia which follows is based on Stanley K. Henshaw, *Camp LaGuardia: A Voluntary Total Institution for*

Homeless Men, New York: Bureau of Applied Social Research, Columbia University, 1968, pp. 1-2, 14-15, 23-32, 43-46, 106-43.

89. Bureau of Shelter Services for Adults, "Shelter Care Treatment Center (Operation Bowery) Annual Report, September 3, 1968–September 2, 1969," New York: Department of Social Services, Shelter Care Treatment Center, 1969, pp. 6-7.

90. Henshaw, *op. cit.* p. 46.

91. *Ibid.* p. 113.

92. *Ibid.* p. 125.

93. D. F. Collier, R. G. Walsh, and G. Oki, *Bon Accord: Milieu Therapy for Public Inebriates,* Toronto: Alcoholism and Drug Addiction Research Foundation, 1969, p. 3. The period reported is 1967-69, and the description does not represent fully the present program. The Alcoholism and Drug Addiction Foundation is now preparing a report on an intensive research year (1971-72) at Bon Accord.

94. *Ibid.* pp. 17-18.

95. *Ibid.* pp. 18, 44.

96. *Ibid.* p. 55.

97. *Ibid.* p. 115.

98. Spradley, *op. cit.*

99. Raymond T. Nimmer, "St. Louis Diagnostic and Detoxification Center: An Experiment in Non-Criminal Processing of Public Intoxicants," *Washington University Law Quarterly,* 1970 (Winter 1970), pp. 5-7.

100. *Ibid.* p. 15.

101. Lee Berton, "Skid Row Cleanup: Some Big Cities Switch from Arresting Drunks to Try Rehabilitation," *Wall Street Journal,* February 14, 1967, p. 1.

102. Nimmer, *loc. cit.* p. 18.

103. *Ibid.* See also Raymond T. Nimmer, "The Public Drunk: Formalizing the Police Role as a Social Help Agency," *Georgetown Law Journal,* 58 (June 1970), pp. 1089-1115.

104. Nimmer, "St. Louis Diagnostic and Detoxification Center," p. 21.

105. *Ibid.* p. 23.

106. *Ibid.* pp. 24-27.

107. Richard J. Tatham, "Detoxification Center: A Public Health Alternative to the 'Drunk Tank'," *Federal Probation* 33 (December 1969), p. 47.

108. Richard J. Tatham, "Detoxification Center—A Public Health Alternative to the Police Drunk Tank," Portland, Oregon, September 12, 1969, paper presented at Good Samaritan Hospital.

109. *Ibid.*

110. Tatham, "Detoxification Center: A Public Health Alternative to the 'Drunk Tank'," pp. 47-48.

111. *In Lieu of Arrest: The Manhattan Bowery Project Treatment for Homeless Alcoholics,* New York: The Criminal Justice Coordinating

Council of New York City and Vera Institute of Justice (no date, c. 1969).

112. Staff of the Manhattan Bowery Project, "First Annual Report of the Manhattan Bowery Project," April 1969, p. 33 (mimeographed).

113. *Ibid.* p. 37.

114. *Ibid.* pp. 39-40.

115. See, for example, Ernest W. Goldsborough and Wilbur E. Hobbs, "The Petty Offender," *The Prison Journal,* 36 (April 1956); Ronald C. Vanderkooi, *Relocating West Madison "Skid Row" Residents: A Study of the Problem, with Recommendations,* Chicago: Chicago Department of Urban Renewal, 1967; New York City Welfare and Health Council, Committee of Alcoholism, Board of Visitors of Hart Island, "The Hart Island Program for Alcoholics in New York City," *Quarterly Journal of Studies on Alcohol,* 14 (March 1953), pp. 140-46. Earl Rubington, "The Chronic Drunkenness Offender," *Annals of the American Academy of Political and Social Science,* 315 (January 1958), pp. 65-72.

116. Robert Martinson, "The California Recovery House: A Sanctuary for Alcoholics," *Mental Hygiene,* 48 (July 1964), pp. 432-38.

117. David J. Myerson and Joseph Mayer, "Origins, Treatment and Destiny of Skid-Row Alcoholic Men," *New England Journal of Medicine,* 275 (August 25, 1966), pp. 419-25.

118. *Ibid.* p. 425.

119. Barry Leach, John L. Norris, Travis Daney, and LeClair Bissell, "Dimensions of Alcoholics Anonymous: 1935-1965," *The International Journal of the Addictions,* 4 (December 1969), pp. 507-41.

120. *Ibid.* pp. 508-509.

121. M. K. Bacon, H. Barry III, and I. L. Child, "A Cross-Cultural Study of Drinking: II. Relations to Other Features of Culture, *Quarterly Journal of Studies on Alcohol,* Supplement No. 3 (1965), p. 46.

122. Irving Peter Gellman, *The Sober Alcoholic: An Organizational Analysis of Alcoholics Anonymous,* New Haven: College and University Press, 1964; Morris Chafetz and Harold W. Demone, *Alcoholism and Society,* New York: Oxford University Press, 1962; *Alcoholics Anonymous Comes of Age: A Brief History of A.A.,* New York: Alcoholics Anonymous Publishing, 1957. See also the excellent bibliography in Leach *et al., op. cit.*

123. Harrison M. Trice and Paul Michael Roman, "Delabeling, Relabeling, and Alcoholics Anonymous," *Social Problems,* 17 (Spring 1970), pp. 538-46.

124. Harrison M. Trice and Paul Michael Roman, "Sociopsychological Predictors of Successful Affiliation with Alcoholics Anonymous," *Social Psychiatry,* 5 (Winter 1970), pp. 51-59.

125. Earl Rubington, "Drug Culture and Treatment Outcome: The HARP Project," *International Journal of the Addictions,* 4 (September 1969), p. 333.

126. *Ibid.* pp. 334-35.

127. *Ibid.* p. 335.
128. *Ibid.* pp. 336-37.
129. David J. Pittman, "The Role of Sociology in the Planning and Operation of Alcoholism Treatment Programs," *British Journal of Addictions,* 59 (1963), pp. 35-39.
130. Blum and Blum, *op. cit.* pp. 261-72.
131. *Ibid.* pp. 270-72.
132. Theodore Caplow, "The Sociologist and the Homeless Man," in Bahr, ed., *Disaffiliated Man,* pp. 8-9.
133. Reginald G. Smart, "The Evaluation of Alcoholism Treatment Programs," *Addictions,* 17 (Spring 1970), p. 42.
134. *Ibid.* pp. 42-43. See also W. L. Voegtlin and F. Lemere, "The Treatment of Alcohol Addiction: A Review of the Literature," *Quarterly Journal of Studies on Alcohol,* 2 (March 1942), pp. 717-803; and M. Hill and H. T. Blane, "Evaluation of Psychotherapy with Alcoholics: A Critical Review," *Quarterly Journal of Studies on Alcohol,* 28 (March 1967), pp. 76-104.
135. Smart, *loc. cit.* p. 43.
136. Allan E. Bergin, "Some Implication of Psychotherapy Research for Therapeutic Practice," *Journal of Abnormal Psychology,* 71 (August 1966), pp. 235-46.
137. Toby Levinson and G. Sereny, "An Experimental Evaluation of 'Insight Therapy' for the Chronic Alcoholic," *Canadian Psychiatric Association Journal,* 14 (April 1969), p. 144.
138. Robert F. Chapman, Warren K. Garlington, and Kenneth E. Lloyd, "A Critical Review of Learning Based Treatments of Alcoholism," paper presented at the State of Washington Alcohol Research Group Meeting, Seattle, October 1969.
139. *Ibid.*
140. S. G. Laverty, "Aversion Therapies in the Treatment of Alcoholism," *Psychosomatic Medicine,* 28 (July-August 1966), p. 664.
141. *Ibid.* p. 663.
142. R. S. Wallerstein, "Comparative Study of Treatment Methods for Chronic Alcoholism," *American Journal of Psychiatry,* 113 (September 1956), p. 228. A comparable success rate has been reported among skid row alcoholics in Atlanta, Georgia. After nine months, approximately half of the groups of voluntary and involuntary patients were still taking disulfiram. See Peter G. Bourne, James A. Alfor, and James Z. Bowcock, "Treatment of Skid-Row Alcoholics with Disulfiram," *Quarterly Journal of Studies on Alcohol,* 27 (March 1966), pp. 42-48.
143. C. G. Costello, "An Evaluation of Aversion and LSD Therapy in the Treatment of Alcoholism," *Canadian Psychiatric Association Journal,* 14, Number 1, p. 35.
144. E. Mansell Pattison, E. B. Headley, G. C. Gleser, and L. A. Gottschalk, "Abstinence and Normal Drinking," *Quarterly Journal of Studies on Alcohol,* 29 (September 1968), pp. 610-33; E. Mansell Pattison, "A

Critique of Alcoholism Treatment Concepts; with Special Reference to Abstinence," *Quarterly Journal of Studies on Alcohol,* 27 (March 1966), pp. 49-71.

145. Laverty, *loc. cit.* p. 664.

146. E. Mansell Pattison, Ronald Coe, and Robert J. Rhodes, "Evaluation of Alcoholism Treatment," *Archives of General Psychiatry,* 20 (April 1969), pp. 477-88.

147. Pattison, Headley, Gleser, and Gottschalk, *loc. cit.* p. 633.

148. *Ibid.* pp. 620-21, 628.

149. *Ibid.* pp. 627, 630.

150. Pattison, Coe, and Rhodes, *loc. cit.* pp. 478-88.

151. *Ibid.* pp. 478, 479. See also E. Mansell Pattison, A Brissenden, and T. Wohl, "Assessing Specific Effects of Inpatient Group Therapy," *International Journal of Group Psychotherapy,* 17 (July 1967), pp. 283-97.

152. Benjamin Kissin, Arthur Platz, and Wen Huey Su, "Social and Psychological Factors in the Treatment of Chronic Alcoholism," *Journal of Psychiatric Research,* 8 (1970), pp. 13-27.

153. It is of interest that individuals who dropped out of the treatment program, that is, those who rejected treatment, had a success rate twice as high as that of the control group. Kissin *et al.* [*ibid.*] suggest that the control group might have had their recovery rate affected by feelings of "rejection" because their peers were receiving treatment and they were not.

154. *Ibid.* p. 26.

155. Smart, *loc. cit.* pp. 45-46.

156. Robert J. Gibbons and John D. Armstrong, "Effects of Clinical Treatment on Behavior of Alcoholic Patients: An Exploratory Methodological Investigation," *Quarterly Journal of Studies on Alcohol,* 18 (September 1957), pp. 429-51.

Chapter 8

1. Colin Wilson, *The Outsider,* New York: Dell, 1956, p. 147.

2. Samuel E. Wallace, *Skid Row as a Way of Life,* Totowa, N.J.: Bedminster Press, 1965, p. 130.

3. *Ibid.* pp. 149-54.

4. Stephen Crane, *The Black Riders and Other Lines,* Boston: Copeland and Day, 1896, p. 10.

5. *Newsweek,* February 17, 1964, p. 26.

6. Robert Adleman, "Where Will Larry Go?" *The Sunday Bulletin,* Philadelphia, June 21, 1964, pp. 1, 6.

7. Ed Wallace, "Sign of the Hojac Hovers Over Bowery," *New York World Telegram,* November 7, 1947.

8. Sharon Curtin, "Aging in the Land of the Young," *The Atlantic,* 230 (July 1972), p. 73.

9. *Ibid.*

Name index

325

Subject index

Abstinence, 277, 279-80
Addiction, 272; addicts, 121, 204, 213, 251
Adolescence, 191
Affiliation, 13, 17-38. *See also* Disaffiliation
Age, 82, 89, 103-4, 109, 113, 120, 191, 241, 287; old age, 15, 21, 37, 92, 97, 104, 121, 170, 255
Akron, Ohio, 219
Alienation, 23, 257. *See also* Anomie
Aliens, 18
Alcohol, 33, 111, 113, 122, 126-28, 144, 160-62, 169, 174, 187, 209, 213; alcoholics, 6, 11, 15, 27, 37, 41, 44-45, 47, 54, 61-62, 66, 79, 86, 95-97, 109, 116, 118, 144, 147, 159, 175, 177, 179-81, 184-89, 191, 197, 200-201, 203-4, 210, 226, 228, 236-37, 239, 245-46, 250, 266-67, 279-80, 285, 287; alcoholism, 14-16, 37, 40, 51-53, 55, 59, 69, 78, 80-82, 85, 90, 100, 103, 110, 112, 114, 176, 178, 183, 192-93, 205, 222-23, 240, 246, 248, 251, 253, 260, 273, 282, 288, 293; disease concept of alcoholism, 81, 83-86, 121, 227, 283, 293. *See also* Abstinence; Detoxification; Recidi-

vism; Rehabilitation; Revolving door; Therapy; Treatment
Alcoholics Anonymous, 53-54, 83, 114, 177, 180, 186, 191, 209, 222, 243, 248, 250-52, 256, 264, 269-72, 283
Alcoholism and Drug Addiction Research Foundation, Ontario, Canada, 58. *See also* Alcohol
American Indians. *See* Indians, American
American Medical Association, 55
Anomie, 192-93, 257. *See also* Alienation
Apathy, 132, 241
Arrests, 39, 94, 120, 188, 222, 226, 228-29, 233-34, 236, 245, 252, 261, 268, 285. *See also* Police
Asceticism, 21
Asia, 21
Assimilation, 12
Athens, Greece, 18
Atlanta, Georgia, 228
Attitudes, about homeless men, 39-86

Barber colleges, 33, 141, 148, 196
Bars, 15, 32-33, 35, 94, 123, 141, 144-47, 151, 161-63, 168-69, 173, 182, 188, 196-97